THE SILENT REBEL

The author S.W.D.K. (Kum) Gandah

S.W.D.K. (Kum) Gandah

THE SILENT REBEL

SUB-SAHARAN PUBLISHERS

First published 2004, by
SUB-SAHARAN PUBLISHERS
P.O. BOX LG358,
LEGON, ACCRA, GHANA

for The Institute of African Studies,
University of Ghana
S.W.D.K. Gandah, The Silent Rebel

ISBN 9988-550-72-3

Acknowledgements: The editors wish to thank Mr Bossman Muurey of the Archeology Department, University of Ghana, for technical help with the photographs.

This publication was made possible by a generous grant from Prof. Jack Goody.

Typesetting, Sub-Saharan Publishers
Cover Design by Anne Yayra Sakyi (Sub-Saharan Publishers)

TABLE OF CONTENTS

EDITOR'S INTRODUCTION

THE AUTHOR, S.W.D.K. GANDAH, has fully explained the genesis of his manuscript, which was unpublished when he died in Ghana on 12 June 2001. I had worked closely with him ever since I started my fieldwork in Birifu among the LoDagaa in 1950 where I arrived in time for the Final Funeral of his father, Chief Gandah. After that we did not see each other for some time as I was working among the Gonja of northern Ghana but we got together again, as he explains, in 1967 when I was preparing my manuscript *The Myth of the Bagre* for publication. Subsequently we returned together to Birifu to make another recording of the Bagre in 1969 and he made yet others ten years later nearby in the administrative centre of Lawra. These recordings we spent years transcribing, translating, then putting on to a word processor. The 1969 versions were published under our joint names by *Classiques africaines* in Paris in 1981 and the last batch came out in 2002 with Carolina Academic Press. This work was carried out at week-ends when I used to travel to North London or occasionally, before his terrible accident, he would come up to Cambridge.

All this time he was also working in his spare moments on his own autobiography which he called *The Silent Rebel* and on an account of his father entitled *Gandaa-yiri: The House of the Brave*. *The Silent Rebel* he had divided into three books, the last of which remained unfinished. If Kum had had the time to complete his autobiography, he would have gone on to recount how he eventually joined British Rail and took further courses in Statistics and the Philosophy of Science. It was at that time that I met him again when he was working as a statistician with Guinness the brewers based at Park Royal in West London. Thanks to Guinness he was able to buy a house and to sponsor the immigration of his children, Kofi and Agatha.

The first volume, which told of his school days, was to be published in Ghana but the arrangements fell through when the printer absconded. When I met him again, Kum was firmly embedded in the Guinness community as well as among the Ghanaian emigrés in London. In 1982 he returned to Ghana and suffered a terrible automobile accident. He came back unable to move and even to eat, but was rehabilitated thanks to the NHS and, while he could only move around in a wheel chair, learnt to work with a computer, which is how he managed to write his book. It was done in difficult circumstances but his great determination kept him going.

What he has presented us here is a fascinating account of early schools in northern Ghana together with the story of how that first generation of school children grew up and blossomed into school teachers, lawyers, politicians, and civil servants of all descriptions. They all knew each other well and their acquaintances stretched from shopkeepers to sanitary officials, from presidents to councillors, from chiefs to commoners. The whole spectrum of 'literate' employment was there, arising out of the school situation.

The story also stresses the determination with which this generation of schooled notherners pursued the educational ladder, some going to England to study for O levels, for the A levels and eventually for degrees, in law and in other fields. Education was the key to their success and they pursued it in a very single-minded way, working to earn money when they had to, but otherwise studying very hard.

Like many in the region, Kum's father, Chief Gandaa I, owed his chiefship to the colonial administration which also encouraged these new appointees to send their children, especially their sons, to school so that eventually they would have a set of 'educated' rulers. That did eventually take place but these families, as we see from the narrative, were heavily split between the schooled and the unschooled. When the political system changed in the 1950s it was the former who were in a position to profit and most of the early Members of Parliament from northern Ghana were the sons of chiefs. *The Silent Rebel* provides us with an insider's account of this first generation of northern politicians, of the early elections and of the formation of the Northern Peoples Party. The author knew very well the first minister from the North (in the government of Kwame Nkrumah), its first leader of the Opposition (S.D. Dombo), and its first (and so far only) President of northern origin, Hilla Limann, with whom he lodged in London.

In editing the manuscript I have changed virtually nothing except a few mistakes of spelling or grammar. In the later version of the manuscript he produced, Kum wrote all local names and words using the International Phonetic Alphabet he had been taught at school. The difficulty for me has been that these were left as blanks on his computer as he did not have the necessary fonts. I have tried to fill in the gaps, which proved relatively easy with the vernacular words but difficult for the personal names, since I did not know all the people concerned.

The author's own notes to his text are reproduced at the bottom of the page and indicated in the text by letters. My own additional explanatory notes are indicated in the text by numbers and appear at the end of the book.

There have been other books published by Ghanaians from the north of the country, but they have been largely accounts of local history. I do not know of any other autobiographical accounts that describe the way the new 'middle class' emerged in Ghana and Kum Gandah's writing gives us an entry into that world that encompasses both the traditional and the 'modern'.

Jack Goody
Cambridge, 2003

AUTHOR'S PREFACE

HAVING WRITTEN AN ACCOUNT OF my father's life story, I had contemplated writing something about myself. But I felt my life was not worth a historical account being of insufficient importance either locally or nationally. As the family began looking to me more and more for leadership, I later felt something about me should be known. The urgency of this became apparent when I was involved in a near fatal car accident on holidays in Ghana.

I was flown back to the UK for medical treatment and while in the hospital, which had a special spinal injuries unit, the patients were introduced to the word-processor and computer games as a therapy for the movement of their fingers. It must be stressed that at this clinic all the patients lacked mobility either in their arms or legs or both. I lost the mobility in both the upper and the lower limbs. For I had fractured the third vertebra of my spinal column and, as most doctors know, this is a fatal spot to damage. Having got the flare for word-processing, I decided to put on paper the simple story of my life. But in doing so it did not turn out to be as simple and straight forward as I had thought. If this book should become useful to the members of my extended family, to the Dagara society in which I live,[1] or to any others who may find something intriguing and worthwhile, then I will have accomplished a useful task.

In my scheme for this work, I have decided to write my life story in three phases. The first part is confined to my life from childhood up to the end of my college life in the Teacher Training College, Tamale, as it affects other people both in the family and outside.[2] The second part contains my life story after finishing with my education in Ghana. This covers several domains such as teaching, family business and local and national politics. The third part will go into my life in the UK as well as my relation with the family and colleagues back at home.

The title of the book describes the tacit revolt nurtured in me from childhood since I have always unconsciously but not violently rebelled against unfair oppression either by those in authority or by individuals. The scope of this first book takes us through childhood, to the primary school in Lawra and then to Middle School in Tamale.

I recount the regimentation and the sadism that was employed by some teachers as well as some prefects in the school. Finally I went to the Teacher Training College where life was tolerable and students were all treated with respect.

I am grateful to my teachers in the Lawra school, Mr Henkel and Mr Montia, for laying down the solid foundation of my education, especially to the latter who continued to keep in touch with me at the Middle School and at College. I am also grateful to my late father, who was initially reluctant to send me to school partly because he thought I was too young to profit from it and he had promised my mother on her death-bed to look after me. I thank him too for his later stand against the authorities when I was about to be dismissed from school for playing truant and finally running away to Wa, despite the heartache I had caused him by doing so. I thank K.J. Dickens for having faith in my teaching ability and Miss Gladstone for her encouragement in the Teacher Training College. Indeed I am grateful to all my teachers and lecturers in both school and college. Last but not least, I take this opportunity to thank Jack Goody who is a personal friend of mine and friend of the Gandah family. I am very grateful because without his personal assistance, financially, morally and physical encouragement, this book would not have been written.

Jack Goody has gone through the manuscript of this book twice over, amending and rearranging passages to clarify the meaning I was trying to convey to my readers. However, where his corrections changed the entire sense of what I was trying to say, I still allowed my original sentence to stand or changed my sentence in such a way as to retain the original meaning. Any errors grammatical or otherwise are entirely mine, not his.

In writing this book I have tried to put events in chronological order. Where this is not possible, I have tried to group them into subject headings. For instance each year of my school life has been chronologically specified in order not to put an earlier event before a later one. Where certain colleagues have changed their names after leaving school or college, I have kept their school name and the original spelling, but have included in the notes to each chapter a short description of the present position of my colleagues and teachers. As a wheelchair bound person, research into any of their lives is virtually impossible especially as I am still living in this country [Britain].

There have been a lot of changes in the vernacular script of Ghanaian languages since these manuscripts were written. I presume the main reason that some of them have been abandoned is to be able to use the typewriter and nothing more. If the vernacular script that was used before I ever went to school had been retained, then there would have been a wider readership than there is today. In my days at school there were two changes. For instance we were introduced to 'tS', to represent the 'ch', in 'church'. Similarly, 'dʒ' which stood for the sound 'j' as in Judge or as in 'George' was introduced. Then just a year or so later, the tS and dʒ were changed to ky and gy respectively. Even in the Dagara regions recent scholars use 'Mw' or 'Mn' instead of the symbol 'ŋm' to represent the sound 'ŋm' in 'Nũũŋmin' which I was introduced to in the mid-1930s. So in the same family, you can have some people spelling their name Ŋmin-yaa and others Mwin-yaa or Mnin-yaa depending on when these new scripts were introduced. Similarly in the same dialect a word such as Nũũŋmin may be spelt as Naamwin or Naaŋmin or Naamnin by different scholars, each of which means God. Surely this must not be allowed to continue otherwise there will be no standardised vernacular script for many Ghanaian languages. I have maintained the use of the script that I was taught in school for ease of foreign readers since I have used that in Jack Goody's the *Myth of the Bagre* and in *Une Recitation du Bagré*.

In this computer age, there should be no excuse for the authorities to keep on changing our vernacular script without any tangible benefit. It would be most appropriate when such changes are inevitable that a wide audience is consulted. The Dagara dialect which is being used in this book has a wide readership in Ghana as well as the Ivory Coast and in Burkina Faso. It should be the aim of authorities of these neighbouring countries to consult one another when a change of script is anticipated, especially when they affect other people with a common dialect but living in different borders.

The Vernacular Vowel Script Used

Symbol	Pronunciation
a	as u in but
o	as o in go
ɛ	as e in bet
ɔ	as o in pot
i	as i in pit
u	as u in you

The Vernacular Single & Double Consonants Used

ŋ	as ng in king
ny	as gne in compagne
gy = dʒ	as j in judge
tS = ky	as ch in church
S	as sh in fish
ʒ	as s inpleasure
ŋm = mw = mn	has no equivalence in English sounds.
gb	has no equivalence in English sounds.
kp	has no equivalence in English sounds.

It will be noticed that I have spelt my father's name as Gandah according to the Birifu dialect instead of Ganda or Gandaa, the latter being the Dagaar pronunciation which was spelt incorrectly by Mr Henkel, the head-teacher, using the Dagaar version, and other people before and after him. So all his children who went to Mr Henkel's school spelt their surname the Henkel way with the exception of the author who later altered it to the right spelling. My knowledge of phonetics at the Teacher Training College made me realise the error in the spelling and I immediately changed my surname to Gandah. Since then I have tried to persuade my brothers change the spelling of their surname but they declined for reasons best known to them. In the entire family, only myself and my children use the correct spelling; and perhaps some of my grandchildren will use the same as their fathers and grandfather. However, for the readers, it is sufficient to know that Gandah is the same name as Gandaa or Ganda and that it is only a disagreement in spelling.

All through in this book I have maintained the spelling as pronounced by the Birifu people of the word 'bɔɔr' instead of Jack's use of the word 'bagre', which is the spelling of Lo'piɛl version of the word, and only appears in the title of his books. I have tried to be consistent by using the Birifu version with the spellings used in the recitation of the myth. In the Kusiele Baɣr, yet unpublished, that was performed in Lawra in 1974/5, I have maintained Jack's spelling as this was recited in Lo'piɛlu.

K.G.

CHAPTER ONE

I WAS BORN IN THE village of Birifu in the Lawra District of Ghana on or about January 14, 1927. Lawra is now in the Upper West Region of Ghana and lies to the north of Wa, the regional capital. My parents were Gandah, the chief of Birifu, and Wule, the head of the women-folk in the village. My childhood was a headache for my parents. It is said that when I was born, I was beset with all sorts of illnesses that could not be cured by ordinary herbal treatment or by any imported drugs available at the time. My father was a very good herbalist in his own right and had saved many lives with his treatment both in the village and in the surrounding districts. However, he could find no cure for my own illnesses. Then one night, in his sleep, a vision came to him which announced that something would happen to upset the peace of the family if he didn't do something positive. The next morning, still shaking with fright or anxiety, he told some of the elders in the house to go and consult a good diviner. Towards evening, the elders returned with the message that it was the Bɔɔr Deity that wanted the Bɔɔr ceremony to be performed by the Naayiile clan; and I was the child chosen to manifest its wish; if I was not initiated into the ritual of the Bɔɔr, the Deity was going to bring disaster to the family.[a]

I was the last of my mother's children; there were also three by a previous marriage and three of us by my father. My eldest brother, Yizɔɔla[b], was about five when he died; then my elder brother who was about three years older than me was called Bizɔɔla and I was called Kuubɔɔnɔ mis-spelt by Mr Henkel, the Headmaster of my first

---

[a] As the Deity is supposed not to be a vindictive god, it does not harm or kill but brings minor ailments on some members of the family so that they realise his presence by going to a diviner and knowing and acceeding to his request.

[b] Yizɔɔla was conceived without my mother having had the usual menstrual period. It was therefore believed she did not have her period before she conceived Yizɔɔla, so he was called a "Tulme", a child born of the reverse process, or "Yuur", a twin.

school, as Kumbɔɔnɔ with a different connotation altogether.[a] My mother became not only my father's favourite wife, but also the most beloved woman in the village; because of her kindness to all and sundry, she got the nickname the "mother of all orphans". Because of my mother, my father would have done everything in his power to save my life from the anger of the gods. Fortunately, the Bɔɔr Deity never kills since it is a deity of happiness, of peaceful gatherings, of good husbandry and of reproduction; it manifests itself only in casting spells in the form of fever and other illnesses on one of its chosen so that its rites will be performed if it considers a section is neglecting the observation of its rites. These rites are a way of life for the Birifu people and in the outlying districts where they are performed, an education in which the initiated are taught to recite the myth from beginning to the end. It is also a religion where ethical and social behaviour is learnt; humility is the essence and the core of the myth. Initiating neophytes takes a year or more as well as a great deal of the resources of the group performing it. It involves the entire clan. I belong to the Naayiile clan which is subdivided into the Sũnkyɛlɛ, Dabɔɔlɛ, Sunkuole and Maarbaalɛ lineages or sections.[b] Each of these subdivisions usually performs the Bɔɔr on a rota basis if the Deity manifests itself in their families or when they feel they have the resources and the neophytes to do so. When one of these subclans performs Bɔɔr, the other three sub-groups play a supporting role. Apart from the Naayiile clan there are about six other clans with their subdivisions that comprise the Birifu community.

So in 1928 Gandah, with his brothers and elders, decided to perform the Bɔɔr. When I was suggested as one of the neophytes to be initiated, Bũyir, a maternal uncle of mine, and also an under-study of Kuusob, one of the Bɔɔr elders of Ŋmangbil but living in Batan, a subclan of Kya at the time, pleaded with my father not to include me, as I might die in the course of the initiation and thus spoil the Bɔɔr performance for the entire community.[6] However, my father, believing in his faith, ignored Bũyir's plea and put me in among the hun-

---

[a] My name Kuubɔɔnɔ means 'those evil doers who think they know where death comes from and will kill other parent's children, they should beware.' Whereas Kumbɔɔnɔ the spelling used by Mr Henkel means 'give me knowledge'.

[b] The other patriclans in Birifu are the Birɛ from Birɔ, Taŋzuule from Taŋzu, the Baapɛri from Bapaar, the Ŋmangbiile from Ŋmangbil and part of Tanziir, the I-iɔlɛ from Silaayir and Tanziir and the Kyaalɛ from Kya, all with their subclans.

dred odd neophytes. The initiation went well during the course of the year and as soon as it was finished, I gradually began to regain my health and put on some weight. For stories have it that I was a mere skeleton and looked like a straw.

Although my health had improved since my initiation, I was still plagued with illnesses such as diarrhoea and dysentery. The diviners were again consulted and their verdict was that I was a mystery-child that was sent to lure other such children back to the land of rebirth. Such a child is known in the Birifu dialect as *kyɛkuɔ*, a concept which has no parallel in English or in modern philosophy. They are identified by the numerous illnesses that besiege them and their unwillingness to live on this earth, however much they are pampered. The doctrine of reincarnation in Birifu thought is quite different from the ideas of Christianity. In Birifu it is believed that there is a kingdom somewhere in the universe (akin to the Hebrew 'sheol' or the Greek 'Hades') to which these children die and return. The chief among these children come into the human world to lure others back to their kingdom. I was supposed to be one of those kings who had come to lure others back to my kingdom. Although I believe in the doctrine of reincarnation, I do not believe in the explanation behind it. My father evolved the idea that if the faces of such children were marked and then they died and returned to the land of reincarnation, they would not be accepted there and would have to return to the land of the living. So if any of his children were supposed to be such a child, his face was marked with a sharp knife and more often than not the supposed child lived.[7] A child that has been reincarnated is called Dɛri (male) or Dɛrpɔɔ (female), or some variant of these names.

I should add that I do believe in the doctrine of reincarnation. Incidents very close to me have given me faith in this belief. My eldest sister, Kuupiirɛ, gave birth to a lot of children but all of them died by the time they had attained the ages of five years. She must have buried over ten of them before she was even in her early thirties. Anyway, Dɛrkpil, whose name was a variant of Dɛri, was born to my sister in the early 1930s and I grew very fond of my little nephew. He was hardly three years old when he died again. One of the elders in the house, Dɔɔr-iɛrɛ, went to bury him and clipped the lobe off one of his ears. My sister became pregnant again and gave birth to another boy; but this time the little baby came back with part of his ear clipped off. This same child died again and Dɔɔr-iɛrɛ again went to bury him. This time he twisted his tongue. When my sister became pregnant again and gave birth, this reincarnated child came back with a twisted tongue. Eventually this child called Nũũ-tomo (Tomo, for short) lived and became his parents' eldest child. In fact this nephew of mine is still living and has a family of his own and in fact is the head of his father's family. These two incidents have convinced me of the veracity of the doctrine of reincarnation.

As years went by, far from being the emaciated and skinny child that I had been, I became a fat and plump little toddler. Being the last born of my mother, I was spoilt by the love which she lavishly bestowed on me. Obviously, had she lived longer to see me grow up, I would probably have been a different person than I am today and might have become a spoilt brat.

My father had many wives each of whom had children by him. In fact thirty-five of his wives survived him when he died on February 8, 1950. So as a child I had over two hundred brothers and sisters alive at the time. My father loved all his children equally, but he was a regular martinet as far as discipline was concerned. So we all had to put on our best behaviour when he was around. However, many a time we became very naughty like any other children in other houses. More often than not I was one of the very naughty ones, taking advantage of my sickly condition and of the fact that I could always run down to my mother who would hide me in one of her rooms. And I wanted to be adventurous like any boy of my age. My father was a very fair man and would only punish you if he caught you in the act of misbehaving.

During the dry season in Birifu, when all farming work has been completed, the men-folk normally went miles into the woods to hunt for game. There are three types of hunting in Dagara society. There is first, the hunt (yɔb), literally a ramble, a walk or an excursion, which normally starts from the compound farms, goes no more than a few miles away and lasts for only a few hours. In this hunt only cudgels are used by the hunters to kill rabbits, wild guinea-fowls and partridges. It can be organised by any member of the clan section, so it does not necessarily include every member in the society. Its objective is to get people to loosen their limbs after the long rest from farming in the dry season and get themselves ready for the more strenuous hunting activities to follow. Only occasionally are bows and arrows used when a duiker or an antelope is disturbed. In this hunt the neophytes are also encouraged to take part so that they can exercise themselves. Of course anything they killed belonged to the Bɔɔr Deity, whose meat they are forbidden to eat.

Then after the Bɔɔr Dance, there is the second type of hunt, *wiɛo* which means literally the 'bush' or the 'wild'. This is organised only by the hunt leaders and the day and place is announced either in the market places on a market day, in pito (beer) houses or by word of mouth. As the name suggests the hunt is done in the bush far away from houses where there is bigger game such as the antelope or wild boar. Hunters leave home at about eight in the morning and return about five in the afternoon carrying their kill and singing their hunting songs as they approach the house.[9] The women run out to meet them ululating and help them carry the kill home. They first place the kill on the altar of the 'hunting gods' where our hunting song is sung three times. They then go up to the roof top and place the kill on the shrine of the Bɔɔr Deity as the men again sing their song three times before dispersing.

Of all the clans in Birifu as far as I know it is only the Naayiile who have a song that was sung when big game was brought home. My father often came home on his horse ahead of the hunt followed by his stable boy who usually carried his gun for him.[10] The sound of his horn would herald the arrival of the huntsmen coming home with big game, especially if he himself was successful in killing one or two.[a] At this juncture the women would ululate and rush out to meet the huntsmen. As a child, Bakyoo Dapla, a cousin from Bakyoo's house, was our solo singer for the hunting song whilst the rest of the group answered the chorus. The song went like this:

Si waana yee si waana
" " " " " (chorus)
Si waana yee si waana
" " " " " (chorus)
Si waana yee si waana
Si waana yee si waana yaa
Laala kuɔra Burŋmaan daa (chorus)
Si waana naa.

which means literally:
We are coming (repeated twice)
We are coming on
You male crown bird[11]
We are coming

---

[a] My father on his return from the hunt normally sounded his horn if he or any member of the clan had killed one or more big animals.

The kill is smoked and the hunt-feast (wɛ-saab) is performed at a later date. During the hunt-feast, the women, except for old ladies who can no longer give birth, are not supposed to touch anything that is used in the preparation of the food.[12] So the men fetch the water from the spring or well, and get the soup ingredients which include the baobab leaves (t'o vaar) ready. Even the guinea-corn is ground on the grinding stones (niɛr) by the males. At about four thirty in the afternoon as the soup and the porridge are being prepared, no woman was allowed within a certain distance of the performance. It was the duty of we, the young boys in the house, to prevent these women from coming near and seeing what the male folk are doing.

We, the children, made improvised bows by tying strings to sticks and using reeds as our arrows. We then shot at sight any woman who came within the vicinity of the performance area. It is the custom so that even the women took it as a joke and did not take umbrage at us. But some of us were so mischievous that we often used needles from thorns as arrow heads. Of course this was very unpleasant for the people shot at since they penetrate the skin. Anyway, my father soon put a stop to such silly and stupid pranks. But as children, we thoroughly enjoyed shooting at our mothers on these occasions, for it was the only time one could do that.

Then there is the third type of hunt (wɛ-gaab, literally, the 'sleep' or 'night' hunt) which takes place any time between March and May or June. Then the hunters go several miles into the bush and even sometimes cross territorial boundaries to hunt big game such as gnu, buck and buffalo.[13] Although it is called night or sleep hunt, the hunt takes place during daylight. They stay there, sleep out and hunt in the woods for up to a fortnight. If they killed a lot, the carcasses were sometimes sent ahead so that the old men who could not make the hunt would smoke them dry. When they do finally return, the reception and performance is the same as for the second type of hunt.

My father was one of the leading huntsmen in the village. One day, there was going to be a communal hunt of the second type about four and a half miles away, at Gũble near the Black Volta.[a] So I wanted to go to the hunt as well, although both my father and mother begged me not to; I insisted and cried until I had my way. However, I was to learn a bitter lesson soon enough. The hunt went on for hours until 2.00 p.m. when the huntsmen gathered at the central point (wɛ-duora)

---

[a] Gũble is one of the parishes of Birifu.

to share their kill. After the meeting the hunt came to an end and we had to retrace our steps home. My father was on horseback and I had hoped he would give me a ride. The sun was scorching hot and the entire path leading back home was as hot as burning embers. Parts of the path were covered with deep layers of sand and in some places my feet were buried ankle deep.

You can imagine the agony I was in, walking barefoot. I began to cry but my father either did not hear my cries or wanted me to learn a lesson, so he paid no heed. The second assumption was probably correct; he wanted me to learn a lesson so that one day, if I was told something by my parents or an older person I would pay greater heed. Luckily, one of my cousins, Dɛrkpɛlɛ, saw I had suffered enough and decided to carry me on his shoulders for the rest of the journey. However, he didn't realise how heavy I was and I could feel he was sweating beneath me as he carried me along. It was only when we were about half a mile from home that my father turned round and saw me being carried that he put me on the back of his horse for the rest of the journey. From then on, I decided I was going to have nothing to do with hunting, communal or otherwise, however near it was to home, until I was really sure I could make the distance there and back.

In Birifu, as elsewhere in the Lawra district, it is the children from five years old to adolescence who look after the sheep and cattle belonging to the family. My father had over five hundred cattle and numerous sheep. Children from five to seven years of age normally tend the sheep and goats in the fields of the compound, while the older ones drive the cattle down to rivers and swamps to let them graze until evening when they are taken back into the kraal. If you were of age to tend the sheep and you didn't go, your mates would tease you for being a mother's child or one who was more interested in the company of girls.

One day, the boys of my age group decided to accompany the older ones to the bush to tend the sheep and goats; and as I did not want to be called a mother's boy, I decided to go along and tend them from then on. The other reason why children of such tender age decide to go and tend the animals is that only those who look after the sheep and the cattle are entitled to the milk from the cows when they are milked the next morning. So apart from avoiding the possibility of being teased by your mates, there is also the added incentive of getting milk to drink. However, in my case, this was not much of an incentive as my mother normally bought me milk from the Fulani cowherds almost every morning.[a] Despite this I started to become a frequent visitor to the swamps to tend the sheep and cattle.

Once I started going to the swamps, I could hardly stop. The cowherds were led by Kũkpi, one of my elder brothers, Kũdɔɔ, a cousin, and by many other older brothers and sisters. The sheep and goats were always left in charge of Volvuu, Bakyaara and sometimes Sɔrkumɔ and some of our teenage sisters who supervised the younger ones at grazing fields near home. Not satisfied with tending the sheep and goats, I decided one day to follow the cows further into the bush. This was during the rains. My father had large farms at Batan, where the adults Sakpi and Kayɛ were asked to guard the crops against birds, monkeys and antelopes. We drove the cattle along while they grazed and arrived at the place where Sakpi and Kayɛ had made a hut. Kayɛ was a brother and my best friend and Sakpi was my brother-in-law. When they saw me following the cattle, they forbade me to go off into the bush with Kũkpi and the others. So I stayed behind and was entertained to guinea-corn beer and at noon with roasted yam and stew for lunch. Towards evening Kũkpi and company returned to take me home. Being the leaders of the cowherds, they rode ahead on the tame cows, while I and my mates drove the cattle on behind them.

I continued to follow the bigger boys to Gbatɛri, a little swamp, down Fofoi way where the cattle are grazed and where the cowherds learn how to swim, fish and wrestle. Very often other herds from different families and clans were brought down at Gbatɛri to graze as well. As soon as they meet, the cowherds begin to sing out, calling the name of their strongest bull. Most bulls and cows are given names which they recognise and answer to. Hearing its name being called out, the bull will go into the space between the groups of boys and prepare to meet its challenger. The other side will sing out the name of their strongest bull to take up the challenge. The two bulls then fight each other until there is an absolute winner.

As soon as they have finished, the two leading cowherds also wrestle until one wins. If there were several family groups who had brought their cattle down for grazing, the challenge would continue until there was an absolute winner, thus establishing an order of hier-

---

[a] The Fulani tribe from Northern Nigeria are a nomadic people who travel into Northern Ghana to herd cattle free of charge to wealthy chiefs and farmers in exchange for the milk of the cattle which they sell in the markets. Of course some of them stole cattle from their masters.

archy. The best wrestler was proclaimed king of the cowherds (naa'kyiin-gbala), and the next best, the second-in-command, and so on. Once the leadership has been established, the leader then nominates combatants among the assembled cowherds to wrestle with one another. These pairs are approximately matched by age. But if there are no competitors in the same age-group, then one could find oneself wrestling with an older or a younger boy. This happened to me on one of my visits to Gbateri. I was picked to wrestle with someone far older than me for the simple reason that I was now well developed for my age. Moreover, this boy came from the community of traders at a nearby stranger settlement (Zongo) in Kuũ-nyu-kuũ, and the erroneous belief was that they had had no training in the art of wrestling. This boy took only a few seconds to put me on the hard ground and that really hurt my pride, apart from the fact that I would be teased by my bigger brothers and cousins as being a good-for-nothing child who could not wrestle but only knows how to eat.

Another pass-time down at the swamp was learning to swim and to dive. There is a water game in which a swimmer dives under water and comes up suddenly behind a fellow swimmer and hits him with one of his legs (*vab*, lit. whipping). The bigger boys go into the deeper part of the swamp while we the younger ones and those who cannot swim stay in the shallow waters. Sometimes the day is spent fishing in one of three ways. Firstly, fishing is done by damming up both ends of the tributary flowing in and out of the swamp into the river. The water is then bailed out into the river itself with calabashes. When the pool is empty, then the fish that are left in the mud are caught and the barriers of the dams are demolished to let the water flow naturally again. The second method used is with bows and arrows. In fast running and shallow streams where the water is clear and the fish can be seen, these are baited with food. As they come up near the banks to eat the bait, they are shot and killed with the arrows. A third method adopted is to use herbs to poison the pond. The fish die, float to the top and are collected from the water. These fish are taken to the rendezvous where the small ones are barbecued and shared out while the big ones are taken home to give to the parents. They are then cured and either used as food for the family or sent to the market to be sold. The proceeds from the market belong to the boy who caught the fish and the money's kept in trust for him. At that time my father abhorred the method of poisoning the pond and made a bye-law in the village forbidding such a practice.

It is a custom of the Birifu people that maternal uncles help their nephews to acquire some property of their own; for we the Birifu people do not inherit on the mother's side.[a] Therefore, as a child, if you visited your uncle's and were about to return home, your uncle would give you a brooding hen as a loan (n'ɔ-guol). It was your responsibility to rear this hen and when it multiplied, you would take the hen and its chickens back to your uncle. Your uncle would decide how many of these fowls to give you. However, if you were a shepherd boy, your uncle could decide to give you a she-goat, a ewe or a cow (bu'guol, pi'guol or naa'guol) depending on how wealthy he is. You would take care of this animal until it multiplied, when you would be given your share.

The idea is for the uncles to train their nephews in the art of animal husbandry so that they grow up to be economically self-supporting. On the other hand, you could also snatch a goat, a sheep or a cow from your uncle's herd as a kind of a loan when the animals were being grazed together with your own. You take these back to your uncle's and get your share as a reward for looking after them. I must admit that I had never been to my uncle's until recently (January 1983) when I decided to get to know my maternal home. For during my father's life-time he forbade us visiting my maternal section of the village, Batan, because they were supposed to be evil-minded and could take our lives by sorcery if we went there. As a result neither Biz nor I (and for that matter, none of his children) had the opportunity of visiting our uncles to be given a fowl or an animal.

Consequently, the only way I could get an animal was by snatching it from their herd if the opportunity arose. As good luck would have it, one day a herd belonging to one of my maternal uncles was brought to graze along with our cattle. The big boys in the group coaxed me into choosing some cows from my uncle's to take as a loan. Instead of choosing one cow, as was the custom, I collected five and drove them back home with ours. Hardly had we arrived when my uncle, Buni-iɔŋ, the uncle of Benima, came and complained to my father, for his boys had gone home and told him what had happened.[b] My father laughed and told me the man was not really my direct uncle and that I could not get a cow on loan from him; and besides I was only allowed one cow, not five. He therefore allowed

---

[a] In some parts of what was then the Lawra district e.g. Lawra and Nandom, the people inherit movable goods matrilineally.

[b] Benima who collaborated with Dr Jack Goody is the son of my maternal uncle.

the man to drive his cattle home. From then on I never asked anything from my uncles, whether a direct or an indirect one.

One day in the rainy season, while we were down at Gbatɛri grazing the cattle, the clouds began to gather. This must have been the first rain of the season. Foreseeing the danger, the bigger boys gave orders for the cattle to be rounded up and driven home. We had hardly reached the Bũũ plateau when the sky became pitch dark with nimbus clouds. As the clouds broke open, giving way to a hailstorm and followed by a howling and hissing wind of hurricane strength, we the younger ones were being carried away by the force of the gale which whipped hailstones and sand onto our limbs and faces.[a] There were cries and yells everywhere. Sensing the danger, men and women came out of their homes and ran to rescue us from the wrath of this fierce and terrifying wind. As good luck would have it, nothing calamitous happened. But from that day on, I did not try to follow the bigger boys to the swamps to tend the cattle or sheep until I went to school and could not care what teasing I got from my mates; and I did not have another opportunity to do so before I went to school.

In Birifu, as in many parts of Africa, both parents take part in farming and other tasks outside the home. Consequently, the bigger children of five and above have the responsibility of looking after their younger brothers and sisters while the mother is away doing chores in the farm or fetching firewood from the bush. They act as nurse-maids to their younger brothers and sisters. Normally this is the work for the girls who have this responsibility until adolescence or until they are capable of doing the work that adults do. However, where a woman does not have a female child in her section of the house, she could go back to her parent's home to bring a younger sister or cousin. I have used the word 'cousin' in the English sense but this is not the same in Birfuɔlu, the dialect of the Birifu people. Cousins (*yɔɔr*, pl. and *yɛbɛ*, sing. for male or *yɛ-puuli*, pl. and *yɛ-puule* sing. for female) regard each other as brothers and sisters; similarly, there are no paternal uncles; my father's younger brother is my 'junior father' and his elder brother is my 'senior father'; and these brothers would have more say over me than my father would. Also my mother would call my father's elder brother her 'senior husband' and the younger brother her 'junior husband'. But neither of these

[a] At this time my brother, Debomo, was one of the little boys who was carried away down the Gbellii valley and was lucky to be rescued before he could be carried further down towards and into the Black Volta river.

brothers would have any access to her body until she is widowed when she marries one of them. It is customary for a widow, more often than not, to remarry into the house, especially when she has some grown up children by the deceased husband and does not want to leave them and go out to remarry into another family. People from the same clan group call each other *yɛbaa* as opposed to *yɛbɛ*. These are distant cousins on the paternal side.

My mother shared her main dormitory section (davura) with six other young wives of my father, each with their own separate rooms. Only the main communal hall (kyaara) and the enclosed open courtyard (davura) were shared with the other wives. Our house at that time comprised about eight of those large dormitories. One of the women in my mother's dormitory was Gɔziɛl who hailed from one of the parishes of Birifu by which name she was called; but this parish was later transferred to Tugo under the Jirapa Division.

Gɔziɛl had a child called Dɛrkpil and as she could not get a girl from any of the sections in our house to look after her little child, she asked my mother if she would allow me to do so. She consented and I was given the responsibility of taking the child outside the house away from the mother, so that she could do her work without any impediment. She could go then to the farm or the bush to fetch firewood, knowing that her child would be taken care of. There was a big thorn tree twenty-five yards from our house where all the nursemaids brought out their little sisters and brothers to sit under the shade and care for them. If your child was feeling hungry or thirsty, you took him or her back into the dormitory to be fed by the mother and you yourself would be fed at the same time.

Although I was a boy looking after Dɛrkpil, this was no problem to me as I was surrounded by bigger sisters, such as Tinyɔi, Sɛnuɔr, Kpaalisa (Hausa, 'Kwalisa'), who could tell me what to do. My only problem was carrying the child down the ladder from the flat roof into the dormitory. Any time I came to the ladder leading down to my section, I called out so that some bigger person could help take the child down for me if the mother was not around. I had become very attached to this my little brother, when sadly he fell ill and died. As you can guess from his name he was one of those reincarnated children; so he had returned to the other world, the world of these mystery children. Dɛrkpil's death had a very profound effect on me and after he was buried, I refused to have anything to do with looking after my younger brothers or sisters.

CHAPTER TWO

The Death Of My Mother

IN THE MONTHS OF JULY and August, farmers in Birifu normally started harvesting their maize and groundnuts. As my father had large farms of these crops to harvest, he usually allowed his subjects the chance to harvest their crops first before he called for their help on his farms.[14] During these harvests my mother was always vigilant to see that all the harvest was carried home and that nothing was taken by the helpers to their own houses. In Birifu during harvest, those farmers who have finished harvesting normally go to other people's farms where harvesting is still taking place and give a helping hand. After the day's harvest, the farmer would give his helpers a portion of the harvest for the day's work. The more you are able to harvest, the greater the quantity of your reward. In my father's case, he usually rewarded the less well off with more, giving less to the well-to-do farmers who came to help.

During one of these harvests in my father's farm at Gũble, my mother supervised as usual the carrying of the harvest home by the womenfolk. One of the women helping was my mother's niece, Pɔɔ-kuu, nicknamed Pɔɔ-bɛru because of her enormous weight of over twenty stones. As they reached Damɔ's house at Silayir, where she was married, Pɔɔ-kuu branched off to her home to put away her reward and then proceeded with her load of harvest to the house. My mother thought she was some one who was trying to pilfer some of the produce she was carrying and went to investigate. In doing so, she trod on one of those long thorns (guɔ-sɔɔla) that grow so well in the rains. She pulled the piece of thorn out but probably left a broken piece in the flesh. She investigated further when she got home but when they could not find the broken piece, she continued with her daily chores. Walking barefoot in the rains must have let in some water and the foot became inflamed causing septicaemia. However, this was diagnosed as a whitlow. Whether it was a whitlow or the thorn, it certainly caused the poisoning of her foot and the poison presumably flowed back into her blood stream and eventually caused her death.

My mother must have known that she was going to die. Consequently she asked that I be brought to stay by her bedside which was in my father's top apartment. Everyday when I woke up, I was there cracking jokes or clowning to give those present something to laugh at, little knowing that she was about to die within a matter of weeks. Early one autumn morning, my mother asked that some fresh maize be roasted for me. The clouds had gathered pitch dark. As they lifted to give way to rain and thunder, my father entered the room. When he saw the pale face of my mother, revealed by the flash of lightning, he must have thought she had given up the ghost. He seized his famous sabre that was hanging on the wall in the room and stabbed himself in the chest. At that moment, the women who were attending to my mother's illness screamed and yelled for help. In fact, many people had expected mother's death sooner than later, so when they heard the yells they thought she had passed away; hence their own yells and screams. However, when the elders rushed upstairs, they found my father with his favourite sabre under his chest, and it had curled up like an overfed viper. They needn't have bothered to raise the alarm since my father had supernatural powers that prevented any knife or arrow from piercing his body. This was a precaution against his enemies in time of war. When he realised my mother was not dead, he must have been glad his powers had worked. But it shows how much my father loved my mother, even being prepared to take his own life for her. From then on, my father was watched with eagle eyes by the elders and his "joking partners" (lũluɔrɛ) were called in to help in case he made another suicide attempt.[a]

Mother might have realised that if she did not leave some responsibility on my father's shoulders, he might try to take his life again. So during the weeks that were left of her life, she implored father to swear to take care of Biz and myself. Mother had acquired some wealth of her own in her first marriage, which she had left behind in the house at Dabɔɔ-yir. When she married my father she also acquired some wealth in the form of cows and some money, mostly in thousands of cowry shells which she buried in large pots under her

[a] Joking partners are based on one matriclan being a joking partner to another. Thus the Kambire matriclan to which I belong are joking partners to the Hiɛmɛ matriclan to which A. Karbo, the present Lawra Nũũ belongs. His father, J.A. Karbo, whom he succeeded belonged to my own matriclan of Kambire. The French colonial system in this part of the area has used the matriclans as surnames instead of the paternal family names. For example if I were in Côte d'Ivoire or Burkina Faso my surname would have Kambire and not Gandah.

granary. She told my father that she was leaving the wealth acquired at Dabɔɔ-yir to her older children whom she had by her first husband, Batiɔr. However, my father should use the wealth she had acquired in his house to take care of Biz and myself until we were grown men. As it was not customary for a man to use a woman's income or wealth to raise her children, my father promised that he would take care of us but not with her wealth. However, he promised that when we became adults he would show us where the money was, and we could do what we liked with it. It must have been this solemn promise that restrained my father from further suicidal actions and also gave my mother the peace of mind to die, knowing full well the man she loved would take care of her children.

Weeks went by. Then one night as the moon was escaping from the clutches of the rain clouds and descending into its fleecy bed over the western horizon, I was awoken by the cries and yells which announced the death of a person in the house. I joined in the weeping not knowing for whose body I was mourning. Had I been a bit older I would have realised that it was no one else than my mother who was being mourned. Anyhow, the wails and cries, mostly by the women, continued for about half an hour to an hour while the gods were being consulted to see if her funeral could be performed or not.[15] While the gods were being consulted, the entire surroundings of our house were filled with human beings from all over the village waiting for their consent, since they could not join in the mourning until the gods had given their permission. All this time my mother's body had been conveyed from my father's upper apartment (bɔɔpiɛ) down to my mother's dormitory where she would be bathed, clothed and prepared to be taken out on the funeral stand (paala). At this point the funeral directors (bɔɔ uune) began digging the grave and getting sticks ready to erect the stand in the event she was to be mourned.[16] At the same time a gate was being opened through the open court-yard so the body could be carried outside the room and placed on the stand or sent directly for burial if she was not to be mourned. When the gods agreed that the funeral should be performed, the xylophones (kuo'-gyile) and the long drum (gaŋgaa) were brought up to the roof-top. As soon as they were played everybody joined in the crying and wailing. That night I cried myself to sleep.

The next morning, the entire compound farm was covered with human beings. People had come from far and wide to mourn for my mother and the whole place looked like a great durbar or palaver. In Birifu during those times, a woman was mourned for four days while a man would be mourned for three. The idea of keeping the body for three or four days was to allow the relatives of the deceased from distant parts, to come and see the body before it was buried. It was also to make sure that the person was really dead before being interred. However, according to our belief the real reason is that our Creator gave the man three chances to sin[a] and the woman four. Consequently, in many performances in Birifu, the ratio of acts for man and woman is three to four. So my mother was mourned for at least four days before she was buried.

Among the sympathisers who came to my mother's funeral were the District Administration personnel, especially Mr Adams, the District Commissioner's clerk and Mr Ribeiro, the dispenser at the Lawra hospital. These officers knew my mother very well since she had often played hostess to them when they visited Birifu or when she was in Lawra with my father. Anyway, these two officers were at the funeral almost every day. On the third day, when they arrived, they had first approached the stand to pay their homage or respects to the deceased as was the custom and were immediately joined by my father and other chief mourners. I was dragged along with some of my age-group. Bavubaa and I stood in front of the stand weeping with the rest of the mourners. Mr Adams must have been told that I was the last born of my mother. Seeing me supporting the back of my neck with both palms of my hands and weeping so pitifully, he came up to comfort me but I reacted rather rudely and shifted away from him. This was more a child's fear than rudeness. I moved to another part of the stand and started weeping again. But then he crept up behind me and started comforting me once more. I could not stand his interference any longer, or so I thought at the time, and so Bavubaa and I decided to move away from this stranger who was preventing us from mourning. We left the area of the stand completely until he had returned to Lawra. When I eventually went to school and knew him properly, I was afraid he would recognise me and remember my rudeness. Fortunately, he never recognised who I was before he left Lawra.

After the burial there were the funeral rites to be performed. This would have occupied at least one year; but because my father had to

[a] The word 'sinning' is used lightly here to mean to commit a crime. For example if one boy insults another, the other boy gives him two more chances before he retaliates. Males would give each other three chances whilst giving a woman four chances.

perform his administrative duties in Lawra as well as Birifu, they had to hurry up with them. Consequently these were performed within a space of a few months. As my mother was an elder in the house, she was buried according to custom in the open court-yard of the dormitory (davura) of which she was the head. The tomb was beautifully made some three feet in diameter and raised about two and a half feet high. There were steps leading to the top where the children who lived in the dormitory could climb and play. One morning there was a quarrel between myself and my elder brother, Biz. He hit me hard and started running away up the ladder to the rooftop. At that time I was playing with a child's bow and arrow. I took aim and shot him, hitting him between his big toe and the next one. He screamed and when my father learnt of what I had done, he was in a rage. He came down to punish me for my naughtiness; but before he could descend to the dormitory, I had already been warned by my mother's faithful maid, Daayel, to run into one of my mother's rooms and hide. I did so and he never got me that time.

That day there was another funeral a few miles away at Tankyɛra, which my father had to attend. Thinking he was still at the funeral, I went up to his room on the roof top, took one pair of his hunting boots, put them on and started dragging them about the floor. Little did I know that he had already returned from the funeral when suddenly I felt a crack on my head. He had caught me in another naughty deed and wished to give out a single punishment for the two mischiefs in the same morning. He warned me to behave and told me that I shouldn't think that because I had recently lost my mother I could misbehave with impunity. Having learnt my lesson I tried not to get myself into trouble so often in the future.

Towards the end of the year, the final funeral rites of my mother were performed so that afterwards everyone could go about their normal business. For then my father could carry out his administrative duties quite freely, without any constraints. This would take place in November or early December. At that time my father was the acting Lawra Nũũ (chief), as Bini, the Lawra Nũũ, had died at the end of June. However, after the funeral rites there was an enquiry as to the cause of my mother's death. For in the Birifu ways of thought, just like those of ancient Greeks, there is no effect without a cause and vice versa. The enquiry had already started prior to her burial, when two people carried her sleeping mat to discover and identify the killers.

In Birifu when a person dies, it is believed he or she must have died of some cause, for example, by the wrath of the gods against the deceased either for some evil deeds committed by him or her or as a punishment to the family for the errors committed against the gods, by sorcery or by natural means. So every effort is made to eliminate each of these causes that is not connected with the death. So when my mother died, the first thing that was done was to use her sleeping mat to see if her death was due to human intervention.[17]

The mat is carried by two people; it is believed the force of the spirit of the deceased would impel the persons carrying the mat to go anywhere the mat compels them. If someone had a hand in the death of the deceased, and lives even nine or so miles away, the momentum of the mat or the bedding of the deceased will impel its carriers to this person's house. This method was used to catch two or three people who were supposed to have had a hand in the death of my mother. When the mat pointed them out as suspects, they themselves confessed that they killed her by witchcraft. Another method by which a witch is identified is by consulting a soothsayer or a diviner. At this time many prominent diviners from near and far were consulted and a few more names were added.

In those days, sorcery was a criminal offence both in Britain and in the Gold Coast. However, those persons who were identified by the diviners refused to admit their supposed guilt. As a result there was nothing my father could do, except take those who had confessed to the District Commissioner's court for trial. These were the three men who had confessed to being witches as a result of the carrying of the corpse's mat and to have had some hand in the death of my mother. But before they went for trial, they also accused certain people of helping them. These persons included my eldest half brother, Dɛn, from my mother's previous marriage and my mother's young cousin, Yɔra, whom she had brought to the house to be my nurse maid and to assist her in her daily chores. There was one Kpɔku, the son of Dɔɔnpuɔ and a nephew of Siilu, who had also been accused. However, these persons denied strongly having any thing to do with the death of my mother.

It is the belief that when we go to sleep at night our souls wander out of our bodies.[a] Our souls (siɛ) do not want to desert us when we

---

[a] It is believed that when the soul temporarily leaves our bodies at night, that is what makes us sleep soundly and become inactive. When the soul does not leave us, we become restless and have insomnia.

are active during the day. Hence their nocturnal wanderings. It is also believed that during these wanderings, the witches come out and turn into flying creatures that look like a ball of fire, crimson in colour, and then go off to meet at their covens. To these covens the soul of their victim is brought. It is turned into an animal usually a cow, and then slaughtered. They then feast on this cow and, depending upon the number of witches that form the coven, it could take months before the meat is finished. It is also believed that as soon as the witches have started eating, the person whose soul it is becomes ill and when the head of the animal which is always eaten last, is eaten by the witches and broken into pieces, the person at last dies.

Witches from one family, it is believed, have no power over the soul of a member of another, unless the coven includes a witch from that member's family. For it is only that witch who knows enough about his relative's spiritual powers and who can disarm him or her spiritually, before luring him to the coven where he is turned into an animal and eaten. It is also the belief that new recruits into the coven are achieved by enticing any soul that may be wandering alone to the coven and given some of the flesh of the animal. Once he has eaten, he becomes indebted to them and is forced to provide a soul at the next coven. This must have been the reason for the three witches to name my eldest brother and his cousin for luring my mother's soul to their coven where she was turned into an animal and eaten.[a]

By choosing them it gives their accusation some credibility. It could also mean that, because my mother was very dear to my father, by naming her son and cousin as her killers they could get off lightly. Anyway, whatever their motive it didn't succeed for they were found guilty and sentenced to three months imprisonment with hard labour at the District Commissioner's Court. My brother and cousin, however, were told to return to their respective houses and later that year my brother, who could hardly bear the public shame that had been brought upon him, left for Ashanti to work on cocoa farms or in the mines and did not return until three years later in 1937. I understood

---

[a] It is also believed that the soul can leave the body of a person permanently when he or she becomes inactive both day and night. The person becomes pale and ashy and is unable to speak. Only people with special powers can see the soul wandering about and alert the person's household. An elder of the household then hires another person with the powers to lure the soul back into the body so that he can regain his normal self. Otherwise the person remains in that inactive state until he finally dies.

that before my brother left for the south, he took an oath that if he was really a witch the gods should kill him within the next three years. So after the three years had lapsed and he did not die, he believed he had been purged and returned to his society.

It is admirable how the early thinkers propounded their theory of witchcraft. This seemed to be based on their theory of the soul and their knowledge about the human physiology. In their theory human life is dependent on the motive force of the soul and the head, that is the brain. For when the head is broken, the brain ceases to function and fails to send messages to other parts of the body and the person dies. Take away the head and there is no life. It is worth comparing their philosophy of life with that of the ancient Greeks, especially Plato's theory of the soul, though such comparison is outside the scope of this book.

After the burial of my mother, my father was still in mourning. In Birifuɔle custom the body of the chief mourner is always smeared with clay or ash immediately after the burial. He was seated under a big thorn tree, Gɔmhara, with a parasite growing with it where the elders from the seven houses of Sunkuol's descendants in the Naayiile clan normally came and gathered during the day, either to talk of family matters of common interest or to drink beer while they gossiped about general topics including reminiscences of the past. It is also the place where the young children who look after their brothers and sisters often gathered. This tree was only about twenty-five yards from our house.

Dɔɔr-iɛrɛ, our sister's son, had had an accident with a cap-gun when he was firing it at a funeral. The barrel of the gun exploded and blew off all the fingers of his left hand. This happened when I was very little or before I was even born. There was a man called Lhee, from Sila-yir, my father's mother's parish. He either did not like putting oil on his skin after taking a bath or he naturally had a dry skin. Whatever the reason, his skin was always dry and scaly. During my childhood I revelled playing in dirt and however many times my mother bathed me, my skin still looked dry and scaly, so I was nicknamed after this man. I did not realise until very recently that I had dry skin. This man was the grandfather of my brother Tiisip's mother, Maar. As a result, Maar always refrained calling me by my nickname but called me her 'grandfather' instead.

Dɔɔr-iɛrɛ's wife, Germuo, the daughter of my father's elder sister, Kpomo, was supposed to be my girl friend. I do not know how and why she came to be called my girl friend, but all I know is that since the time I could comprehend things, she had always called me her boy friend when she visited my mother's dormitory. Anyhow, on this particular day, Dɔɔr-iɛrɛ, who had always taken me as a playmate or joking partner, jokingly started to insult me saying that my buttocks were scaly like those of Lhee or those of a monkey; and so I could not call his wife my girlfriend. I retorted with my own teasing insult, saying that because his hand was like that of a leper, his wife jilted him and took me as her boyfriend. It was rude for a boy of my age to insult an adult that way even though he was a brother; but because it was a joke no one took any offence. In fact everyone under that tree was laughing and I could see my father killing himself with laughter on his easy-chair. This abusive dialogue between Dɔɔr-iɛrɛ and myself kept everyone there in stitches. But when my father felt that I was going too far he gave me a chiding, telling me to refrain from my rudeness. It was then I realised my folly and stopped.

CHAPTER THREE

The Opening of the Lawra Primary School

PRIOR TO MY MOTHER'S DEATH, my father had been one of the signatories to the rebuilding of a new school in the district. The two divisional chiefs, Gana, the Jirapa Nũũ, and Kũnkuu, the Nandom Nũũ were loathe to sign an agreement with the government for the building of a school in the district because of a previous bitter experience. In 1919 a school was built but a child died there in suspicious circumstances and therefore these two chiefs feared that the same thing could happen again.[a] In order of seniority the two chiefs should have signed the agreement before my father; for my father was acting as the Lawra Nũũ because the new chief had not yet been enstooled. However, as my father did not see it in the same light as they did, he consented and signed the document first; and as the two chiefs didn't want to look conservative in the eyes of the District Commissioner they too went forward and signed the document which authorised the Government to give a grant for the building of the school.

In early 1935, the headteacher-to-be went round from village to village selecting his pupils. His name was William H. Henkel, whose father was a German administrator and whose mother was a Wangara;[18] for the senior Henkel was stationed at Kete Krachi in German Togoland before the first World War.[19] Mr Henkel came to our house one afternoon in the harmattan or the dry season to select his new pupils. He was accompanied by Mr Adams, the District Commissioner's clerk. We had just returned from grazing the cattle when we were called to gather around so he could make his selection. The criterion which Mr Henkel used to choose the pupils from our house was to let each of us put our arms over our heads and if the tips of the index fingers passed over the lobes of the ears he or she was said to be too old for school and if the tip of the index finger did not reach the lobe he or she was too young.

By this criterion, four of my brothers were selected to join the first

---

[a] The date when this school opened differs from scholar to scholar or researcher to researcher. This was the school that my brother Zoi and his uncle Miiru and the late J.A.Karbo, the Lawra Nũũ, and the late Dasɛbri, the DC's interpreter, all attended. (This was the 'Hausa school' started by A.C. Duncan-Johnstone to train the sons of chiefs. Ed.)

new intake; that is, Nuũnatuo (Nana), Bizɔɔla (Biz), Gyubunu (Gyub) and Debomo (Deb). It seemed a very arbitrary method of selection to adopt. For Nana was older than Tiisip who was rejected for being too old and I for being too young; even though he accepted Deb who was no more than a month or two older than me. However, since children's births were not recorded in those days and even still today in many parts of the country, that was one of the only means by which he could have selected his pupils. I do not think, however, it was the same criterion he used in selecting from other villages; for some boys in their early puberty were recruited into the school, most of whom were made school prefects.

One of our sisters, Kɔnzɔl, was selected as well; however when she went to Lawra with the aim of going to school, she was not admitted but stayed in Mr Henkel's house as a maid- servant. I understand he was grooming her to be his wife when she grew up. Anyway, when holidays came and Kɔnzɔl went home, she refused to return the following year to work as a maidservant instead of learning. All Mr Henkel's frequent visits to our house failed to get her to return.

Mr Henkel did not get his full intake of pupils for the first year. And as a new man in the district, he probably consulted the District Commissioner about what to do. When my brothers who had been selected went to Lawra, they found that the school buildings were not ready to accommodate them; so they were put up in town while the workers carried on with the construction work. Lessons were carried out in town until the middle of April. Then on April 15, 1935, the school in Lawra was officially opened. A few months later Deb had guinea-worm and was sent back home for treatment. [a]

This depleted Mr Henkel's intake still further. He needed forty-five pupils for a full intake but he had only forty including Deb whose name was still on the register and no other parents were ready to send their children for enrolment. The District Commissioner, Mr Elison, was a friend of my father, so he approached him and asked if he would like to send more children to school as there were still five vacancies to be filled. He intimated that since he was the initiator of

---

[a] Debomo later acquired the name David (Dave) when he went over to the U.K. for further training. (Debomo became a Clerk of Works and building contractor, constructing the Black Star Hotel at Bolgatanga. Nana became a medical orderly and succeeded his father as Chief, Bizɔɔla and Gyub became teachers, the first tried his hand at politics, the second became an officer in the Army. Ed.)

the building of the school, its failure would reflect on him as having sold a white elephant to his people. Because my father ardently believed in education, he told Mr Elison he would think about it. It should be remembered that children in the rural areas were and still are economically valuable to their parents in farming and the herding of cattle. Unless it was someone like my father, who had a lot of children, they would not like to let any of their children go to school. So initially it was only the relatively wealthy parents, most of whom were chiefs, who allowed their children to go to school and in most cases those were children who were orphans (anyone who had lost their mother).

Months passed by and I was longing to see my elder brothers in Lawra. One day, my father with his faithful linguist, Sakpi, was about to go to Lawra for the usual administrative duties. Itɔ, an elder brother, and I wanted to follow them but the bigger boys were told to hold us back whilst my father and Sakpi cycled off. When they had ridden about half a mile away from us, to the plateau of Kuor-zu, the boys released us from their clutches.

Itɔ pursued them using short cuts across Kuor-zu and was able to catch up with them, so they gave him a ride to Lawra. Even if they had not done so, Itɔ knew the way to Lawra and had been there on several occasions for injections at the district hospital. Anyway, I was not that lucky; for I had lost sight of the party. However, I persevered until I came to Pũ-yi-teŋ at the top of a hill where there was a T-junction. This was about four to five miles from home and half way to Lawra. The road on my left led to Dapla which was a custom's post in the French colony of Ivory Coast, and the other led to Lawra where I wanted to go. I could see the zinc roofs of the District offices as well as a Catholic church on a hill in Tuori next to the school buildings; this was about five miles.

Unfortunately, I did not know which way to take since I had never been outside Birifu except to Fofoi, which marks the boundary between Birifu and Kuũnyukuũ. There was no one near I could ask. As a result, I sat down and wept bitterly for almost half an hour. I had never been that far from home. Apart from being tired and thirsty, there was nothing I could do but retrace my steps home. When I reached there, I fabricated a story, which I would later regret, in order to make people believe I had actually walked to Lawra and back.

I told them that I reached Lawra and that my sister Kɔnzɔl had gone to fetch some water in a calabash. She brought it to me, knelt down, and gave it to me to drink. I should say it was and still is the custom in the area for women to kneel down when offering water or food to a person, especially to a male or a visitor. I also told them I returned on the back of Sakpi's cycle and I was dropped off to come home while they passed to the zongo (strangers quarters) at Kuũnyukuũ to see my father's friend, Malam Sissi. Any time my father travelled, his younger brother, Dɔɔtaa, who was given nick-name of Gaziere by Hausa speaking people because of his short height, would be left in charge of the house. So when he heard my story he asked some women to go to the pito houses and buy some pots of pito (sorghum beer) to await the arrival of my father. Not only did he order pots of pito, he also asked that a guinea-fowl be slaughtered and plucked for in preparation for my father's meal.

Little did I know that my father was not returning home that day since the meeting in Lawra was going to take up to three days. When it was about 9.00 o'clock in the evening and my father did not return, Gaziere knew I had told a lie. So he called me before him and if I had not just been recently orphaned, he would have given me a hiding I would not have forgotten. I was really very lucky to get away with a lashing of his tongue. When my father returned on the third day and was told the yarns I had spun about him, he laughed, pulled me by his side and asked if I wanted to go to school. My face lit up with pleasure and my reply was some rapid, emphatic nods. So with his tongue in his cheek, he told his younger brother that I should be included in the batch of my brothers that was to meet him in Lawra to be taken to the school for admission. This was because he had to leave for Nandom for another gathering of chiefs and did not want me to repeat my escapade. My uncle took my father's word literally and so included me among the brothers that were to be taken to school.

It was not until the early hours of one August morning that I was to be awoken from sleep and told I was going to school that day. You should have seen the joy that came to my sleepy face. I immediately got up and joined my other brothers. This must have been about three or four o'clock in the morning. My other brothers were Sɔrkumɔ, who died in his penultimate year of school in 1944, Dɛri, who was an Agricultural Assistant and died in about 1968 and Tiisip, who is now a retired bank manager from the Agricultural Development Bank, Lawra.[20] There were about five women carrying pots of pito which my father had ordered to be brewed and brought to him in Lawra. We set out on the nine mile walk to Lawra.

I was the youngest in the group but the excitement of going to school made me forget the pain of walking those nine miles. I chatted away, telling them of the distance I had covered during my last escapade, especially any time we arrived at a hall mark I had set myself during that journey. This was getting on my uncle's nerves and he told me to shut up or else he would cane me thoroughly. So I stopped talking until we reached Lawra at about seven o'clock in the morning. My father was expecting the party, though not to see me among them. After giving us a good breakfast and some of the pito the women had brought with us, he tried to persuade me to return home with him. But I would not listen to his persuasions. I did not say no but my facial expression of dissent told it all. Seeing that he would break my heart if he forced me to return, he eventually relented and said I could go to school with the rest of my brothers.

The reason my father did not want me to go to school at that time was because I had recently been orphaned and was the youngest of my mother's children; having such a baby face he thought I was too young to assimilate my lessons. But I was to prove him wrong in the not very distant future. Anyway, my father had made an appointment that day with his colonial friend, the District Commissioner of Lawra. We went to the District Commissioner's office before going to the school for registration. For it was Mr Elison who advised him that as there was a high rate of infant mortality in the family, it might be to his best advantage if he sent most of his children to school. Besides, it would make no difference to my father whether the children died at school or at home. After being introduced to the District Commissioner, we set off to the school, which was about one and a half miles from town. We had not gone far when a torrential August rain began to pour down without the least warning. By the time we got to the school, the whole party was drenched to the skin.

My father introduced us to the Principal Teacher of the school (at that time Headmasters were called Principal Teachers). After the introduction our names were entered in the school register and the Principal took my father and his entourage to his quarters to entertain them. Then they all left for home and he returned to the class. There and then we were put into the 'Lawra compound' for pupils from the Lawra Division. It would seem Mr Henkel was aware of our impending arrival since he was not the least surprised. He immediately wrote the vowels followed by the consonants of the vernacular alphabet on a card for each of us to learn, and he assigned some of the boys who were already there to help us do so. I found it easy to memorise my vowels by associating them with names of animals or objects in my tongue. So that evening I knew all my vowels together with the consonants.

At that time no pictures were used to represent letters in the way we were later taught at the Teacher Training College. The only letter I could not say properly was the letter "r" which is pronounced with the rolled tongue. I found it difficult to roll my tongue and pronounce the letter; so I always pronounced it as "illi-lili" and got slapped for it even on my first day at school. Indeed I got a great deal of knocks from Yakuu Karbo, a relation of the late chief of Lawra, and from Manuɔr Gaŋ-man for the mispronunciation of this silly letter. This was to be a subject of teasing which my brothers, especially Nana and Dɛri who were great teasers, continued to use at home; and even illiterate brothers like Kpaari, Zumɔka and others teased me with it, just to annoy me, even though they did not understand what all that was about.

The next day Mr Henkel asked us to read to him and was surprised to find me able to read the whole alphabet except the wretched "r". So he caned Gaŋ-man who was supposed to teach me and of course I later bore the brunt of it from him from then onwards. However, it was not long before I was left on my own as I could read without being able to pronounce the letter nonetheless. For once I started reading words and sentences I could recognize the word containing the letter without being called upon to pronounce the letter alone.

In the 1930's the Native Authority system was introduced into the Gold Coast. This was developed in Northern Nigeria by Lord Lugard, the then Governor, and it was thought that since the cultural and social organisation of the peoples of the Northern Territories (N.Ts.) of the Gold Coast had some affinity with that in Northern Nigeria, the system should first be tried there. Consequently, the N.Ts. were divided into Native Administration areas. That of Lawra was called the Lawra-Tumu Confederacy Native Authority which comprised the Jirapa, Lawra, Nandom and Tumu Divisions, each headed by a Divisional Chief. As a result the Principal named his school dormitories by these divisional names. All boys from the Jirapa Division were housed in the Jirapa compound, those from Lawra were housed in the Lawra compound and those from the Nandom Division were housed in the Nandom compound. As there were then no boys from Tumu at that time, the Tumu compound was left unoccupied. But Mr Henkel discovered that the Lawra compound had more boys than any of the two other compounds and the Nandom compound had the least. So my brothers Tiisip and later Debomo were housed in that compound even though they were from the Lawra Division.

CHAPTER FOUR

At The Junior School

AFTER BEING ASSIGNED OUR DORMITORIES, we were introduced to our respective compound captains or prefects, called 'chiefs' (*Naminɛ* or *Nũũ* singular). The first school and dormitory prefects and other office holders were:

Dakura Nɔnɔ[a]	School Nũũ
Yakuu Karbo[b]	Lawra Nũũ
Yiryele Baanyɛ[c]	Asst. Lawra Nũũ
Ŋminyɛla Diepɔɔ[d]	Jirapa Nũũ

---

[a] One of the Colonial Officers stationed in Lawra had presented the school with a small table-top printing machine which Mr Henkel taught a few boys including Dakura Nɔnɔ how to use. When the Native Authorities started imposing taxes in their areas tickets were first printed and paid for from the south. Mr Henkel decided that the school could save the Authority some money if it was allowed to print these tickets for the Authority. Dakura and a couple of boys were detailed to do the printing of these tickets with the supervision of Henkel himself. At the end of 1939 when Nɔnɔ was considered too big to go the Middle school in Tamale, he was employed by the Native Authority as full time ticket printer. He later became the Gbari Nũũ and died in 1992.

[b] Yakuu Karbo is a relation of the late Lawra Nũũ, J.A. Karbo. He trained as a Native Authority sanitary overseer after his standard three education. He resigned from the Native Authority service and opened the family shop in Lawra. He became a court bailiff in the District Commissioner's court in Lawra and later a bailiff in the magistrates' court from which service he has now retired.

[c] Yiriyele Baanyɔ, the son of the chief of Kalsaɣri in the Lawra division, trained at the Native Authority Agricultural School in Tamale after his middle school education. He was appointed as an Agricultural Instructor to the farmers. On the death of his father, he succeeded him as the Kalsaɣri Nũũ.

[d] Ŋminyɛla Diepɔɔ was the son of the chief of Siɣri in the Jirapa division. He was one of those big boys who could not go to the Tamale Middle School. He trained as a ploughman at Zuarungo Agricultural Station and later returned to demonstrate ploughing with bullocks to the farmers in the district. He resigned from that position and joined the Medical Field Unit (MFU) and became the Siɣri Nũũ when his father died until his own death in about 1989.

Dakura Ŋminwule[a]	Asst. Jirapa Nũũ
Kele Gyiɛlɛ[b]	Nandom Nũũ
Ar-iɔŋn Paga[c]	Asst. Nandom Nũũ
Diedɔŋ Dɔmbɔ[d]	Dining hall Chairman
Maanuɔr Gaŋ-man[e]	Asst. Dining hall Chairman
Darmaani Dakura[f]	Office boy
Nibɛvuur	Dispensary orderly

There were other appointments such as those to the school police force, which caught culprits for going against school regulations, for being late at roll calls or for not having taken a proper bath. This police force was headed by Ŋminyɛla Diepɔɔ assisted by Pusaŋwiɛ who was greatly feared by most of the smaller boys for his false arrests. The judges were made up of the compound prefects headed by the school prefect. This was a system I hated all through out my junior school days. The so-called accused, called prisoners, were arraigned before the judges and if found guilty, were given a heavy punishment that was not commensurate with the crime. In any case

---

[a] Dakura Ŋminwule was the son of the Tiza Nũũ and like Ŋminyɛla he was sent to train as a ploughman in the Agricultural Station in Zuarungo. He worked for the NA for a while and when the Agricultural Station in Babile was built they were both taken over by Mr Hinds, the first Agricultural Officer there. Dakura resigned and did the ploughing in his own farms complementing that with hunting big game. He succeeded his father as the Tiza Nũũ and is now dead.

[b] Kele Gyiɛlɛ was the son of the chief of Guo in the Nandom Division. After his standard three education he joined the Tsetse Control Unit (now MFU) in 1940. What has become of him I do not know.

[c] Ar-iɔŋn Paga after leaving school at standard three was sent to Tamale to train as NA sanitary overseer and when he returned was employed in that capacity until his retirement and death.

[d] Diedɔŋ Dɔmbɔ (S.D. Dombo) is the son of the late Duori Nũũ, and was a founder of the Northern Peoples' Party.

[e] Manuɔr Gaŋ-man was son of the chief of Lisa. After his middle school education he trained as a Native Authority Agricultural Instructor and was soon gazetted as an Agricultural Assistant. He rose to become an Agricultural Officer in charge of the Babile station. He died a premature death through a car accident.

[f] Darmani Dakura was the son of the Han Nũũ. After his standard three education, he went to the Mampong Trade School to train as an artisan. From there he joined the army and was demobilised immediately after the war. On his return he was employed as NA foreman but died prematurely in the early 1950s.

they were presumed guilty until proved innocent. No wonder they were called prisoners and not the accused. I could not remember any person ever being freed once they had appeared before this court of "star chamber", to borrow a term from English Legal History.

If you pleaded guilty at first, you stood a better chance of getting a lighter sentence than if you pleaded not guilty. I presume there was an appeal to the Principal Teacher but to the best of my knowledge nobody had ever taken this course. In the first instance, one was never aware of his name having been taken until the day of the judgment when one's name was called out and one was frog-marched before the judges; so one had no time to prepare one's defence. Secondly, the judges were biased in favour of the prosecution and so even if you had a defence, it would be fruitless presenting one. Thirdly, there was no appeal from this star chamber court to any higher court. As a result, many boys including myself would plead guilty even if they were not. It was a system that was full of cruelty and injustice from which there was no appeal.

After only about a few weeks in the school, my right foot had been affected by whitlow (gbɛr pla), which was one of the ailments that was supposed to have killed my mother. As a small boy, I did not know what was wrong with me. I thought it was a needle from a thorn tree that I had stepped on, and which probably broke and had left a part in the sole of my foot. My foot became septic and contained pus. It was therefore the duty of the dispensary orderly to cut open the swollen foot. Fearing that I would squirm with fear and therefore struggle if the wound was cut open, some big boys were asked to hold me down, while Nibɛvuuri cut open the wound with a razor. He was surprised how well I took it and called me his brave little boy. I was given a hot dressing with lint that had been boiled and in a short time the wound healed. From then on he called me his little brave friend.

The first year, which was a short one for me, passed very quickly. We were sent on vacation about December 19 for two months. In February 1936, we returned to school. On our return, at the onset there were many changes. Dakura Nɔnɔ was dismissed from his post as the School Nũũ and was replaced by Diedɔŋ Dɔmbɔ. His crime was only known to a few as no one was told publicly what he had done to merit the dismissal from his post. To me he seemed an efficient and fair School Nũũ even for the short period I had known him in that post. However, in that school, ours was not to reason why, ours was to do as we were told. Dakura Nɔnɔ was reduced to a commoner. This must have sapped his confidence a great deal in many of his school activities. For Dakura was very brilliant in his first year but in later years that brilliance dwindled away. His exuberance was no longer there. As a result of his demotion, Manuɔr Gaŋ-man was promoted to be the Dining Hall chairman and my eldest brother, Sɔrkumɔ Gandah, and Bɛsuɔ were appointed as his deputies.

As far as classes were concerned, some of the early entrants were promoted to class two. Those who did not pass their test and the five of us who came to school at the latter part of the year were asked to repeat a class. However, in about June of that year I and my brother Deb, whose first year of studies had been interrupted by his illness, were promoted to class two to join the other pupils. On the very day of our promotion to class two, Mr Henkel was giving the class an English spelling test. I was seated near my school chum, Abayifaa Karbo[a] who was very good in English spelling as well as other subjects. He spelt out the words and allowed me to copy his spellings. When our slates were marked by Mr Henkel, he got twenty-one marks and I scored the same. This amazed Mr Henkel and he wanted to cane all those pupils who scored less than I did. That would have been the entire class except Ar-iɔŋn Paga and Abayifaa.

However, to save them from being caned for nothing, I owned up that I had copied from Abyifaa's slate. Mr Henkel was so pleased with my honesty that he caned neither me nor the other pupils. Having become ashamed of what I had done, I learnt all the words that were given us for the spelling test and any that were subsequently taught us in class. So for the next test I had a very high score and Mr Henkel wanted to know if I had again copied from my chum. I answered in the negative but some of the pupils claimed that I had done so. So Mr Henkel asked for all those who thought I had copied to raise their hands. Ar-iɔŋn, Diedɔŋ, Biz and Manuɔr raised their hands claiming that I had copied the spelling from my friend. To prove that I did not copy from anyone, Mr Henkel placed the four of us at each corner of the classroom and the fifth pupil was placed in the centre of the class. We were then given a fresh spelling test there and then

---

[a] A. Karbo trained as teacher after which he opened the ɛremon Day school. He was the first to return to the Teacher Training College with E.A. Mahama in order to obtain his Certificate A training. He entered Parliament in 1954 under the ticket of the Northern Peoples' Party (NPP). He had a formidable opponent in the person of my brother, Nuɔnatuo Gandah, the late Birifu Nũũ III who opposed him on a Convention Peoples' Party (CPP) ticket.

whilst the others watched. Lo and behold! it was only Ar-iɔŋn who managed to beat me. So Mr Henkel caned each of them for falsely accusing me. As the year progressed, I began to compete with some of the brightest pupils in the class and by the September quarterly examination, I became fourteenth in the whole class of about twenty-eight or thirty boys. I still remember that position well because I was able to beat my brother, Nana, whose position was fifteenth. I was proud of myself for only having been in that class for just under three months. In any case this was a respectable position to achieve out of about thirty or so pupils.

We took our final tests in December before we left for the long vacation. When we returned in February, 1937, I found that some of the boys I had beaten in the test the previous year were promoted to standard one, an example par excellence being my brother, Nana, while I was only promoted to class three. I could not understand at that time how these promotions worked out; but even if I had, I would not have dared challenge any of the decisions, however wrong they might be. Tiisip and others who were in class one were promoted to class three to join those of us promoted from class two. Apart from Abayifaa, I was the whizz-kid in arithmetic problems. So although I was in class three, I was constantly called upon to standard one classroom to answer problems of arithmetic when none of them knew the solution. I was also very quick in mental arithmetic, which gave Mr Henkel the excuse to cane all of them for allowing a junior to solve their problems. For that reason I was not very popular with some of the big boys in standard one, especially with the prefects.

The normal day in the school ran like this. There was the reveille at 5.30 in the morning when the whistle was blown and we got up and cleaned our dormitories. At 6 a.m. there was the roll call, when we paraded in front of our dormitories and marched to the tune of xylophone music from there to a central point in front of the Union Jack; this was hoisted on the flag pole at six o'clock every morning and taken down at six in the evening. The xylophone players were Pɔlkuu Kũnkuu[a] and Nana. The roll was checked and each compound prefect reported to the School Nũũ who in turn reported to Mr

---

[a] Pɔlkuu Kũnkuu trained as a teacher after which he opened the Nandom Day School in 1946. He later returned to the college for his Certificate A course as a specialist teacher in Agriculture and married my late sister, Pɔɔpla. On Imoru's death he succeeded him as the Nandom-Nũũ and later became member of the PNDC. He died in 1984 with cancer of the pancreas.

Henkel. After the roll call, Mr Henkel drilled us (this was later known as physical training) to some tunes of xylophone music for at least half an hour until 7 a.m. The big boys were then marched to the school farm where each dormitory was allotted some acres of land to cultivate and tend for the farming season.

The smaller boys were asked to go to the bush to fetch firewood, which the cooks could use to prepare our food. More often than not I was asked to lead the group. I was more or less like the firewood prefect on those days. So I usually marched them to the bush and returned within an hour to get back before bath time. At 8 a.m. there was another call when we ran down to a pond, which was probably created when the school was being built, to take our baths. Breakfast was at 8.30 a.m., and at 9 a.m. there was another roll call for classes when we again assembled in front of our compounds to march to the flagstaff. However, prior to that, the senior prefect would go round from dormitory to dormitory to see if it had been kept clean; if that was not the case, woe betide the pupils responsible.

They were either given instant punishment, which meant a caning, or their names were taken to appear before the school court. When the roll was taken at the flagstaff, Mr Henkel inspected each child's nails and hair to see that they were cut short and also that each child's teeth and uniform were kept clean. He looked for short cut hair, combed and well parted, or heads shaven for those of us with ringworm. Everyone's teeth were inspected to see that they had been properly cleaned after breakfast and after lunch. If a child was found not to comply with all these rules, then the compound prefect was in trouble. Mr Henkel would cane the prefect and if he did so, the child was in greater trouble, for the prefect would then cane him twice as much. On the other hand, if the senior prefect was caned for your error, then he would cane your compound prefect for allowing you to commit the misdemeanour; and your compound prefect would in turn cane you for allowing him to be caned. So in the long run you ended up receiving four times the original punishment meted out to the senior prefect in the first place. This was the brutality to which we were subjected in that school, a legacy that left its print for a very long time.

After Mr Henkel's inspection of the parade, we were marched off to our respective classrooms. Although there were four classes, Mr Henkel was the only teacher teaching them. Lessons finished for classes one, two and three at eleven-thirty in the morning whilst standard one finished their lessons half an hour later. Lunch was between twelve noon and twelve thirty in the afternoon and after lunch everybody was supposed to be in their dormitories for the afternoon rest or siesta, except those who were undergoing the punishments that had been meted out by the school court. If you were not undergoing any punishment and wandered out of the dormitory and were seen by the school police (or rather I should say a 'provost', since this was more like a military camp than a school), your name was taken down for the next court.

At two in the afternoon there was another roll call, from whence we were marched to our classrooms for the afternoon lessons. Those lessons finished at about three thirty and we again went to the farm to return at four thirty for games. However, when there was enough farm work to be done, the games were given a miss. Games finished at five thirty and we rushed down to the pond to have our baths. Although we had communal bath cubicles for each compound, seldom did we use those except in the dry season when there was no water in the pond. Between six and six thirty in the evening, we had our dinner and at seven there was another roll call when we gathered at the flagstaff to tell stories or have a singsong. Those in standard classes went for private studies in their classrooms. At eight the day's activities came to a close and we were marched to our dormitories to sleep. If anyone was found not to be in bed within a short time, the provost would take his name or the compound prefect would give it to a provost so he could be called before the school court on the next Friday.

On Saturdays we washed our clothes at the pond. During the dry season when there was no water we went down to the Black Volta river at the shallow crossing called Man gbulu that divided the Gold Coast from the French colonies of the Ivory Coast and Upper Volta. This was about four to five miles from the school and we normally returned at about three in the afternoon. After an hour's rest, we went for firewood or did some general cleaning around the school or beat some sisal hemp for our handicraft lessons. Saturday evenings were for dancing after dinner. One was supposed to enjoy dancing but how could that be achieved when one's belly was either too full to dance or one was too tired to enjoy it. In any case if the prefects felt we were not enjoying the dance they would collect gravel from the ground and throw it at us or they would whip us while we were dancing. This must have been one of the reasons why I did not enjoy dancing until I went to a senior school. For I do not believe in pretence and could not pretend to enjoy dancing when indeed I did not.

On Sundays, after the morning roll call, there was a general march past in different sorts of formations when Mr Henkel stood on the pedestal of the flagstaff which was raised to about thirty inches from the ground. There he took the salute under the Union Jack like a General taking a salute on parade. The Union Jack was the symbol of the British Monarchy and every child was supposed to salute it like soldiers saluting their commanding officer when they met him; that is, the child was supposed to salute the flag from three paces before and three paces after in their daily walk whenever they happened to pass by it. Any child who was caught violating this rule underwent a trial at the school court. The day was thus full of parades and roll calls. With so many rules in the school, it was impossible for any child to escape being caught for infringing some of them except for some of the bigger boys who were feared by the school provosts. Moreover the only people who escaped arrest were the prefects; they could not do any wrong except in front of the eyes of the principal teacher. After the march past there was the general cleaning to be done on the school grounds. After breakfast the entire school went to fetch firewood, or went to beat or fetch sisal hemp if the stock was exhausted. Public Holidays took the same form as Saturdays or Sundays. We never had any rest; it was work, work, work, and punishment on top of that.

The year 1937 was the Coronation year of King George VI. For King Edward VIII, who succeeded his father King George V, had abdicated for his love for a divorcee before he could be anointed king. So a lot of preparations were being made in the school as the pupils had to entertain all the chiefs and people of the Lawra-Tumu Confederacy District who were going to attend. The entertainment consisted of sports both for the school pupils and for men and women who wanted to take part. Besides the sports, the school had prepared songs and dramas, a sort of revue, for the public. Since the re-opening of the school, Mr Henkel had devoted all his energy to rehearsals of drama, songs and recitations. Those in standard one were given recitations and short plays to learn.

Diedɔŋ in particular was given recitations to learn and recite because he had that projecting voice that most actors would love to have, and indeed the more recitations he learnt the more his voice improved. No wonder he became a good speaker in later years. Apart from the rehearsals, we were engaged in constructing sheds for the distinguished guests since the week's program was all to take place in the school. As the days approached, the police, who were under the command of Sgt.

Nɔga, with the prison warders who had some part to perform, came to the school to rehearse. The school children were engaged in lining both sides of the road leading to town with stones and whitewashing these with clay together with all the compounds in the school. Bunting was hung along both sides of the road that led to the town; stones were also placed along the streets in town by the school children. The chiefs and people of the four divisions had been gathering in town about three days earlier. So for the three days prior to the Coronation day, the town was buzzing with tribal drumming and dancing. There was great excitement among the school children even though we were up to our necks with last minute decorations so as to finish the work before the day.

On the eve of the day of the Coronation there was a heavy downpour of rain that washed off almost all of our whitewashing. As a result we had to get up very early that morning to re-paint all the stones and dormitories and we kept our fingers crossed in the hope that there would be no further rain. Prior to the day, we also had fetched firewood that we piled mountain high to be used for a bonfire. The fire from the bonfire was to ignite and throw the rockets into the air, one of which displayed the portrait of the new King and Queen. We were indeed lucky that we had no further rains throughout the entire week. The events were spread over a week and more. On each day's celebrations the arrival of the chiefs at the school was heralded by drumming and music. As the chiefs rode on their horses showing their expertness in horsemanship, their subjects trotted behind them.

Once they had arrived and were seated, the whole area became filled with a sea of umbrellas and palanquins of different sizes and colours. Before the advent of the Native Authority system, there were more than four divisions in the Lawra-Tumu district. Each divisional chief had been given a standard with his own colours. My father had his own standard hoisted on a pole which he took along at each chiefs' meeting. It was also used as a symbol of his authority to summon any person to his court. These banners were still carried by these chiefs even though their positions had been merged into four larger divisions. These banners added extra colour to the splendour of the place.

At the end of each day's event we were allowed to visit our parents or relations who had come to celebrate the Coronation with us. The climax of the events was the fireworks display. The eight Gandah brothers trooped to town as soon as we were dismissed to see our father who entertained us lavishly as though we were at home. Every school child was presented with a coronation mug which had on it the heads of the King and the Queen to commemorate the event. We presented our eight mugs to my father.

After the hectic fortnight of celebrations and excitement, when all the chiefs and people had returned home, the town was left desolate and lifeless. Life at school became very dull and was never the same again for me. I felt homesick the moment my father and his entourage had gone home. I thought of my younger brothers who were tending the sheep and cattle and wished I could join them.

Even though the school duties were very strenuous, up to this point it had not been at the back of my mind to run away from school. We returned to our school duties as soon as the celebrations had finally ended. Because of the preparations for the Coronation, the school farm had been neglected; so we spent all week there whilst Mr Henkel and some clerks in town who had formed a tennis club, travelled to Wa for a tennis tournament against a local team. All this time it did not occur to me to plan my escape, even though my desire to be home became stronger and stronger every day. Then one day I was asked to lead the smaller boys to the bush to fetch firewood. Where we went to fetch the firewood was beyond Tuori, the present site of the Lawra Secondary School. We were almost near the Lawra-Birifu main road and I could see the famous hill, Sobaal-tɔŋ. The sight of this hill increased my longing for home instantly.

At that moment I took my chance like a flash. I gave my command to one of the boys and told him that I wanted to free my bowels in the bush. I then went further into the bush towards the main road and when I was totally out of their sight, I took to my heels in the direction of my village, into Kuol, a settlement mentioned in the Kusiele Bagre recital, crossing little swamps and rivers to get there. I was lucky it was not the period of the heavy rains; for then I could not have gone far and might have drowned in attempting to cross some of these rivers or streams. Anyway, within half an hour I had hit the main road leading to my village and I left Sobaal-tɔŋ behind me. As I walked home, I often ran into a side road to hide myself any time a cyclist came from behind in case I was discovered missing and was being looked for.

I followed the road until about four o'clock in the afternoon when I hit the ridge on which the Birifu rest-house was situated. At the village rest-house, boys of my age were herding the sheep and goats in the meadow on the plateau and were paddling in a water hole. I joined them until evening when those in charge of the cattle came from Gbatɛri to meet us and we brought the animals home. I was too scared to approach my father but somehow I had to tell him I had run away from school and was no longer interested in schooling. Surprisingly enough, he was very calm about it and not annoyed with me as I had feared. He pampered me that evening and sent me to bed as I was very tired after having walked nine miles.

When the school could not trace my whereabouts, they must have reported the matter to the Lawra Nũũ who despatched one of the Native Authority policemen to report my disappearance to my father. Meanwhile the whole bush around the school was searched in case I had been caught by a wild animal. For the surrounding bush was full of hyenas and leopards. By the time the policeman arrived in Birifu through torrential rain, I was fast asleep when he broke the news about my absence to my father; my father laughed and told him I was safe at home and that he would return me to school the next day. The next morning the cowherds had milked the cows and filled a very large basin which my dad was sharing among all the kids in the house. I was given my share since he knew I loved milk very much for my breakfast. When I had finished drinking my milk mashed in thick porridge, he gave me some pocket money and asked his linguist, Sakpi, to take me on his bicycle to Lawra.

As I was aware of what was awaiting me in Lawra, I refused to sit on the bar of the cycle that would take me back to school. It was then that my father lost his temper, came down from the roof of his house to the forecourt and gave me a good whipping. I quickly got on to the bar of the bicycle and Sakpi rode off with me. But as soon as we were out of sight of my father and of the palace, at the edge of the plateau sloping down to Fofoi, I stood astride on the bar of the cycle thus preventing him from pedalling. Sakpi called upon one of the farmers from Kɔntɔ Wura's house who was farming in his compound farm just by the roadside to come and help him put me on the bicycle. As we descended the hill and came to Fofoi, as soon as he had crossed the bridge and was ascending another hill, I again got myself astride on the bar of the bicycle. Being his brother-in-law he was shy and loathe to hit me as my dad did. Indeed from my childhood I cannot ever remember Sakpi using his hand on me or even scolding me.

So he begged and begged until I decided to go with him only after he had told me he would take me to the school and bring me back again. For if I told the teacher I did not like the school, I would be allowed to return with him. I believed him and accepted his word. Within a couple of hours we had arrived at Lawra and he took me to the Lawra Nũũ's palace and reported to him that he was returning me to school. After refreshing ourselves with the pito which was offered to us by the grace of the chief's hospitality, the Lawra Nũũ told me of his own little escapade when he was a school boy but which he now regretted. I paid no heed to what he was saying and his words passed through one ear and out at the other; I was so determined to leave the school which seemed like a prisoner-of-war camp to me. After his advice and when the pito had been drunk, we rode off to school

When we got there, the entire school was doing general farming. I was taken to see Mr Henkel at his house where I was prepared to beard the lion, in this case Mr Henkel. He asked me whether I did not like the school any more and I replied to him in the affirmative. He then told me that he would cane me before dismissing me from school. I was pleased about that remark so I quickly seized my brother-in-law's walking stick and gave it to him to cane me with so that I could return home with him. This rude behaviour must have shocked and incensed Mr Henkel a lot, since no boy had ever been so rude to him even though most of them were young men. He called out to Diedɔŋ, the school prefect, to Dakura Ŋminwule, nicknamed Broad, who was the Asst. Jirapa Nũũ, and were in the vicinity at the time, and told them to carry me off to the school farm. Diedɔŋ picked me up like a feather and put me on his shoulders without any effort at all. I struggled to get down but he would not release his iron grip. So I put my arms round his throat and started strangling him so that he would release me.

Sakpi had ridden far off and Mr Henkel shouted to them to put me down and to cane me all the way to the school farm, which was about three quarters of a mile away. However, Diedɔŋ found it difficult to release my hands from his throat. So he virtually lay on the ground with me and instructed Broad to press my hands on the ground against the gravel. That did the trick for I quickly let go my hold as soon as Broad pressed my hands against the gravel with his foot. When he got up, there were some young acacia trees near by and they both cut branches from them and started caning me while I ran to the farm.

Diedɔŋ vented his anger on me; for as he whipped he commanded me to run faster. Mr Henkel followed on his bicycle telling them to cane me harder and more often. I wailed and yelled, hoping that Sakpi was still nearby to rescue me from such brutality. But that was a forlorn hope. By the time I got to the farm, there were no more tears left in my eyes and the wails sounded like those of an old Dagara lady approaching the funeral stand of a relative, mourning the dead. As we reached the farm, all eyes were gazing at me. I was ordered to do tasks far beyond my capabilities, and if I could not do them I was whipped. My brothers, Dɛri and Nana, who were great teasers, often took great pleasure in my plight, imitating my cries and wails and mocking me whenever I annoyed them or they wanted to annoy me.

The next day after the morning roll call, Mr Henkel told me that since I told him I did not want to stay in the school any longer, he was going to cane me in front of the whole school before expelling me from the school. For he wanted to use me as an example to frighten any other boy who might want to emulate me. For my school chum, Abayifaa Karbo, and a cousin of his at a later date, did run away during that year or the preceding year. I was called in front of all the pupils at the parade ground and six big boys were asked to hold me and to stretch me out about two and a half feet from the ground. This allowed Mr Henkel to give me about one hundred and fifty strokes on my bare buttocks without ever having to bend down.

Although my whole posterior was covered in blood, I did not feel a thing after twenty or so lashes due to the numbness of the skin. The only time I reeled and writhed with agony was when Nibɛvuuri, the dispensary orderly, was asked to rub iodine onto my badly bruised bum. For two weeks I could hardly sit down. After this brutal punishment, I thought, since I had been punished for my impertinence, Mr Henkel would keep his word and dismiss me from the school. But no, he did not. On the contrary, every child in the school was asked to watch me with eagle eyes in case I attempted to run away again. Perhaps I would have done so immediately if only I could walk, so that I could show my father the bruises which were mercilessly inflicted upon me. I was now more determined than ever to escape if and when the opportunity arose and I bade my time for it.

In this year there was an outbreak of chickenpox in the school and almost every child contracted it. One of the dormitories, the vacant Tumu compound, was used as a quarantine station. There was no cure other than our bathing ourselves in water with carbolic lotion to stop the pox, which had broken into sores, from getting septic. But because of the pus in the sores, the stench that was emitted fouled the air all around. I am sure it must have come as a relief to Mr Henkel when the epidemic abated and eventually had vanished completely. Among the Gandah brothers at the time, Biz and I were badly affected and up to date one can still see the scars left on my skin by this horrible disease.

After this epidemic, the school returned to normal until one night Biz found out he could not breathe and felt pains in his chest. He was rushed to the hospital where his illness was diagnosed as pneumonia.

At that time there was no cure for pneumonia even in the United Kingdom until in the early forties M & B was discovered to be a cure for cerebro-spinal-meningitis (CSM) and other diseases such as pneumonia. So Biz's life was left in the laps of the gods. No doubt my father was told of the perilous situation in which Biz found himself. His temperature rose every day until it hovered around 104 degrees Fahrenheit. The entire school was told that if his temperature went above 105 degrees he would die.

From this moment, Biz's food was prepared from Mr Henkel's house. The senior wife of Mr Henkel, who is a sister of R.B. Braimah, was called by the name of 'M ma buba', a Hausa phrase meaning "my senior mother", and was in charge of the preparation of the food. The big boys in the school were chosen to take his meals to the hospital morning, noon and evening. Except for Deb and myself, my other brothers had gone to the hospital with his food and to see his condition. Biz was almost given up for dead. Then one evening, to my great surprise, I was called and told by the prefect that I was to accompany those boys taking his food down to town and I was to spend the night there with him. I thought this was a gentle way of hinting to me that this might be my last time of seeing my brother alive.

When evening came, I followed the two big boys to the hospital and we went into his ward where he was isolated from the other patients. After staying there for a while, the two big boys returned to the school that night while I was left to keep vigil over my sick brother. There was no possibility of my being awake all night. After a couple of hours I started to nod off. Biz, seeing my plight, urged me to lie down on the floor and go to sleep since there was no spare bed in the ward. So I lay on the cold floor without a blanket or anything to cover myself from the cold of the rainy season except the clothes I wore going to the hospital. I kept tossing here and there until daybreak when I returned to school.

My uterine brother, Dɛn, had returned from Kumasi where he had gone into voluntary exile at the time he was accused of taking part in killing his own mother by sorcery. When he returned all was forgiven and he was allowed back into the house where he had grown up. He told my father that when he was accused he had sworn to the gods to take his life within three years if he was shown to be a witch and had taken part in the death of my mother. But if he was not a witch, he would return after the three years to clear his name. So when he returned and learnt that Biz and I had been sent to school, he gave both of us a shirt. I remember mine was a green one.

When Biz was ill, my father was worried and sent his elders to diviners near and far to find out the cause. Eventually, they came back with the news that Biz's illness was caused by his uterine brother. My father was livid and told Dɛn to return to his father's house at Dabɔɔ-yir. He did so and we were ordered to return his gifts to him because it was believed that it was through these that he managed to make Biz ill. Soon afterwards Biz began to recover and his temperature began to fall below the 100 degrees level until it reached normal again. He was eventually discharged from the hospital and returned to the school where he carried on with his work.

CHAPTER FIVE

AFTER THE CORONATION CELEBRATIONS OF King George VI, we had a short break for our mid-term holidays, all of which was spent in the school, doing general farming. When school re-opened, not only did we have a new intake of pupils but also a new teacher. Mr Imoru Egala was a Native Authority clerk in Tumu at the time and as the Tumu Division did not send any pupils when the school was first opened, it was decided that an effort had to be made to include some pupils from that part of the district.[a] The authorities transferred Mr Egala from his post as a Native Authority clerk to that of a pupil teacher. Mr Egala brought with him a number of pupils from Issala land at the beginning of the second half of the school year. Consequently Mr Henkel taught classes one and two while Mr Egala taught standard one initially and later, in the course of the year, class three as well. As a pupil teacher, Mr Egala's lessons were constantly supervised by Mr Henkel, for he normally came to his classroom to give all the help he needed. The following year, the authorities sent Mr Egala to the Teacher Training College at Achimota, near Accra.

---

[a] Imoru Egala was the son of Sgt.Major Egala of the Northern Territories Constabulary Force. He hailed from a village of Pina, about twelve miles from Tumu town. He was educated in the Tamale Middle School and became one of the first senior prefects of that school. He was appointed as a Native Authority clerk in Tumu and was appointed a pupil teacher in Lawra. He then trained as a teacher at the Teacher Training College at Achimota School from 1938 to 1941 where he was given the nickname 'N.T. horse' because of his athleticism. He taught in Lawra and later opened the Tumu Primary School. He became a local councillor for the Tumu Local Council and shortly after was sent to the University College at Legon for a course in Education. On his return he was appointed to teach at the Tamale Teacher Training College. Mr Egala first entered the Legislative Assembly in the 1954 General Elections in which he stood as an independent candidate. However, as soon as the results were declared, Mr Egala declared himself a member of the Convention Peoples Party (CPP) and was immediately called to Accra and appointed Minister of Health, a post that was promised to both him and my brother, the late Birifu Nũũ, if either of them won. For this matter some of his constituents never forgave him and he lost his seat in 1956 to Mumuni Dimbie, the Headteacher of the Walembellia Day School and now chief of the place - the Walembellia Koro. He was then appointed Chairman of the Cocoa Marketing Board. Anyway when Mumuni Dimbie was disqualified from taking his seat in Parliament, Egala was elected unopposed.

As we were harvesting some bambara beans on our farms in November of that year, I suddenly heard my name being called by almost every child in the school. This was the custom during Mr Henkel's headmastership that when he called out for someone every one immediately did so too.[a] For when Mr Henkel coughed or sneezed, everyone trembled. He was the monarch of all he surveyed, at least in the school which he governed. So I appeared before him in no time, pondering what fault I had committed now. For no child was wanted by Mr Henkel without his being at fault.

He was standing there with his pupil teacher, Mr Egala, in one of the plots of the Jirapa compound farm. He looked stern and peered straight into my face and asked if I still wanted to leave the school. I looked into his eyes timidly thinking of what to say to him when it suddenly dawned on me that if I answered affirmatively, he would cane me and would still not dismiss me from school. For as he had not honoured his word the first time, what guarantee was there that he would do it on this occasion. He only wanted to satisfy his sadistic passion that morning since he had the brain wave to cane some one. Then I told myself I was not going to give him that pleasure of caning me when he had not the slightest intention of sacking me from the school. So I answered in the negative. He then said to me 'You billy-goat' (budau ŋa) and told me to clear off, which I did, with some hidden feeling of satisfaction of putting one over on him.

At mid-December we were sent home on holidays. But during that period Mr Henkel frequented our house on social calls since he had won the confidence of my father and had become his good friend. His draconian methods towards us even during our holidays frightened us all the more. If he came to our house and found the surrounding area or the top of the palace dirty, we were in trouble. He would ask us to return to school the next day even though the others were still enjoying their freedom. Knowing that he was likely to visit

---

[a] During Mr Henkel's period in the school when he called out for a boy, all the boys went into hysterics and started shouting the boy's name. However, when the new headmaster, Dawson Andoh took over in 1940, when we were returning from games one evening, he shouted the name of one of the boys whom he wanted to see. I believe the boy was TSoo Gai, the Jirapa compound captain. At that moment, all the boys went into hysterics and shouted his name. Mr Andoh was so annoyed that he gathered all those boys who took part in this performance and gave them each six lashes. And my word, six strokes of Dawson were equivalent to Mr Henkel's twelve.

our house at any time during our holidays, we did all we could to clean the top of the palace and its surroundings reasonably well every morning.

During this particular holiday, Mr Henkel had visited Birifu and found that the palace was littered with leaves and rubbish blown about by the harmattan wind. He immediately ordered us to return to school the following day. As the result of my father's plea, he gave us three days to pack up and return to school. So on the said day, we were sent back to school. When we arrived we were the only pupils there and every morning we were asked to clean the entire school grounds as well as to fetch some fire-wood. By the time the other pupils returned a week later there was a mountain of fire-wood piled high at the back of the school kitchen.

On another occasion, my father had visited Lawra on his usual chiefly duties after which he paid a social call on Mr Henkel at the school. Perhaps in their discussion over a drink, my father must have let slip the fact that we had been very naughty since we had been back home. This took place almost at the end of our holidays. Mr Henkel was very incensed and he told my father to make us return to school within the next two days. When my father intervened he agreed that we could return within the next ten days. However, we knew that our holidays had less than a week to go. So when my father returned he told us what he had spoken to Mr Henkel about our behaviour, and that the latter wanted us to return within the next two days but that he intervened and it was agreed we should stay on the rest of our ten days. We tried to tell him that there were only four days left in our holidays but he said emphatically that Mr Henkel told him there were ten days left. So that we must have been wrong in our calculations of the days, in which assertion he was supported by his faithful linguist, Sakpi.

When the ten days had elapsed my father packed us off back to school, only to find that we were six days late. The boys were already doing general cleaning. The next morning after roll call we were arraigned before the whole school and were told of our misdemeanour while on holidays, in addition to which we were six days late in returning to school. None of us had the nerve to tell him that he misled our father in telling him about the number of days left, lest that person would get the greatest punishment. Anyway, we were each given six hard strokes for being both late and naughty at home.

When the school was first opened in 1935, the fees were supposed to be ten British West African shillings per pupil. By 1938, the fees had doubled to one pound. However, it was felt that since most parents could not afford such an amount, fifteen shillings could be paid in kind and five shillings in money. After a heated debate among the chiefs during their meeting to decide the financial estimates in April, it was agreed that each parent should provide a sheep, either a ewe or a ram in addition to the five shillings which could be used to buy soup ingredients from the market for the preparation of our food.[a] But it had previously been decided a year earlier that scholarships be awarded to some of the brighter boys of each class so that their parents would not have to pay fees.

The outcome of this decision was that three Gandah brothers were among the recipients of these scholarships, namely Gyub and Biz who were in the upper class and myself in the lower class. Consequently, from 1937 to 1939, my father had only to send five sheep and one pound five shillings to the school in payment of the fees for his other five sons. However, after 1939 the fees of those going to the senior school in Tamale were automatically taken over by the Native Authority, who were reimbursed by the Education Department. When Mr Henkel told my father that I was awarded one of the scholarships along with Gyub and Biz, he could not believe his ears. In fact during one of our annual holidays, he confided to me that Mr Henkel had told him that I was the brightest child among his eight sons in the school and yet he had often thought I was the dunderhead among them since he felt I was too young to grasp my lessons. For as a child, because of my baby face, I often looked like a fool even though I was not. No wonder Mr Henkel took me for a five-year-old when I went to school instead of my real age of seven. From then on, any time we were on holidays and he wanted some clerical work done, my father would call upon me to do it for him. This took the form of writing letters to the Lawra Nũũ or to the DC informing them either of some problem of which they should be aware, or asking them for

---

[a] The Financial Year in the Gold Coast used to end on April 5th of each year. The chiefs who were responsible for preparing their Native Authority budgets met at Lawra to discuss their proposals under the auspices of the District Commissioner. Here the chiefs told the DC what developments they wanted in their areas. At one of these meetings, the Kaan Nũũ told the DC that he wanted a well in his area. The DC tried to dissuade him by telling him that Kaani had an ample supply of water. But the chief retorted by saying that it is the well water that he wanted (A bule kuɔ la ka miɔ buɔrɛ). This brought great laughter in the congregation and livened up the proceedings a bit. When completed, these estimates were forwarded to the Chief Commissioner for his approval.

some advice. I was also called upon to interpret from English into the vernacular and vice versa, when he had a European or any other visitor that could only speak English.

Another task included the Bɔɔr dance which invariably took place in December each year and my father was often given some Bɔɔr gifts;[a] or he would give some to other people depending on which section was performing the Bɔɔr that year, and whether there were any persons in that section who had previously given him some Bɔɔr gifts. Bɔɔr gifts, unlike Christmas gifts, are reciprocal and increase in geometric or arithmetic progression between friends or relations. As he received gifts from several of his subjects, he asked us to keep a detailed account so that he could reciprocate when they performed Bɔɔr in their section. For only those from the section performing the Bɔɔr that year can expect to receive anything.

In 1938, three of my senior brothers were promoted to standard two whilst I and three other brothers were moved to standard one from class three. Our eldest brother, Sɔrkumɔ, was promoted from class two to class three. In standard one, Mr Henkel had transferred his daughter, Susanah, from a school in Tamale to his own school in Lawra.[b] Her junior brother, Friedrich, who was one of the first to join the school, was promoted along with us to standard one. Susanah's real class at that time should have been standard two but because initially she could not cope with the lessons in that class she was sent down to standard one, since the standard set by her father in the school was very high indeed. In that light Mr Henkel and his staff must be praised. Susanah shared the same desk with me initially. Our new teacher was Mr Gonna Montia. There were now five classes in the

---

a Bɔɔr gifts are given to those members of the patriclan performing the Bɔɔr that year by other clan members. These gifts are reciprocated when it is the turn of their patriclan to perform the Bɔɔr. The gifts increase in arithmetical or geometrical progression according to the whims of the donors and their social relationships with recipients of these gifts.

b Susanah Henkel, after passing through the Tamale Middle School, trained as a teacher at Achimota College. She later opened the Middle Girls Boarding School in Bolgatanga in the middle of the 1950s. She married Alhassan Gbanzaba (Edmund Alhassan), her former class teacher in the Tamale Middle school, when he returned from the U.K. having taken a degree and was then appointed an Education Officer. She became an MP when special seats were created and allocated to women during the Nkrumah regime. She was a member of the PNDC and then a member of the Council of State.

school with only two teachers. Mr Henkel opted to teach classes one to three whilst Mr Montia taught standards one and two. Even then, Mr Henkel occasionally interfered with Mr Montia's lessons by taking some himself so as to maintain the high standard he had set himself to achieve. No doubt Mr Henkel was a brilliant teacher but it was his sadistic nature that frightened me.

The year 1938 was not as interesting as the coronation year that had just passed. It was decided that all the chiefs in the Northern Territories of the Gold Coast should meet at the end of the year in Tamale, the Provincial capital, for a durbar with the Chief Commissioner. Usually, the CCNT went round the province at least once a year to meet the chiefs and people in each district. But this durbar was an innovation started in 1938, I believe by Mr Eyre-Smith, whereby the chiefs went to the CCNT instead.[21] It was also decided to hold an inter-school competition in football and in drama. The idea of bringing the schools along, in my opinion, was to provide entertainment for the chiefs and their people as well as for the distinguished guests invited for the occasion. In order to get his school well prepared for the occasion, Mr Henkel used most of the games and physical training periods to prepare his team for the competition, whilst most nights and afternoons were used for the rehearsals of the play. To be able to qualify for the football competition, the players had to be not more than 5ft tall. This was so that no school was at a disadvantage. It was a crude way of assessing children of a certain age. Consequently, the choice of players was limited, especially in Mr Henkel's case, since most boys were already teenagers or young men.

Although I was good in all subjects, my handwriting was awful. Both Mr Henkel and my class teacher gave me extra lessons in handwriting; but this yielded no good results. My handwriting was still probably the worst in the class, if not in the entire school. However, I believe that had I been given a bit of encouragement rather than being made to write under duress, my writing would have improved a little. For instance, at one time I was suffering from conjunctivitis and if I looked into the page of my exercise book, it caused my eyes to water and drop onto the page when the sunlight reflected on to it. I would at that moment be caned for messing up the page.

I was not only untidy in my class work but in my bodily appearance and my clothes as well. Mr Henkel was a stickler for finding faults and ways to cane children. As a result when written or mental tests were conducted, he would cane first for errors, then for untidiness and after for any other faults he could conjure up. Apart from caning for faults, marks were also deducted from one's work for those same faults. For example, if one had say twenty-five errors in dictation or essays and the marks were out of ten, one would be given a mark of minus fifteen. If this was in exams, one lost fifteen marks in the aggregate besides the caning. As a result, I was constantly in the firing line for untidiness. So when tests were done, I usually ended up having hundreds of marks deducted for untidiness and for all sorts of other reasons. Despite all that no classmate of mine shifted me from the first position. It was this high standard of mine at that time that made my teacher, Mr Montia, give me the nickname of 'Dr Aggrey of Africa'.[a] Dr Aggrey was the first African philosopher from Anomabo in Cape Coast.

By the end of the first quarter of the year, Susanah had picked up in all her subjects and was almost a challenge to my supremacy as the top pupil in the class. In fact not only were we challenging each other, but we were also a challenge to the top pupils in the upper class since we were all taught together in most of the subjects. Despite the marks her father usually deducted from my work, my top position was in no way seriously threatened by her or by any other of my mates. When the Inspector of Schools, one Mr Wentworth, came round for school inspection, Susanah and I were put forward for promotion to standard two to take effect from the second half of the school year; at that time pupils in the standard classes needed the sanction of the school inspector before any promotion could take place.

However, when the school inspector had given his permission and had gone, only Susanah was promoted to the next class while I was left behind at the beginning of the second half of the year. I could not believe this since I was told by my class teacher that the inspector had authorised the two of us to be promoted to the next class. The only reason offered at the time was that Mr Henkel said my handwriting was awful. But to me, that was a very lame excuse as I was being punished many times over for the same crime. At the time I did not think much about it, but as I grew older I felt that Mr Henkel had

---

[a] Dr Kwagyir Aggrey from Anomabu was the foremost of African philosopher of the time. When Achimota School was opened in 1927 he returned to the Gold Coast to teach in that school. It was he that designed the school badge using the black and white keys of the piano. His philosophy was that as the black keys alone could not be used to form a piece of music neither could the white keys. Consequently the black race cannot do without the white race nor could the white do without the black.

done me some injustice and I had difficulty in understanding why he did it. After this latter incident I was more than ever resolved to leave the school and return home to be a farmer or a shepherd boy.

There was one incident that took place between Susanah and myself which has plagued my mind and I still feel terrible about it even to this day. Susanah and I shared a desk together. Towards the course of the year, Kuupone Yirbɛkyũũ replaced me and I shared a desk with my brother, Debomo.[a] We were seated just behind Kuupone and his new partner. Then one day we were set an examination by Mr Henkel but supervised by our class teacher. In the course of this examination, I caught Susanah copying from her notebook. Both Kuupone and I threatened to report her to her father. The poor girl was terrified of what he would do to her and begged us not to report her. She promised to give us her share of the meat from her lunch.

For Mr Henkel's children did not take part in the school meals but ate at their father's house. So they had meat with their meals everyday whilst we the boarders had meat once in a blue moon, as when the medical officer, school inspector or the Director of Education was visiting the school. Anyway, at lunch time I forgot all about it and went to eat. After lunch, I returned to the classroom to revise for the afternoon paper. Then Susanah appeared with the head of a guineafowl wrapped in her hand and offered it to me. I felt very guilty about accepting it, since it would seem like a sort of blackmail on our part. It would have been blackmail if we had asked for it, but she insisted that we must have it. Maybe it was to bribe us to keep our mouths shut forever. But up to this day I still feel disgusted any time I think about it.

During the mid-term holidays, Mr Henkel left again for Wa with his tennis team to play a tournament against their local team, as he had done the year before. The school was then left in charge of his assistant, Mr Montia. As usual the holidays were spent on the school farms. On one of these farm days there was a scuffle between Yakuu Karbo and Mr Montia, but with the other big boys present this was not allowed to develop into a major crisis. However, on Mr Henkel's return, the matter was reported to him by the senior prefect. Mr Henkel was livid because he felt that a challenge on his assistant was a chal-

---

[a] Kuupone Yirbɛkyũũ became the first literate Native Authority Police Constable (GP) in the district and rose to the rank of a sergeant before his untimely death. The Native Authority Police system was abolished some time after Ghana became independent.

lenge on his own authority. Besides if he did not take severe action against Yakuu, maybe other big boys might emulate him and possibly challenge he himself as well.

I am sure had Yakuu not been a relation of the Lawra Nũũ, after setting an example of him before the entire school, he would have expelled him. However, one evening after our dinner, we all came together in the infants' classroom. On receiving the report, Yakuu was arraigned before us and we were told of his crime. Mr Henkel then birched him by first giving him thirty-six hard strokes which was followed by another six for King George and a further six for the Kaiser. I should stress that Mr Henkel, from his behaviour at the time, could be said to be a diehard German Nationalist and must have sincerely believed in the return of the Germans to a united Togoland. For every punishment he gave to a pupil, there must be one for the Kaiser; if he was giving a pupil a dozen lashes he normally issued thirteen lashes which he called a German dozen but which is known in Britain as a baker's dozen. I often wondered whether he was oblivious to the rise of the Nazi party in Germany at the time. All his children were given German names with German spelling.

Having completed his side of the punishment, Mr Montia was asked to cane him, then followed the senior prefect and his lieutenants and after that the big boys. When it came to we small boys who were asked to give six lashes each, Yakuu must have received over three hundred. With my experience, I do not think he would have felt any pain after a couple of dozen strokes. After the brutal punishment that was inflicted on him, Yakuu was stripped of his compound prefectship. So Yiryele, his deputy, was made the Lawra Compound Nũũ and Manuɔr his deputy. As a result Bɛsuɔ and Sɔrkumɔ became the chairman and assistant chairman of the dining hall respectively.

Mr Henkel had ordered some games equipment amongst which were cricket materials and boxing gloves. He tried to teach the game of cricket but this never caught on. Instead he used the bats in hitting us any time we violated school rules. The culprit was asked to hold on to one of the pillars in the classroom while he used both hands to hit him with the bat. In fact the wrists of one or two boys were broken by his vicious use of the bats. As for the boxing gloves he never taught us how to use them. They were kept in his office all the time. However one day during our morning recreation, Mr Henkel had gone home to his quarters for the break and to have his 'elevenses', while we played about in the classroom. In the course of this fifteen minutes interval, Debomo and I had a fight when Mr Henkel returned and caught us at it. He asked everyone to sit down while Debomo and I stood in front in a narrow strip between the blackboard and the first tier of concrete platform seats to battle it out.[a] The gloves were put on us and we were asked to hit each other with them irrespective of whether we hurt ourselves. There we were, two brothers, hitting each other madly until we were both worn out. He asked if we were both now satisfied and would not fight again. Debomo replied affirmatively, but as I was still fuming with anger, I said nothing. Mr Henkel thought I was defiant and ordered another boy, Kuupone, to put on Debomo's gloves and challenge me. Kuupone and I started hitting each other for some time until he too became tired. I was very tired myself but still would not pledge that I would not to fight against my brother in the future. For if I did, and was caught fighting him one day, my punishment would perhaps be greater than what I was getting now. However, he must have seen the weariness in me, so he asked me to sit down and told me he would get another boy to challenge me on another day.

I was greatly relieved to hear those words. For at another date, I would have a fair challenge. Days went by and I was not called upon to challenge another mate. Then one evening, while we were shelling some groundnuts at Mr Henkel's, he called me and asked the prefects which boy they thought could challenge me. Lɔŋtuo, who was a bit older than me but the same size, was named. Although he was older, physically I was capable of beating him. To Mr Henkel's better judgment and to my relief, he did not allow us to challenge each other. I knew within myself that if it came to wrestling, I could beat Lɔŋtuo; but I was not very sure of out-boxing him. I have again won the day with my passive resistance; or should I say my silent rebellion against tyranny.

This sort of tyranny or sadism was not only typical of the Lawra School or of Mr Henkel but of many junior schools and their headmasters as well. For when I did eventually go to the Middle School at Tamale, other names like Mr Haruna of Wa School or Mr Cockra of

---

[a] These were raised platforms that were about 5ft. long, 1ft. wide and about 1½ft. high. There were about five of these in a row separated by 1½ft gaps between them. There were two of these rows separated by 1½ft alley way. When these were not used to write on as desks as with us kneeling on the floor, we sat on them as seats and listened to our lessons.

Bawku School were mentioned by pupils who came from those schools. At the same time Mr Henkel mitigated his cruelty with some sort of kindness. He had bought himself a double-barrelled shot-gun. Almost every week-end he went out at nights with Broad and Darmani Dakura to hunt small game such as duiker, wild guinea-fowl and partridge. Some mornings, they would return with as many as fifteen duikers and after giving some to his friends in town he would sometimes give to the school two or three duikers for our meal. The pupils appreciated his generosity, so did I at the time. But today, I wonder what happened to the meat budget provided by the Education Department. Was that spent on our food as well? Despite my scepticism, I have to give Mr Henkel the benefit of the doubt, for I have no reason to question his honesty. I only despise him for his cruelty and sadism, not his honesty.

As the year progressed and with the help of Joshua Annobil, Mr Henkel introduced a sort of spiritualist Christianity into the school. I call it a sort of spiritualism because boys were asked to look into a calabash of water where they were supposed to see spirits and to interpret back the messages which these spirits had brought. This resembled a practice in some Islamic sects but was accompanied by Christian hymns and psalms. The entire school, especially those in the upper classes, were compulsorily recruited since they could sing the hymns. I was much taken with this credo and I ardently followed everything that was taught about it. We were taught to fast and pray several times a day. The younger ones who could not fast the whole day were allowed to fast for only half the day. Indeed when one fasted, one found a sort of purity and serenity in one's soul and mind; at least I did. So I enjoyed fasting. And on those days when fasting took place there was peace and tranquillity in the school as there was no beating either by Mr Henkel or by the prefects since this would go against the grain of the whole concept of fasting.

One time I was the curator for the dining hall in the Lawra compound for the week and was responsible for bringing the food from the kitchen to the dining hall and washing the bowls afterwards. Unfortunately for me I was late in doing my dining hall chores and was unable to say my morning prayers before the roll was called. So I tried to make up by saying my prayers to myself while we were on parade. As I was saying them in silence I saw in the sky, and still believe that I did, the picture of a bearded man, golden in the rays of the hazy morning sun—a picture which I took to be God Almighty. I must have been in a momentary trance when I saw this beautiful picture, for at that moment the pupils were ordered to march to their respective classes and I was still dazed, gazing into the eastern sky that still glowed golden with the fantastic picture of God.

Even now I can still visualise the beautiful picture as I saw it at the time; it was a wonderful experience. To the non-believer, this would seem incredible, but if this was my own dream, surely I must have had a great imagination to reproduce such a picture in my mind. Anyway, my tranquil silence was suddenly broken with a whack on the head from Mr Henkel and that picture immediately vanished from the sky and from my eyes. Surely, the psychologist and the atheist would both have some explanation for my experience. From that day, I blamed Mr Henkel in my mind for interrupting my presence with God. But honestly, I could not put the blame on Mr Henkel since he could not have known why I didn't obey the command when it was given. But for the fact that it was compulsory to attend these services, I would have given up his method of Christianity. I had to attend these services that were conducted in his house where one of the rooms was converted into a sort of a church with altars and almost all the paraphernalia of the church.

One day, during one of the evening services, I was asked to look into the calabash of water and tell them what I saw. Of course I saw nothing other than my own shadow and told them so. On several other occasions, my friend Abayifaa Karbo was asked to look into the calabash and tell them what he saw. He was able to see something and told them what he saw. From then on he would be used to do water divination for them. I call it water-divining although it may have another name. Rumours had it that Mr Henkel used such a medium to predict the chances of his school succeeding in the forthcoming competitions in Tamale and thought he would win both competitions but he erred against one of the prohibitions given by the spirits.[a]

---

[a] Rumours had it that the spirits Mr Henkel was invoking during our religious meetings told him that if he abstained from sex during the period of the competitions, he would win both. It was presumed that because he did not comply with the wishes of the spirits his school lost the football match. I believe this was nothing but an old wives' tale.

CHAPTER SIX

THE JUNIOR SCHOOL IN LAWRA was vacated early in December, 1938 so that those going to Tamale for the football tournament and the drama competition between the schools of the Northern Territories could do so. Among the Gandah brothers, Sɔrkumɔ the eldest, Debomo and I, couldn't go. But Sɔrkumɔ and Debomo were asked to remain in the school and keep watch over Mr Henkel's wives and children. So I was the only one who went home for holidays. Those going to Tamale were to travel by lorry to Wa where they would meet up with the Wa school children. So on the day school term ended, I took the long wide road towards home alone. I had hardly passed Sobaal-tɔŋ (the 'Hill of the Humble Road'), that features prominently in the Kusiele version of the Bagre myth, when the vehicle in which Mr Henkel and his pupils were travelling swept past me, leaving a thick cloud of dust trailing behind them. The dust was so thick that I could hardly breathe, let alone see the way. I waited for some minutes to allow the wind to blow away this horrid cloud of dust before I could continue with my journey.

An hour or so later, I was at the brow of a hill, known as Pũyi'-teuŋ, when I heard a continuous boom which I first mistook to be thunder. That was very unlikely since it was the dry season. In fact it was the vehicle in which Mr Henkel and his pupils were travelling that was making such noise. After ascending this steep hill, I decided to call a halt and take a rest under the big silk cotton trees that lined the road opposite the house of the chief of Pũyi'-teuŋ. Although I was thirsty, I dared not walk across to beg for some drinking water for fear I could be poisoned if they knew whose son I was. This is because we were told not to accept anything from strangers. Even in the house itself, when visitors were served with pito, if you happened to sit far away from the person pouring the drink, and a visitor passed it to you, you were loathe to accept it unless an elder from the house told you to do so. It was the belief at the time that if your parents' enemies could not harm them spiritually, they would try to harm the child in order to get at them.

As I was about to sit under the shade, the truck approached from

Dapla and turned right towards Wa. I saw Mr Henkel sitting in front with the driver who stopped the vehicle when he saw me. Everyone got down to stretch themselves and to empty their bladders. I was half way from home and so Mr Henkel decided to put me on his lap and drop me at the zongo in Babile where I could make the remainder of the journey home, one and a half miles up the hill. When I arrived my father enquired about the rest of my brothers and I told him that Sɔrkumɔ and Debomo had been asked to stay behind and keep company with Mr Henkel's wives and children while the other five were on their way to Tamale. Little did I know I was only to spend a week with my father at home before he too left for Tamale with the other chiefs from the District.

As my father did not want to travel with the other chiefs in the same truck, for reasons best known to himself, he usually hired his own vehicle[a] to take him and his entourage to Tamale. The size of his retinue then depended upon his own wishes and was not determined by the administration, which would have limited the number of his followers. On the day of his departure, even though his eldest son, Kũŋkpi, was ill, he wanted to go along too but was advised to stay behind and help Dɔɔr-iɛrɛ and Gaziere keep guard on the house. While my father was trying to talk Kũŋkpi out of going, his mother, Kpɛrɛ, added her support. When he found that my father was adamant, he reluctantly agreed to stay behind.

My father had hardly left when Kũŋkpi pounced on his mother and wanted to beat her up. For he was incensed with her because he felt she was interfering when father was advising him and, as an adult with his own wife, she had no right to scold him. So he started to go for her and but for Dɔɔr-iɛrɛ and Gaziere, would have beaten her up mercilessly. In the event, with his only usable hand Dɔɔr-iɛrɛ seized him by one leg as he hobbled on the other, and tried to toss him like a caber, telling him he had no right to lay his hands on his mother, however enraged she might have made him. For it is against the moral and social attitudes of the Dagara for a son or daughter to fight a

---

[a] The DC normally hired vehicles to convey the chiefs to these durbars from district funds, later to be re-imbursed by the CCNTs from Tamale. In the Lawra-Tumu Confederacy district four vehicles were hired for the four areas: Lawra, Nandom, Jirapa and Tumu. My father disliked travelling in a cramped vehicle with the other chiefs and their retinues. So he often hired his own vehicle where he could take as many followers as he pleased, for the use of the government vehicle would have limited the size of his retinue to two or three.

parent.[a] If this happens he or she would have to find animals and fowls to go before the ancestral shrines and pacify them. So Kũŋkpi was very lucky he did not get to lay his hands on his mother.

Before my father left for Tamale, one of his wives, Yɔɔra, was given the responsibility of cooking for me and for my younger brothers and sisters who had no mothers to look after them. Yɔɔra's cooking was awful and she never provided the food on time. I urged my other brothers and sisters not to eat her food; and we went on strike for the two weeks my father was away. I decided to do the cooking myself. My father had not taken along Debomo's mother, who normally cooked for him, because she had a young child to care for. When she heard of my plight she came to my father's quarters where I was doing the cooking to give me the help and the advice I needed to be able to make thick porridge (saab). As for the cooking of soup I needed no guidance since I had had that training from my father himself. Yɔɔra was very apprehensive of the outcome if and when my father returned. She did everything to compensate for her failings but we refused to call off our strike. When my father returned and learnt what had taken place, he was furious with his wife. Unfortunately,Yɔɔra had no child in the house at that time and my father probably felt she had no maternal feelings towards his children. That ended Yɔɔra's obligation to cook for my dad, for she was relieved of her duties and returned to her own dormitory where she cooked for herself alone.

After receiving my report of Yɔɔra's behaviour towards us, which was supported by my junior brothers and sisters, my father decided to appoint five of his young wives to be responsible for cooking our food. Every day during our holidays two guinea-fowls were slaughtered for our lunch and two for our dinner.[23] We were paired off to

---

[a] The word Dagara was originally used to differentiate between the human beings and the beings of the wild. Hence we had what were called *Dagara zu sɔɔla*, " the beings with the black hair", that is the black race, and *Dagara zu ziɔo*, "the beings with the red hair", that is the beings of the wild. As they did not meet any race except the black race, that phrase referred to Africans. However, as transport facilities opened and different peoples invaded the area and they themselves travelled out, they soon gave names to other tribes. Hence other races whose languages they did not understand were termed *nibuli* or *bɔɔni*, which means the gibberish people or the knowledgeable people. Later it was used to embody the entire area that speak various dialects of Dagaare. So I have been loathe to use Jack Goody's classification of the area. See *The Social Organisation of the Lowiili* by Jack Goody, London. 1956.

share one bowl. At first I was to pair with Debomo but later Sɔrkumɔ decided that I should eat with him. After a while, Sɔrkumɔ must have felt it was unfair for us to be treated differently from the rest of the brothers who were unfortunate not to go to school, especially those of his own age group. As a result he normally invited the eldest Kũŋkpi and Volvuu who was a few months younger, to join us at meal times. My father must have thought that by eating with such big boys, I was not getting my fair share of the food. So he decided that I should eat with him. Thus, any time his meal was ready, he would shout for me to come and eat. The reason he gave was that the way I ate gave him some appetite to eat too.

A few days after my father's return, my other brothers who had gone to Tamale came back for the holidays. Sɔrkumɔ and Debomo, who had been guarding Mr Henkel's family while he was away at Tamale, also returned.[a] When it was time for us to go back to school my father distributed some clothes among us. There was a pair of yellow shorts which both Tiisip[b] and Gyub[c] wanted. My father gave

---

[a] After finishing his Middle School education Debomo Gandah was recruited with some of his classmates to re-open the old Trade School in Tamale and stay there for a further two years. After his training in 1948 he was employed by the Lawra Native Authority but resigned after a few months. He worked for the Public Works Department in Wa from 1948 to 1949 and in 1950 was then employed as a Station Foreman when the Tumu District was opened and needed their own Station Foreman. In 1952 Dr Kwame Nkrumah offered scholarships to one hundred artisans and he was one of those chosen. He took a two year course in Building Construction at the Bristol College of Technology. On his return from the UK he was employed by the Regional Administration as Foreman of Works from 1954 to about 1958 when he resigned and set up his own business as a contractor and a hotelier. He died in January 1965 leaving behind four boys and two girls. (One in England (where he had also married) and the others in Ghana. Ed.)

[b] After leaving school Tiisip Gandah joined the Agricultural Training School in Tamale for a two year training course. When he had finished, he was posted to the Lawra District in the employment of the Native Authority as an Agricultural Instructor. In the early 1950s he was gazetted as a Government Agricultural Assistant. Not long after he was awarded a scholarship to the Agricultural School in Kwadaso near Bantama in Kumasi. In the early part of 1960s he won a scholarship to go to California and on his return was made the Principal of the Nyankpala Agricultural Training School. When the Agricultural Development Bank was formed he was recruited by the bank and trained as a banker. He was made Birifu Nũũ IV and Gandah III in 1973 while still an employee of the Bank. He retired to run his own beer bar in Jirapa.

[c] Gyubunu Gandah (Gyub) trained as a certificate A teacher at the Tamale Teacher Training College. After teaching for a couple of years he resigned and joined the

the yellow pair to Tiisip and gave Gyub a pair of a different colour. But Gyub would not accept a different one. So he asked Tiisip to exchange his yellow one. But Tiisip too would not have that and started to cry. This annoyed my father very much and he decided enough was enough. He therefore ordered us to go to school refusing to give us any pocket money.

Our illiterate elder brothers and cousins, who normally accompanied us to school carrying our foodstuff and luggage, were asked to inform Mr Henkel that we had been very naughty and that we should be caned for our bad conduct at home. As we took the road to school, we did not wait for one another as we normally did. We each took our own way and I suddenly found myself alone whilst the others were some distance away with our illiterate brothers and cousins carrying our luggage. As they distanced themselves from me I contemplated what steps to take. There were so many options open to me. I could return home but would be put on a bicycle and taken to school. If I was sent back to school, I would be caned by Mr Henkel for the naughtiness of Gyub and Tiisip.

This I was not prepared to accept. I followed the bush path which I thought my elder brothers had taken but suddenly found myself at the main road crossing the strangers' settlement at Kuũnyukuɔ. I paused for a few seconds and decided to turn right on to the main road instead of the left. This brought me to Babile about two and a half miles due south. Here at the crossroads there was a signpost pointing west showing the road to Birifu and another pointing east showing the path to Jirapa. The third signpost pointing south showed the way to Wa and the fourth pointed north to where I had just come from, showing the way to Lawra. Again I was tempted to turn right and go home but the thought of being caned for something I had not done appalled me. With some hesitation I decided to take the road to Wa.

So I continued southwards and walked over seven miles before I could hear the booming of a lorry. How glad I was to hear that noise! I waited by the roadside and when it was about two hundred yards from me, I started hailing it down. It stopped just by me and the driver asked where I was going. I told him I was going to Wa, having

---

Mass Education Team. After a couple of years he resigned from that job as well. He enlisted with the Ghana Army and in 1958 he was sent to Britain for a short course. He was one of those sent to the Congo during the Congo crisis. He returned from the Congo and a few months later in October 1961 died in Accra as a Second Lieutenant.

seen the signpost in Babile, and he asked me to jump in. I did so with difficulty, but with the help of the driver's mate, I managed to scramble in. If the driver had asked me for my fare, which he said was one shilling and six pence, he would have realised I had no money and would not have taken me. Luckily he did not. So in the lorry I was planning what story I would tell when we got to Wa, since in his anger my father had refused to give us any pocket money (although later on he sent it after Sɔrkumɔ and the other brothers). The only luggage I had consisted of a few clothes which I tied in my sleeping cloth. I deliberately undid the cloth before we arrived at Wa and when we got to the lorry park between two and three o'clock, I told the driver that my luggage had come undone and my money had dropped down to the bottom of his truck.

The lorry was laden with bags of shelled groundnuts, each bag weighing approximately 240lbs. They shifted the bags from where I sat but could find no money. The driver asked me how much money I had in my luggage and I told him I had five shillings since that was the amount my father normally gave us any time we were returning to the junior school. He asked where I was going to and I told him I was going to Wa School. But as ill-luck would have it, there were some Wa school boys at the lorry park and he asked them if they knew me and they answered in the negative. My secret was nearly exposed; but with quick thinking I told him that since I was a new pupil, they would not know me. So I escaped paying the fare with only his insults.

At that time I knew nobody at Wa except an aunt, Pɔɔziɛ, and her husband, Dɛri, but I did not know where they lived. For I only knew them when they visited Birifu and were guests of my mother. I asked these school children if they could direct me to her house. Unfortunately they directed me to the house of the wrong Dɛri, a brother of one Tuure, a chief collector of passengers and cargo (a motor union official).[a] I was later to find out that Tuure was a rival of my father

---

[a] The collector system was introduced by the Motor Union. Their duty was to solicit passengers and loads for lorry owners going to different destinations. This was well organised in Kumasi and the North. To become a collector one had to register with the Motor Union for an annual fee. The loads and passengers solicited are then paid for and invoiced to lorries that are ready to travel and a commission of ten per cent in the pound was charged in those days. Before any lorry owner or driver could load, a fee had to be paid to the chief collector of that station and you still had to oil the palms of the chief collector and his lieutenants.

who had intended to marry one of Wa Nũũ Pelpuo's widows. Anyway, I believe I was lucky to be alive for my father thought he would have poisoned me if he had known I was his son. If he had that killing instinct in him, then I was saved because I said I knew his brother, Dɛri. Luckily for me, that Dɛri was not in Wa to deny or confirm my knowing him. For I was told that Dɛri had left for Kumasi the previous day and would not return until a week later. It was surprising to me that I did not see my aunt there in the house. Nevertheless, I was treated very kindly indeed and furthermore I met a man from Vuuna Bayɔɔ's house in Tanziir, Birifu, who was also staying there to be treated for hernia. I was therefore at home.

Every day Vuuna Bayɔɔ's son, who was also called Dɛri, showed me round the market stalls where we looked at the goods on display. Then one day, I met an Ashanti man who had come to the north to recruit labourers for his kola nut farm. At that time kola nuts were selling much better than cocoa since this was one of the depression years in the industrialised countries. Consequently, nobody wanted to buy the cocoa crop. Anyway, this Ashanti man wanted to recruit me so that I could be his clerk and time-keeper. He took me round the market asking me to show him whatever I wanted so that he could buy it for me. However, I did not want to be indebted to him and to find myself bound to him forever for the few small things he would have bought for me. So I tried to put him off, but he was such a persistent person and at last I relented.

I told him that if by the next day my host did not return from Kumasi, then I would let him buy me whatever I wanted. The next day Dɛri had not returned from Kumasi and as I did not want to break my word we decided we would go to the market the next day. The following day he did not call on me until the afternoon when we went to the market and I saw a small table clock that was made in Japan. I fancied the clock and said that since I was going to be both a time-keeper and his clerk, I would not mind if he bought it for me. That clock cost only one shilling and sixpence in Wa at the time. As soon as we returned with the clock, Vuuna Bayɔɔ's son told me he had seen Sakpi riding towards the back of the Zongo settlement. This was about four o'clock in the afternoon. The news of Sakpi's presence in Wa put me on the guard. I immediately left Bayɔɔ's son and the Ashanti man and made a run for a hiding place.

There was a gully north of the town running parallel to the town centre about a quarter of a mile away and I made my dash there, not knowing that I was being watched by Bayɔɔ's son, who was suspicious of my sudden dash. I hid in that gully for nearly an hour and was congratulating myself that no one knew where I was. When Sakpi and the Dɛri I knew, together with a Police Sergeant, rode into town, Bayɔɔ's son must have told them where I had hidden myself. Just as I was gloating about my success and playing in the sand waiting for darkness to fall, two faces appeared on the bank towering over me. I felt I was betrayed. Sakpi asked me to come out of the gully, but I refused.[a] I told him I was not going back with him. But when Dɛri told me that, since I said I was coming to him, why could I not come out so we could go home to meet my aunt. That won my confidence and I stood up in the gully and managed to scramble up the bank with the help of the two of them pulling my arms. I wonder what would have happened if they had not found me.

When we got back to Tuure's house, a Police Sergeant was already there grilling Tuure for not reporting my presence to the police. When I approached, without any questions he immediately used his walking stick to give me a whack on the head. I was stunned and annoyed that a stranger I hardly knew could hit me so hard. I held his stick and told him in no uncertain terms that if he hit me again I would hit him back. He must have been taken aback by my arrogance and told me that he knew I was his father (uncle) but he would hit me first and then pay his debt to the ancestors. However, he did not hit me again. It turned out that this police constable was Sgt. Bɛri Lobi, who was married to one of my aunts, and was then in charge of the station in Wa.[b]

I packed my few belongings from Tuure's house and went home to Dɛri's. I was fully entertained that evening but my aunt made me realise how foolish I had been to have run away from home, giving heart-aches to the people there. The next morning Sakpi and I went to the Police Station where the Sergeant took us to his quarters and I was given breakfast and some pito while we waited for the next avail-

---

[a] It is said that in a vision Sakpi saw that I had travelled to Wa and not within the district. So he got up before dawn and rode off on his bicycle to find me. I wonder what explanation those sceptics who do not believe in such supernatural powers, would give for this.

[b] Sgt.Bɛri Lobi hailed from Dikpɛ about three miles from Lawra on the banks of the Black Volta river. They claim to be the first settlers in Lawra. Sgt Bɛri Lobi led the murder investigation into the famous Kibi ritual murder where the culprits were eventually arraigned and brought to book. He was very useful to the Scotland Yard detectives who were brought in to investigate the case.

able transport to Babile. In those days all lorries passing through a district had to report at the Police Station on entering and on leaving. So by between ten and eleven o'clock we found a lorry loaded and ready to proceed northwards to Lawra. Although this lorry was fully loaded and the people packed in like sardines, Sakpi was squeezed into the back while I was asked to sit on someone's lap in the driver's cab. We then set off for home as soon as the police had given the go-ahead to the driver.

For the week since my absence had been reported, the entire district had been engaged in searching for me, in the swamps, by the riverside and in groves and ditches. The search was carried out in the Nandom Division by the Nandom Nũũ, Kũnkuu, in Jirapa by the Jirapa Nũũ, Yelpoi, and of course by the Lawra Nũũ, Karbo. None of the adult males in Birifu had any rest whatsoever. They searched everywhere from dawn till dusk through the entire week. But according to Sakpi, he saw in a vision that I was in Wa. That vision was manifested by the beings of the wild (in Gold Coast English, "fairies"). Hence he got up at dawn and travelled by bicycle to Wa to verify the truth of his vision. It was a good thing he did so, for otherwise I would not have been sitting here today to write my tale.

It was on a Babile market day when Sakpi and I arrived. Earlier in the day my father had called off the hunt and was resigned to the possibility that I was dead. He was refreshing the thirst of the searchers with pots and pots of pito when our lorry pulled up at the market square. As soon as I alighted, my father saw me and instantly came towards me. I was terrified for fear that he might give me a hiding there and then. But when he approached me and I looked into his sad eyes, which were as red as fire and bloodshot with restrained tears, I saw the mischief and sadness I had caused him. He simply stretched his hand and held mine, pulled me gently to where he was sitting and ordered some more pots of pito for the searchers as well as for Sakpi and myself. But the melancholic look of my father and the realisation of the heart-ache I must have caused him during the past week, made me swear to myself that I would never run away from home again. When I had drunk one or two calabashes of the pito, he ordered some bean cakes (sinsɛɛ) and meat and gravy from the market for me to eat. For it was about three o'clock in the afternoon when we had arrived at Babile and I was more than hungry. When I had finished eating my food, he put me on the back of his horse and we rode home.

I was still apprehensive that he might cane me when we got home but nothing happened. Maybe in his own way he blamed himself for my running away like that. Anyway, my unusual behaviour was attributed to the beings of the wild. Sɔrkumɔ was sent home to report back to the school as soon as I was found. He went off to school the following day while I stayed behind so that the beings of the wild could be pacified through sacrifices. I had a pleasant stay for the short extra time at home. Either Sɔrkumɔ did not hear properly of Sakpi's story about my being in the gully or the boys in the school misunderstood him. For when I returned to school, it was said that while in Wa I was living in gullies with nowhere to go. I tried to explain but no one would believe my real story. So I let them believe what they wanted to.

While in Wa, I learnt the tunes of some Koranic recitals but not the words. So every night at home, I sang these tunes in gibberish, but my mates enjoyed it and asked for more. After about a week or so I was returned to school. As I approached the school, I had the feeling that Mr Henkel would cane me severely for my misdemeanour. But neither he nor the other teachers raised their hands against me. No cross words were used and the prefects did not even punish me for any of my failures. So from February to the beginning of April, I had it easy at school; but little did I know that there was something else in store for me.

After about a week there was a singsong one night and I was called upon to give a song. The Koranic tunes were still fresh in my mind. I sang one tune with my own version of the Arabic words and everyone lapped it up. I was asked to sing more. As I continued with my gibberish, Mr Montia[a] happened to come in and knowing that what I was singing was nothing but rubbish, he scolded the prefects for encouraging me to blaspheme, as he termed it. The singsong came to a close that night. Months passed, but I was still not brought before the school to be taught a lesson.

---

[a] Mr Gonna Montia trained as a teacher, taught for a while but his services were terminated and he was suspended for quite a while. It is believed that he and one Mr Bayensi went straight from Standard V into the Teacher Training College. He was re-instated in 1938 and stationed in the Lawra Primary School until the end of 1941. In 1942 he was transferred to the Tamale Middle School where he taught until the end of 1944. In 1945 Mr Montia was transferred to the newly opened College as one of the African masters. It was in this college that his proper salary scale was re-instated. I understood he got a lot of back pay dated to the year of his suspension. He was later made an Education Officer and when the Pusiga Teacher Training College was built he was made the first Principal of the College.

In April, the chiefs met in Lawra to discuss their annual estimates and the pupils in standards one, two and three were asked to go and listen to the proceedings. So every morning after breakfast, we were marched down to town to the District Commissioner's court-house that adjoined his office. There the meetings took place. We returned for lunch after the morning sessions only to return at two o'clock for the afternoon ones which lasted till about five o'clock when we went back to school for dinner. These estimate sessions usually lasted a week and this one was no exception.

At the end of the last morning, the District Commissioner announced that during the afternoon session one of the school boys, namely myself, would be birched before the chiefs and the pupils present so that it would be a lesson to the other pupils so they would not emulate what he did. In addition, after I had been caned, I would be removed from the school. I was very delighted that I would be caned and sacked from the school. So on our march back for lunch I prayed to God to let the District Commissioner's words come true; for on many occasions God had listened to my prayers. However, it seemed that this decision was taken by the three divisional chiefs of Jirapa, Nandom and Lawra, the DC and the headmaster without consulting my father. When he heard the District Commissioner announcing this to the congregation, he was annoyed and after the session went straight to the Lawra Nũũ, telling him that he would not sit down and watch his child and that it would be done over his dead body. He also warned that if I was sacked from the school, he would remove all his eight children. Immediately there was a conference between my father and the three divisional chiefs. He told them that since none of them would sit and watch their sons caned in front of them, he could not understand why they agreed with the District Commissioner that this should happen.

When we returned for the afternoon session, I was ready for my punishment but was greatly disappointed when Kũnkuu, the Nandom Nũũ, got up on behalf of the chiefs and told DC Elison that they had changed their minds after speaking to the boy's father, and decided that it was wrong for me to be caned in front of his father or removed from the school. Both the Lawra Nũũ and the Jirapa Nũũ agreed. It must have been a relief to my father but it was a great disappointment to me. After the session I was disgruntled and moody because I had not been caned or expelled. As we marched back to the school I was scolded all the time by prefects. Their conduct towards me had changed. During the following days I was now on the receiving end of all sorts of punishment. Had I not pledged to myself that I would no longer give my father any more heart-ache, then who knew where I would have gone.

In the course of the preceding chapters, I remarked that parents were asked to pay some of the school fees in kind and some in cash. The payments included sheep which needed tending. From 1938 I was often chosen to be a shepherd boy for the day. However, my nomination either as a shepherd boy or as scarecrow was now becoming more frequent than ever. I was not sure if this was a deliberate ploy by the school prefect but by 1939 I was sometimes absent from the class as much as three times a week. When I was not dismissed from the school and was constantly chosen to be either a shepherd or a scarecrow, I loved every minute of it. For that was the reason for my running away from school so I could go home and tend my father's cattle and sheep. But this state of affairs did not continue long without someone noticing it. Mr Montia, the class teacher, had seen that I had missed a lot of lessons in the week and he queried why I was always chosen. He laid down that I should not be given those tasks any longer since I was not the only boy in the school who could look after sheep or drive away birds from the school farm. But I enjoyed it while it lasted and it kept my mind too occupied to plan another escape.

CHAPTER SEVEN

IN 1939, THERE WAS A third intake of pupils from the four divisions. Among the boys from the Tumu Division was one Dei[a] from Pulma, a subdivision of Tumu. This child did not like the school any more than I did. But Tumu was a long way to escape to, since it was 69 miles from Lawra. So in order to get himself sacked he declared himself a witch. At that time one of Mr Henkel's wives had given birth to a baby boy, Horus, who died in infancy; Dei claimed that he and certain members of his coven were responsible for the child's death. He named my class teacher, Mr Montia, as one of the members. The news soon spread around the school like a wild fire that teacher Montia was a witch; for there was nothing better that school children liked than to have the character of their teacher stigmatised. In those days a man was called a wizard and a woman a witch.

One night while I was fast asleep in the dormitory, in which those of us who wet our mats were grouped in one room, I was awoken by Diedɔŋ[b] with four other big boys. They shone their lantern into my face and then told me to go back to sleep. It turned out that Dei had

---

[a] Dei was among the second intake of boys from the Tumu District and hailed from Pulma. He was about five when he came to school in 1939. So when he was sacked I did not set eyes on him until later when I resided in Tumu and became a District Councillor in the early 1950s. One day he was ordered with other men to bring thatch to the council for roofing purposes when one Issaka Kanton pointed him out to me. Not very long afterwards I learned he was crushed under a roof during a heavy storm. So I wondered why he did not use his sorcery to escape his untimely death

[b] After leaving school, Diedɔŋ, popularly known as S.D. Dombo, trained as a teacher and was first posted to Eremon. He became the chief of his village when the position became vacant and still taught for sometime. He was a member of the Northern Territories Council and later served on the J.H. Coussey Committee on Constitutional Reform, 1949. He became an appointed member of the Legislative Council with J.A. Braimah and Yakubu Tali in 1950 and then he was elected from the Northern Territories Electoral College in 1951 into the new Legislative Assembly with Nkrumah as Leader of the House. When universal suffrage was extended to all people in the North, in July 1954 he formed and led his party, the Northern Peoples' Party (NPP) and became the first leader of Her Majesty's

been brought along to identify me and those other boys whom he had accused as wizards. This was kept secret from me until the appointed day when we were all called to the school room for Mr Henkel's class, the room for classes one and two. The Lawra Nũũ was asked to address the school and he broached the subject, saying that there were certain witches in the school and he had come to warn them that the Lawra Earth shrine would not tolerate witchcraft.[24] Up till that time I still did not know who these witches were, apart from Mr Montia whose participation was the subject of rumour.

I am sure that he too was not aware of what the Lawra Nũũ was talking about. He told the rest of those present to leave except for Mr Montia, Dei, Dɛri Kuyen[a] and myself; we had to stay behind since we were the supposed wizards of the school. Mr Montia was prepared to swear by his own fetish or any they cared to put before him but the Lawra Nũũ would not listen. I was flabbergasted when my name was called and did not know whether to vanish into the thin air, bury myself under the earth or even kill myself instantly. We all denied this trumped-up charge and there was nothing the Lawra Nũũ or anybody could do about it. When he had his say, he allowed us to go for lunch; but lunch that day was far from my thoughts. I had been humiliated and did not feel like eating. I leant against the dining hall wall when we came out, weeping until one of the cooks, Maalzie-ma, came up to console me by saying she knew I was not a witch.

But that was no great consolation since my character had been scarred forever. This stigma followed me to the senior school where children from other schools had been told of my supposed witchcraft. What baffled me is why Mr Henkel, who had introduced Christianity of a sort into the school, should have believed that his baby son, not more than three to six months old, could have been eaten by four witches. After all the baby's mother had always treated me like a son any time I was ill by giving me a dish of my own from her cooking. Why should I repay her by killing her son? If it was to punish Mr

---

Opposition in Parliament. After the 1956 elections all the opposition parties united to form a strong party, the United Party (UP), when the new leader was the late Dr Busia. When Ghana became Independent, Chief Dombo with many of his opposition leaders were interned without trial and was only released after the 1966 coup. In 1969 when civilian government returned he became a minister in the Busia regime until the 1972 coup.

[a] Dɛri Kuyen hailed from Zambo, a village three miles from Lawra. After leaving the Lawra Primary School, he joined the Medical Field Unit.

Henkel, why did we not go for one of his bigger children like Susanah or Friedrich, both of whom were in the same class as me and who were taught by Mr Montia? I do not know what reasons Dei had to frame the three of us with this charge of sorcery but there are two or three reasons I could think of.

One day, while rumours were rife that Mr Montia was a witch, Dei's brother, Abu Nankpa, had asked me to cut his hair short for him. Dei was sitting by his brother while I was cutting Abu's hair. In the course of this haircut, I mentioned an incident that happened to me one morning between four and five o'clock. I had woken up to go and empty my bladder in the flower beds outside my dormitory so as not to wet my mat and be punished for doing so. For those of us who wet our mats were forced to kneel and smell our own urine while the school and the compound prefects gave us a number of strokes. While I was urinating, I saw some flying creatures somewhere in the vicinity of the school well where our vegetable garden was situated. I was terrified and ran into my room. When I was cutting his brother, Abu's hair I asked Dei if he and my teacher were the people I saw as balls of fire flying about in the early part of that morning. He did not reply and I forgot all about it until I was named as a witch.

The second reason is that from 1938 I had been developing some sort of psychic power without knowing how I came by it. I put it down to my prayers and to my faith in God. It all started when Mr Henkel was preparing his team for the football competition in Tamale. He used to match his own team against the best eleven in the school while the rest of us watched. As they played, I used to forecast which team would win and which players would score the goals. I was right in my forecasts most of the time, so I was taunted by my mates who wanted me to make my predictions before the game started. What they did not know was that as soon as I made my predictions, I prayed continuously to God to let my predictions come true so that I would not be disgraced; and more often than not my predictions were correct. I was soon hailed as a magician (Tiisob) by my mates who did not know it was the will of God. This ability to forecast correctly continued into 1939 when Dei came to school as a new boy. He must have seen me make forecasts from time to time which had come true.

The other possible reason which could have influenced Dei was my escapade to Wa. The stories that were told in the school about me and my adventure was enough to make him believe I was capable of being a witch, stories which were exaggerated and most of them unfounded.

I could only guess that these three possible reasons might have made him conclude that I was a witch, and in order to make himself believable, especially with the current thought of the day on sorcery, he had to name me as a member of his coven. Once I had been disgraced in front of the entire school as a witch, I gave up making such predictions since I did not want to aggravate the situation any further. I prayed to God to kill the powers in me that made me often forecast so correctly. Since I never predicted again, I did not know whether or not God accepted my prayers.

In 1939 the Bɔɔr deity manifested itself in Heyi, later Dr. W.H. Gandah, one of my junior brothers, who was only a couple of years old. This was to make the elders aware that the Bɔɔr myth must be performed by the Naayiile section. So about one hundred and four men, women and children were selected (Bi'-ir, literally, "Selection of Children") as the neophytes-to-be among whom was Heyi. The Bi'-ir Ceremony heralds the beginning of Bɔɔr when the neophytes are given their first taboos to follow and from then on are referred to as children; Debomo who had not been initiated at the same time as me, was also included even though he was in school with us. Each time the next phase was about to begin, he was sent home a week ahead while the seven of us were allowed to go home on the eve of each performance.

It was on one of these visits which coincided with our mid-term holidays that we were allowed to go home for a fortnight. My father had already been informed of my being proclaimed a witch in school. Before the "Bɔɔr of the Beans" (bɔɔr biɛ) performance was carried out, he brewed pito for the annual sacrifice to the Ku'kpɛnibiɛ shrine, which normally took place about that time of the year.[25] Before he went into the temple he told me that he had heard I was a witch and asked what I had to say to that. I told him I had never been a witch and it was lies told against me. So he asked me if I would like him to give me a fowl to take into the temple and make an oath (pɔl) that I was not a witch. I was elated at the chance to clear my name of such a preposterous accusation. He believed me, and therefore gave me a black fowl and we went into the temple where he spoke on my behalf and the fowl was slaughtered. It turned on its back, signifying that I was not a witch. My name had not been tarnished for ever.

I was very interested in learning everything about the Bɔɔr and the only way you can do so when you have been initiated is to act every year as a guide to other neophytes or to be a keen attender and observer at these performances. I might have chosen Debomo as my neophyte but instead chose one of my favourite brothers, Wanizama. However, as I was not at home, Dunfaa, one of my cousins, was given Wanizama to look after. Dunfaa was a second-grader[a] (bɔɔ-sɔɔla) while I was only a first-grader (bɔɔ-pla). So it was Dunfaa who taught me, for the first time, how to feed my neophyte in a ritual manner. Before a neophyte eats or drinks at these performances, he or she must go through the ritual feeding first (*to*). Indeed, I learnt a lot from Dunfaa; for when his duties as a second-grader coincided with those of mine, he showed me what to do as a first grader whilst he performed his part as a second-grader. (For duties of first and second graders see the *Myth of the Bagre* by J.R.Goody).

After the "Bɔɔr of the Beans" performance we returned to school for the third and fourth terms. In the eyes of my school mates I was still a witch and when I had tiffs with any of them out came the insult or taunt, "You wizard, you cannot eat me". If he was a boy I could beat, I beat him up even though it did not stop him still insulting me the more. If he was a bit older than myself, I would still fight him to purge the anger from my system even if I lost. However, on one dark evening all the children had gathered at Mr Henkel's house to shell his groundnuts which he bought from the market to retail in the south or to take down to Kete Krachi with him.[b] I was the curator of bowls (laa pɔɔrɔ, literally, dish washer) for the dining hall in my compound for this particular week. So when I had finished washing the bowls I was walking over to Mr Henkel's house. Hardly did I reach halfway between the flagstaff and the house, when Pusaŋ-wiɛ met me but said nothing to me. He passed me and went to his compound and quickly retraced his steps and we both returned to the place where the children were shelling the groundnuts. When we arrived he told

---

[a] First graders (bɔɔ pɛlɛ pl. and bɔɔ pla sing.) are the initiates who have not yet been initiated into the second grade and act as guides to the neophytes. These are carefully vetted by the Bɔɔri mothers because they do not want inexperienced guides to take charge of their neophytes. Women are automatically made second graders as soon as they pass through the first initiation. Second graders (Bɔɔ sɔɔli) have special duties apart from overseeing and coaching the new guides in their duties.

[b] Mr Henkel was born and bred in Kete Krachi. Being transferred there was like going to one's home town. Kete Krachi was part of the Northern Territories and under the Gonja traditional area. Because they spoke a dialect of Twi, they fought hard to be separated from the North and put under Ashanti. [In fact, the Krachi language is a variety of Guang, more closely related to Gonja than Twi. Ed.]

me that Diedɔŋ wanted to see me. I went to where Diedɔŋ was sitting and he asked me to sit down. I was hidden between him and the other big boys from the view of Mr Henkel who was seated in his verandah watching us as his tilley lamp shone out into the patio. Diedɔŋ told me that they had seen me change into a ball of fire flying towards them. When I denied this, I was slapped on the face and was told to shut up. He was joined by Yiryele Baanyɔ, my compound captain, Manuɔr Gaŋ-man, his assistant, Ŋmin-yɔla, the Jirapa compound captain, and two others. I was pinched and hit in the face and on the head by all of them simultaneously. All this torture was going on under the nose of Mr Henkel, though I must admit he did not see what was happening to me. But that was not all. As the moon rose above the eastern horizon, the darkness opened to silvery brightness, making it easy to pick out any minute object from the ground, especially on this particular night when the sky was cloudless and blanketed with azure blue. Mr Henkel therefore asked us to go down to the flagstaff and have a singsong. When we got there, they asked for branches of the acacia tree to be brought. I was caned with these branches and any time I cried or winced they said I did not feel the pain of my torture, that I was only feigning because I had hidden my real body (the soul)[a] somewhere else. They wanted me to confess to a crime which I had never committed. Even if I had been a witch, it was too early in the evening to turn myself into a flying ball of fire since witches do not start flying at seven o'clock in the evening; I believe they wait until everyone is in bed before they go out to meet in their coven. Anyhow they started to beat the ground around me in order to find out where I had hidden my real body in the form of my soul. As they did so I winced as Yiryele was about to hit the ground, for I thought that he was going to beat me. When he observed that I cowered, he then said that my movement implied that where he hit the ground was the place I had hidden my body.

They all started frantically beating that area and then hitting me afterwards. Then I got the idea to feign. When they began hitting the ground, I pretended I was feeling the pain and started reeling and writhing about. But when they hit me afterwards, I braved it out and pretended not to feel the pain at all. Then they would return hitting

---

[a] The soul (siɛ) is believed to be shed and hidden somewhere else by the witches when they are being beaten or whipped so that they do not feel the pain of the punishment.

the ground. In this pretence, I got them fooled and made them use their energy on the ground. But that did not stop them, for they turned to a different method of torture. They all fetched some pebbles, and Yiriyele and Ŋmin-yɔla each took an ear of mine. They put a pebble on each side of my lobe and began pinching my ears between the pebbles. This was the most painful part of their torture and I grew taller and taller every time they squeezed. While this was going on, Diedɔŋ and Manuɔr did the same to my body. With this second method of torture, it was impossible for me to feign that I was not feeling the pain. And so this torture continued until the whistle went for us to go to bed and I was left alone.

The mental and physical torment I suffered in that school for being branded a witch was very great. I was the object of scorn from the smallest boy to the biggest. It was worse in that I was being taught with the biggest boys in the school all of whom held school posts. So any time I excelled in the class I was accused of using my sorcery to gain the answers from the teacher's handbook. At one time I did not know what Gyub or one of my brothers did to Mr Montia. But they must have been whispering in the class about his being a witch. Anyway, he was very angry with them and instead of punishing them for being rude to him, he alluded to the fact that if they were rude to him because he was accused of being a witch what about me sitting there, for after all, I was also accused. At that moment, I did not know where to hide myself as the whole class burst into laughter. I felt that was an uncalled for remark from my teacher but it must have been frustration that forced him to make it since it was with the connivance of the headteacher that we were both disgraced as witches. So he could not punish a boy for calling him a witch. Whatever degradation I suffered in that school, I blamed no other than Mr Henkel. It was he who brought public disgrace to us and not Dei or the Lawra Nũũ. So I could not blame Diedɔŋ and others for their torture partly because witchcraft was the belief of the day and partly because Mr Henkel encouraged the belief in the school.

A month or so later we were sent on holidays and I was glad to see the back of the tormenters. For they were sent to Tamale to the Middle School when schools reopened. Mr Henkel was also transferred to open a new school at Kete Krachi which was then part of the NTs, the Gonja District. The next senior prefect was to be Sɔrkumɔ while Dɛri, another brother, was to be my compound captain. So I did not suffer that torment as much as I did with the others. Our new headmaster was to be Dawson Andoh who had been a teacher at the Wa junior school.

Before the school was vacated, Mr Andoh[a] came to Lawra to acquaint himself with the school. He witnessed the appointments to the posts that were to be held by the different boys. Then we had our annual school feast. Every year the Lawra Nũũ presented us either with a pig or an ox, and pito was brewed by the cooks for the occasion. Some of the mothers of pupils were invited to attend these feasts. Although this was supposed to be a happy occasion, we were forced to eat and drink everything that was put in front of us, whether we were full or not. Failure to do so meant that one was flogged or forced to eat and drink not even caring whether or not one's belly would burst. More often than not the smaller boys were at the receiving end while the big boys got away with it. While the feast was going on we sang the song "Come landlord fill our earthen bowl until it just runs over", an English folk song in which the word "landlord" was substituted by the word "teacher". This was most appropriate as we were eating from earthen bowls in the school. The night did not end with just eating and drinking. Having filled our stomachs with food and drink, one was then made to do vigorous local dancing. If this was not enthusiastically done, then the prefects gathered gravel from the ground and threw into our faces and on our bodies. The next day between ten and eleven we were sent on vacation.

---

[a] Mr. Andoh hailed from Cape Coast. He taught in the Wa primary school under the headmastership of Mr Haruna, a Dagomba. He was promoted to be the next Headteacher of the school. Mr Andoh was in Lawra for nearly nine years as the head master. He was transferred to the Tamale Middle School for a short while and was then promoted as an assistant Education Officer and stationed in the North-West. In 1952 he was sent to the University College, Legon, to do a further course in Education. On his retirement he taught at the school in the Kumasi College of Technology (now the Univerity of Kumasi). From there he went to Nigeria to teach and earn some hard currency. He returned to Ghana and died.

CHAPTER EIGHT

WE WERE SENT ON HOLIDAYS about mid-December and as Debomo was a neophyte he was allowed to go home some weeks ahead of us for the Whitening Ceremony (Bɔɔpir, literally, the Bɔɔr crowning). Unfortunately because of our examinations we missed the ceremony. After the performance, the neophytes normally travel with their guides, usually women who are capable of carrying the baskets full of guinea-corn which have been presented to the neophytes, on their rounds from house to house. Within a house there could be two or more family units farming separately; and in that case, it was possible for a neophyte to get two or more baskets full of guinea-corn. A popular neophyte might have three to four guides following him or her to carry back the gifts of sorghum, perhaps even returning to carry more. Apart from the sorghum, the neophytes are also given money which they keep in their goat skin bags (bɔɔ wuur) that they had been given during the ceremony. If a child was too young to travel, his Bɔɔr gourd (bɔɔ kuɔr) and bag were taken over by an older initiate who acted for him. All these gifts are kept separately for each neophyte until the next ceremony.

The three weeks of the Whitening Ceremony are followed by the Beating of the Malt Ceremony (Kɛɛŋmier)[a] in which I understudied Dunfaa who was the guide for Wanizama (Wanzam). After this ceremony the neophytes are again let out to roam around and beg for

---

[a] At Kɛɛŋmier (the Beating of the Malt) the neophytes are led to a heath (gbal) where they are seated in a circle with second grader sitting in between two neophytes. Each guide fetches a small pot of pito with two or three ears of guinea-corn. The white bɔɔr is recited up to the stage when the Kɛɛŋmier is being performed. After the recital the ears of the guinea-corn are thrashed; and the grains collected and winnowed. The neophytes are then led to a special spring where they are bathed. Each guide filled the pots with water from this spring and and takes them home where the grains are put together in a big vat and the water from the spring is poured in to let it steep. When this is well steeped, it is drained and the grain taken upstairs, spread on the roof top and covered with leaves and mats for three days to malt it. Prior to that, however, the white bɔɔr is repeated at the ancestor shrines (kpiin) and also at the Bɔɔr shrine (wen). *Wen* is interchangeable with *Nmin* especially in the Kusiele myth where the wen is called the *Bag' Nmin*.

fowls, or to snatch some when they are refused. As Wanzam's guide, I went out with him to beg for the fowls. During the morning we went down to his uncle's parish at Mal where we were generously given fowls and shell money. My fowl coop was full when we returned home at about 11.30 for the neophytes to be fed. After lunch we rested till about 2.00 when the neophytes and their guides were called over by Dɔɔr-iɛrɛ, one of the Bɔɔr Mothers, to prepare to go out for the afternoon rounds. In this instance Dɔɔr-iɛrɛ was both a Bɔɔr Mother and Father. A Bɔɔr Mother is an initiate whose offspring is a neophyte, while a Bɔɔr Father is a Bɔɔr elder. As the Bɔɔr was being performed by the Naayiile clan, we hired the Kyaalɛ elders, Kuusob[a] and Bũyir, to be our Bɔɔr fathers. However, as they would normally need expert help, Dɔɔr-iɛrɛ and Yinku among others were in turn hired from our house to assist them. Hence the dual role of Dɔɔr-iɛrɛ and Yinku.

I went out again with my neophyte, this time taking the path to Baapar and so covering all the parishes to the east. I went from house to house and nobody was interested in giving my neophytes a fowl. The practice is, if you go to a house to beg for a fowl and you are refused, the guide tries to lure the fowls with grains of guinea-corn and then catch one to hand over to the neophyte. Once the neophyte touches it, it is supposed to have been spoilt and becomes Bɔɔr property. So as I was getting nowhere with begging and the sun was descending fast, I resorted to the method of enticing the birds with some grain. I caught over ten birds from that one compound alone and handed them to my neophyte to put in the chicken basket. We went to a few more compounds to beg for fowls before I decided it was time to take my neophyte home for him to quench his thirst and get ready for his dinner, for there are special times when these neophytes must be fed and go to sleep.

I had hardly arrived at the outskirts of our house when my father, who was lying in his hammock under the shade of a shed on top of which the feed for his horses is placed, beckoned me to come. I went over and saw the man whose house I had raided being served with beer. I knew he had brought a complaint against me but I was not worried because I thought I had done everything according to the

[a] Kuusob belonged to the Ŋmangbiile patriclan, but settled in Batan among the Kyaalɛ patriclan. It would seem he was often hired by the Kyaalɛ to lead them in their Bɔɔr performances when they did not have an elder old enough to do so.

Bɔɔr rules. When my father asked me if I had taken ten birds from the man's house, I answered confidently and affirmatively. He told me I was only allowed one bird per compound and I then explained that as my neophyte had already touched all the fowls, they consequently belonged to the Bɔɔr deity, the wen. He laughed and told me to let the man take his birds home. So the man looked into the basket and selected his birds. My father may have allowed this man to violate the Bɔɔr rules because he was a non-initiate and therefore was not bound by those rules; if that was not the case, then the matter was between him and the Bɔɔr deity.

After another three weeks, the Bɔɔr Dance (Bɔɔsiɔr) was to be performed.[a] It was at this time that my cousin, Dunfaa, most needed my help. For as a second grader (Bɔɔsɔɔla) he had his own tasks to perform, and was relieved to have me as his assistant. From the eve of the Bɔɔr night (Bɔɔsiŋgbile) till the last day of the dance, my father had hardly seen me except at meal time when he expected me to eat with him. From Bɔɔr eve, no guide or Bɔɔr elder who was actively taking part in the performance was allowed to have sex; he could forego either his sexual pleasures or else the spoils of Bɔɔr. As for the neophytes, they had been forbidden to have sex some time before the Whitening Ceremony until the end of the Bɔɔr performance (Bɔɔgbelme).[b] But in Birifu at that time custom forbade casual sex before marriage. Even if you were married and the bridewealth had not been paid, you restrained your sexual urge until this had been done. As I was only about twelve years old, rules about sex hardly affected me. But another rule about not eating pepper was observed by everyone in the house including my father and all non-initiates.

---

[a] The Bɔɔsiɔr (the Bɔɔr Dance) takes three days. The eve of the Bɔɔsiɔr, the eve of the Bɔɔr Night, Bɔɔsiŋgbile, (the Bɔɔr of the bambara beans) where the guides are busy boiling the bambara beans and the black-eyed beans as well as roasting pieces of yam for the next morning's performances, is not counted as days of Bɔɔr dance. At the first crow of the cockerel, the guides get up to prepare for the wailing of the wen; and at the second crow of the cockerel at three o'clock in the morning, the wen is called down. The first day of the Bɔɔsiɔr, known as the Bɔɔtisɔɣ, the Bɔɔr Night, is the busiest day of the four days when the fowls of the path and of the bag are sacrificed (sor nuɔ and wuɔ nuɔ) and the killing and reviving of the neophytes take place. It is the day when the real dancing and merry-making start.

[b] Bɔɔgbelme (the washing of the Bɔɔr bells) is the last of the Bɔɔr ceremonies when all prohibitions are removed after a year of strict observance. The neophytes are sent to the local market and circle round.

At about three o'clock in the morning (at the first cock crow) on the day called Bɔɔr Night (Bɔɔtinsɔ), we were awoken by the elders to perform the ceremony of calling down the deity (Bɔɔwen Kon). This was the first time I had ever taken part and it was very frightening as I was told to expect. When it was time to call the deity, the initiates with their neophytes went to the side of the house and then we stood on the top of the flat roof facing the east. Dunfaa had already briefed me that when the deity was called I should cover the face of my neophyte with my left hand and get ready to run with him for dear life without looking back after the deity had responded and was descending to earth following the third call. My heart was in my mouth as we went there wondering whether or not the deity would catch up with me since I was a poor runner. My neophyte was also shaking like a leaf under my armpit. I could not tell who was more terrified, he or me. We chanted the first call but nothing happened and we waited for a few seconds. Then the second and again there was no response. After the third chant when everybody expected the descent of the deity, we all turned and raced on the rooftop with our neophytes, their eyes still closed, towards the Bɔɔr shrine before the deity could come down. When we got there the second graders took out their fowls and sacrificed them to the shrine of the deity.

After the call to the deity, no one goes back to sleep, so we made our neophytes sit by log fires to keep them warm against the cold of the harmattan wind whilst we went about our chores of boiling the bambara beans, cow peas, groundnuts, and yams that would be needed for the morning performance of the Fowl of the Bɔɔr Bag (Bɔɔwuɔ nuɔ).[a] The women too were busy preparing food so the neophytes could break their fast. By four o'clock everyone had eaten. At about five in the morning (at the third cock crow) there was the Fowl of the Path Ceremony (Sor nuɔ)[b] when we went to sacrifice to the paths

---

[a] Bɔɔwuɔ nuɔ (the killing of fowls to the Bɔɔr bag) takes place at about nine o'clock in the morning on the Bɔɔtisɔɣ day. This lasts for an hour or two. After the ceremony, the neophytes are fed with the bambara beans, the yams and the black eyed beans, thus revoking the taboos under which they have been placed for so many months not eating these items.

[b] The Sor nuɔ performance takes place at about five in the morning of Bɔɔtinsɔ, where sacrifices are made to the gods to guard all the roads or paths leading to the Bɔɔr house and to ward off any evil spirits that may threaten anybody coming to enjoy the dance for the rest of the three days and to keep at bay any evil person intending to do evil at the Bɔɔr house.

leading to the Bɔɔr house. By about nine o'clock we made our neophytes assemble in the Bɔɔr room for the next stage of the performance at which sacrifices are made to the Bɔɔr Bag. After the killing of the fowls to the Bɔɔr bag, the morning Bɔɔr songs are sung to the accompaniment of drum rhythms. As Dunfaa and my father normally played on the big drums whilst Zoi[a] and Yinku played the smaller ones, I was left to do Dunfaa's remaining duties as a guide.

On this particular day, Yinku was a Bɔɔr father and had to help lead the singing of the Bɔɔr songs. His place as a drummer was taken by another player. Dunfaa made sure he showed me what to do when the time came and even when he was on the drum he constantly cast his beady eyes in my direction watching what I was doing, so that I would not make a mistake. After the killing of the fowls, the guides and all those initiates present in the room chanted and danced for almost two hours whilst the neophytes sat motionless throughout. After the morning ceremony, I left my neophyte in the hands of the Bɔɔr Mothers and went off to join my father, who praised me for taking so much interest in the Bɔɔr. By five in the evening we brought our neophytes together again in the Bɔɔr room (bɔɔdio) because the evening performance involved their killing and resuscitation of the neophytes and lasted from about eight in the evening until four the next morning. After the killing of the neophytes,[b] I was left on my own since Dunfaa had to play the big drums to the tunes played by father and Tɛku Dɛr on the xylophones when the congregation sang the evening hymns.

---

[a] Zoi was a nephew of my father whom he brought up as his son. He was the first of my father's children to be sent to the school that was opened in Lawra in 1919. As an older boy he used to lead the late Lawra Nũũ, J.A. Karbo, by the hand to school and prevented other boys bullying him. They became good friends in later years. However, he was sent back home for treatment by my father because he had a bubonic boil on his head that was contagious. His uncle Miiru replaced him at the school.

[b] The killing and resuscitation of the neophytes takes place between eight o'clock in the evening till about three in the next morning. On this particular day one of my cousins, Kuletaa, from the old chief's house, heard that he was going to be killed, so he escaped from the room and would not return. It was with great persuasion that he was brought back for the killing process to start. It is also believed that some Dagaar clan (in the Lawra version they were supposed to be Dɔŋmiinɛ, people from Dɔŋmin) who did not know how to kill and resuscitate their neophytes used cudgels to beat them to death and failed to bring them back to life. Hence they have refused to perform Bɔɔr ever since.

After that the guides travelled from house to house throughout the entire clan settlement, from about four in the morning, catching adults in their beds by surprise, taking hold of their hands and legs and swinging them from side to side and up and down while they sang the songs of praise. Eventually when they were given some money or a payment in kind, they left them in peace. Dɔɔr-iɛrɛ was the first to be caught in the Bɔɔr room and treated in that manner but he would not give in to them; for nearly half an hour, he was tossed up and down and sideways until he at last agreed to pay. Sakpi, Yinku and Gaziere did not want to go through the same ordeal and paid up before they were even held.

We then moved up to the top of our house, on the second deck on which my father's apartment stood. As we respected him as a chief, we did not go up to the roof top on the third deck where he was sleeping but stood singing outside by the wall of his apartment until he gave us some money. In this way we collected from almost every adult in the house, both from the initiated and the non-initiated. Then the group turned on me, wanting to swing me in order to get some money. But Dunfaa intervened and told them they couldn't do that since I was not an adult. Some of them replied that though not an adult I had money of my own; I suppose they thought that as a school child I had money.[a]

When they had finished with our household and had gone on to the other houses in the settlement, I decided it was time for me to turn in. After putting in some three hours sleep, I got up again to get ready for the day's task. In the Shaving of the Head or Bathing Ceremony, known as the Bɔɔr Noon (Bɔɔmunaa), the neophytes were stripped of their old clothes, their heads were shaven as soon as the White Bɔɔr had been recited, and they were bathed. Their old clothes together with the shaven hairs were then buried in the Bɔɔr "'tomb" (Bɔɔyaa), for which a hole (grave) had been dug. After that the neophytes were fed and about eleven they were all made to run into the room in the special manner, each preceded by his or her guide. At that time there were about nine cap-guns (Dane guns) in the house, apart from those brought by the relatives of some of the neophytes. Repeated volleys were shot into the air as the neophytes ran in. I ran

---

[a] It was presumed that we school children (called bɔɔni bibiir) earned some money when we were away from home, not knowing that our father provided us with pocket money.

inside followed by Wanzam who copied the manner of my running[a] as the women ululated. As they entered, the neophytes were seated on the Bɔɔr "stools" which consisted of rolled mats.[b]

The senior elder, the Speaker (nuɔr sob),[c] was placed on his high "stool" (dakɔ-kpɛ̃ɛ̃), in a special manner, this stool being just an ordinary Dagara one. He then began the Bɔɔr proceedings. The Black Bɔɔr was then recited until about 4.30 in the afternoon. This incorporates the themes of both the White and the Black. At the end of this long recital, the neophytes were clothed in their best attire and ready to emerge for the outside performance. The gunners were again at the top of the house and let off several volleys of gunfire as the leader appeared with the neophytes, while their each guide and second grader, danced behind their neophyte and sang more hymns while circling the xylophones.

At that juncture, my father and his colleagues took over from the general players to play the Bɔɔr tunes while we sang and circled round the xylophone three times. When we stopped we went and seated our neophytes for them to receive their presents from the public. At that juncture, I was called upstairs by Sɔrkumɔ to make a record of my father's Bɔɔr presents (bɔɔ tuor). When I went up, he and Biz were already recording in their notebooks the gifts people had given. I was given three or so parishes and asked to write down the names of the people and their gifts. Gifts also came from places outside Birifu such as Lawra, Tankyɛra, Tugu and so on. Consequently, I did not carry out many of the guide's outside duties for the rest of that day. As there were few duties to be performed the following day, I was again engaged in recording more names of people and the gifts they had brought. This work continued for the following three or four weeks until everything concerning the Bɔɔr was over, at which time we had to return to school.

---

[a] This is not a rushed or hurried running but a slow and majestically executed run.

[b] After sitting on these rolled straw mats no initiate would from henceforth be allowed to sit on a fully rolled mat; it has to be unrolled a little before an initiate can sit on it. This is a taboo for all initiates to follow for life.

[c] Nuɔr sob (the speaker) is the leader or senior of the Bɔɔr elders responsible for leading all the recitals in the room. Before he starts to recite he must be seated on his seat in a special manner when he pretends to reject his role; just as the Speaker of the House of Commons pretends to refuse his post when first elected.

My father valued our future contribution to the development of the village so much that he took great pains to make promises to all the principal gods as well as the demi-gods (tibɛ) in the house in order to secure prolonged lives for us. As a result, when we came home and were about to return to school, he took us around all the shrines and made sacrifices on our behalf so that our lives would be protected while we were away. This procedure went on throughout our school lives and when we had all finished, he made his final sacrifices to the gods to free himself of his obligations to them. We have been told that the many deaths in the family in the sixties and seventies were attributed to my father's failure to fulfil his promises to the gods. I find it incredible to believe that he did not do what he had to do before he died.

As Nana, Gyub and Biz were now attending the middle school in Tamale, they left over a week early in order to travel there on foot. They went to Wa by lorry to join the schoolboys from that town and took the same route to Tamale which they had followed for the school competition only a year previously. They went through Bulenga, Dusie, Munwele, Konkore, Daboya in Gonja and then to Tolon in Dagomba land. A fortnight later the rest of us packed up and went off to school too. While I was at home during this particular holiday, I had to be on my best behaviour towards my elder brothers since Sɔrkumɔ was to be the School Nũũ (senior prefect) while Tiisip and Dɛri were to be compound prefects. Any deviations in my behaviour and I would probably have suffered at school from their wrath. There were now new prefects as well as a new headmaster, all trying to feel their way around, so I did not suffer as much torment as I had done under the previous regime.

The school was staffed with four teachers, Dawson Andoh, the headmaster who hailed from Cape Coast and later became an education officer, Gonna Montia, Benin Duori, and finally Kuunũũ-i-ŋmin Bini (C.K. Bini), the son of the late Lawra Nũũ, Bini, who later became an Executive Officer in the Ghana Administrative Service but met with an untimely death through drowning in a flooded river near Bolgatanga. The latter two were then pupil-teachers. Mr Montia taught standards two and three, Mr Andoh, standard one, while Mr Bini took class one and Mr Benin Duori, classes two and three.

It was the practice in that school to have tests every Friday in the lessons that had been taught. In Mr Henkel's time he set the questions for every class. When Mr Andoh took over, the teachers moved round and set the questions for the class they were going to examine.

As Benin and Kuunũũ-i-ŋmin were pupil-teachers they set questions and tested the lower classes, while the exchange in the upper ones was between Gonna and Dawson. These tests became less frequent because the new headmaster was slow in marking the papers before the next Friday; and since he was the headmaster, he could not blame the other teachers for not setting tests when he was behind with his own. So their frequency tapered off during the course of the year.

In one of these tests, Mr Andoh was to examine both our class and standard two. Among the subjects to be tested were the three R's. So in English, Mr Andoh set us an essay topic to write on the celebration of the Empire Day. It took him a fortnight to mark the papers. On the Monday morning before we marched off to our respective classrooms, to my amazement he read out my essay to the entire school and exhorted them to write vividly in this way in the future. For if one student could write such good English, he saw no reason why the rest of them could not do so. I was pleased with myself but dared not show it. From then on he encouraged me by giving me long recitations to learn, or roles in plays that contained such passages. He nurtured in me the desire to learn plays, which became useful to me in my later life.

On September 3, 1939, Britain had declared war on Germany, and the Dominions and the entire Empire were involved. Mr Henkel took this opportunity to teach the upper classes, especially standards two and three, the Morse and the semaphores codes. DC Amherst, who was then stationed in Lawra, was very much impressed by Mr Henkel's war effort and came almost every evening to watch us practice semaphore on the school playground. When Mr Andoh took over in 1940 he did not continue either with the Morse or with the semaphore, but nevertheless he wanted to help the war effort in his own practical way. When British East Africa was under threat from Mussolini, the West African Frontier Force was sent to defend its interests. These soldiers came from the Gold Coast, Nigeria, Sierra Leone and the Gambia. As colonies these countries had no say whatsoever in whether to join the war or not since they were supposed to be fighting for "King and Country". The Dominions, on the other hand, were not obliged to join except with the approval of their respective parliaments.[a] Later on, the Japanese became a threat in the

[a] Former British colonies that had attained dominion status were not compelled to join the war and in any case they had to seek approval from their respective parliaments to enter the war. Hence Eire refused to join the war with Britain.

Far East and our brothers were sent there to stem their aggression in Burma and other places. So it was decided that we could help these soldiers by sending them some home comforts. Those boys who could walk nine miles to Birifu and back were sent to cut a certain shrub (dol) that flourished in the Batan hills and valleys and which is very good for cleaning teeth. A powder from this herbal shrub is also used to arrest gum decay in children.

Those of us who were selected to go and cut this shrub in Birifu got up one morning before dawn and took the long road to the village. By about nine or ten o'clock we arrived at my father's palace. There was a shed on top of which the fodder for his horses was stored and under which he sometimes rested, made his xylophones or held court. We were dismissed by Sɔrkumɔ the School Nũũ, and ordered to fall out and sit there while he and the teachers went up to greet my father. A few minutes after they had gone, we saw women coming down with dozens of pots of pito and calabashes for us. As we drank word was sent round to the nearby parishes for able-bodied young men to come with some cutlasses. By the time we had finished drinking, these young men had arrived and were also given pito to drink. They were then ordered to go with us and help cut the shrubs.

Mr Andoh did not anticipate such help and pleaded with my father to let us go there alone. But my father would not have it and we went all together along the Bũũ plateau and descended down Fofoi valley into Batan. We were in the bush until about three o'clock before we returned, each boy carrying a bundle of the branches. Once again we were entertained with more pito but did not know that father had ordered the women to make lunch for us as well. By four o'clock the food was ready and both teachers and pupils were entertained to a delicious meal of "fufu" (kapala or nyusaab), which is a dish prepared from pounded yam. As I was about to eat with the rest of the boys, my father called me to join him at his table. By five we had finished our meal, and set off with our loads of sticks back to school, arriving there at about eight in the evening. Within a short time the sticks were prepared, dried and dispatched to Accra where eventually they were shipped to East Africa and Burma. I understand the school got a letter of commendation from the Governor himself for its war effort.

One day during the course of the year, my class teacher set us some homework in arithmetic which included finding a square root.[a]

---

[a] The syllabus for standard three did not include the solution of square root problems. It was only taught in standard five at that time.

However, Mr Montia had not taught us the method of doing this. On the Sunday afternoon, I was busy doing my homework on these problems to be ready for the Monday morning, when one Toyie Maalɛ, a senior brother of Tɔrwan[a] and a cousin of Kuunũũ-i-ŋmin who had been visiting the school that same day, came into the classroom and saw me doing my work. Toyie and Kuunũũ-i-ŋmin had finished their middle school education in Tamale together, and when Kuunũũ-i-ŋmin came back to the school as a pupil teacher, Toyie was attached to the Lawra hospital as a trainee nurse. Intrigued to find me alone in the classroom engrossed in my work, he asked me what I was doing. I told him that I was doing some arithmetic homework. Then he asked if I had done all the sums that were set. I told him I had finished all except for one, which I showed him. This he showed me how to solve but his explanation was not very clear to me. Although I did what he told me, I was a little apprehensive that, should my teacher ask me how I got the answer and I was unable to tell him how, he would possibly cane me for copying.

On the Monday, we had two new trainee teachers in the school, Mr Assibi Mahama and Mr Imoru Egala. They had been sent from Achimota College to do their teaching practice in Lawra. Assibi, who was either a Builsa or a Grunshi, was sent to Lawra with Egala because his father was a sergeant at the District Police Station.[26] Assibi was assigned to take our two classes under the supervision of Mr Montia who instructed Assibi to go over the homework he had set. A number of the children were able to solve some of the questions set; but none except me was able to do the problem of the square root. When he came to that, he asked if there was any one in the class who could do it.

I was terrified of raising my hand in case I could not explain properly how I did it. In the end I had to raise my hand because if I had not done so, I might have been accused of copying. Assibi asked me to go to the blackboard and solve the problem for the class. I went there, took the chalk, and my whole hand began to shake like a leaf as if I was having a spasm. My voice trembled too, but in the end I solved it. Mr Mahama was pleased with my effort but disgusted with

---

[a] Tɔrwan Maalɛ was an executive officer in the Ghana civil service; it is the counterpart of the District Commissioner of the British Colonial Service or the Government Agent of the early Nkrumah regime as distinct from his later political party appointments of District Commissioners.

the rest of the class for he did not know that we had not been taught the topic. He ordered the entire class to carry me shoulder high to the dining hall and as a punishment to grind the maize for flour to make our breakfast the next morning.[a] But when lunch time came and he had left the class, I refused to be carried on their shoulders.

As a matter of fact I could not understand why Mr Montia had included that problem in the homework, since square roots were not in our syllabus. For when I went to the middle school I realised that some boys in standard seven could not even solve these problems and my mates were taught it in either standard five or six. Maybe he intended to teach us the topic after discussing the homework with us, which is what he did when Mr Mahama had finished with his teaching practice and had returned to college. He also taught us how to solve cube root problems which at that time was in the standard seven syllabus.

---

[a] During Mr Henkel's time he bought a hand-driven grinding machine for the school, which was worked by two big boys for the grinding of maize and guinea corn to make our porridge. Prior to that our flour was ground by women from nearby villages such as Touri, Kalsaũri, Zambo and Yaatugri.

CHAPTER NINE

ABOUT AUGUST 1940, THE NANDOM Nũũ, Kũnkuu, met with a sudden death. His death was a shock to the district since no one had previously heard of his illness. According to the stories he had gone to his farm on his moped, and on his return went off the road, either before or after having a heart attack and died on the spot.[a] On the eve of his death there were several shooting stars northwards in the Nandom direction, which fell from east to west. According to the belief of the day, shooting stars portend the death of a prominent person. So everyone expected someone important to pass away in the Nandom area. By mid-night persons bearing the funeral messages (kuo'-yele) had arrived from Nandom to deliver the sorrowful news of Kũnkuu's death. As he was not only a divisional chief but also the President of the Lawra Confederacy Native Authority, messages were sent to all the chiefs in the district.[b] As our family was related to the deceased, my father was informed according to the custom, not only because he was a chief. Early at dawn, all the chiefs with their people headed to the funeral where most of them would stay for the entire three days of mourning.

One of Kũnkuu's nephews, Yaani Kũnkuu, the son of Bɔrɔ, whom Kũnkuu had succeeded, was one of my classmates and a compound prefect as well. So he had to leave that night with his cousin, Nuɔtiɣ Kũnkuu, later both a midwife and a mother, to go to his uncle's funeral. The next morning the big boys who could walk the eighteen miles were chosen to represent the school at the funeral together with some of the teachers. Those of us who could not walk there and back

---

[a] In 1940 there was no doctor in charge of the only hospital in the Lawra District. For Dr B.B. Waddy who had been in charge of the hospital was sent away to the war. As a result there was no autopsy to ascertain the cause of Kũnkuu's death. Dr Waddy worked at Kintampo with the Medical Field Unit and later at the Hospital for Tropical Diseases in London.

[b] The Presidency of the Lawra Confederacy Native Authority was always occupied by the most senior Divisional Chief, that is, the longest serving one. Under the Native Authority system, Gana of Jirapa was the president, to be succeeded by Kũnkuu when he died in 1936.

stayed behind and were made to do general farming and cleaning around the school. After three days of mourning the boys and the teachers returned from Nandom and school resumed as usual.

Once or twice a year, the school inspectors paid visits to select pupils for the only Government Middle School in the North, which was located in Tamale, and then reported to the Director of Education on all the various schools in the province. Consequently, a school inspector's trek normally took him several weeks to visit all the schools, of which at that time there were about ten in all excluding the schools run by the Missions. At the end of 1939 the Lawra School had sent ten pupils to the Tamale Middle Boarding School, which was the first opportunity that they ever had. However, at the end of our year, 1940, there was to be an intake of only six from our school even though we were thirteen in the class at Lawra. Towards the end of the year Mr Flynn, the Provincial Inspector of Schools, came to Lawra to inspect the school and to select the six boys who were to be promoted to standard four at the beginning of the next session.

He spent three to four days in Lawra and one afternoon he came to take our class personally in order to assess our ability and to choose those boys he thought should go to Tamale. He asked our teacher what page we had reached with the *Companion to the New Method Reader*, which was called the *New Method Reader, Book Three*.[a] Our teacher told him that we had finished the whole book. So Mr Flynn asked us to open our *Companion*s at page 78. When we had done so, he asked the pupils who were sitting on the row to my right and nearest to him to complete some sentences from the book. The first sentence read like this:

"A soldier is best able to ..."

and underneath these incomplete sentences, was a list of words including "fight". The gaps were supposed to be filled with the appropriate words. Unfortunately, all the seven pupils seated on the row failed to spot the right word. He turned to my row and as I was seated in front and nearest to him asked me and I answered,

"A soldier is best able to fight".

That gave the clue to the other boys and they chose the appropri-

---

[a] The readers in all the schools in the North at that time were the *New Method Readers* I to VII, by Michael West, each with its own supplementary reader called the *Companion to the New Method Reader*. Class III was introduced to English reading with the *New Method Primer*.

ate words for their sentences. At the end of the lesson, Mr Flynn left to see what was happening in the other classes. I had saved the face of my class teacher for we had never even looked at the Companion, much less worked through it, so none of us knew what to do.

At the end of the afternoon session, Mr Flynn left for the headmaster's office while we got ready to go to the school farm. I was halfway there when I heard my name being called out and I was told I was wanted at the headmaster's office. Thinking that I might have broken a school rule, as I ran back I started ruminating in my mind as to what I might have done wrong, but nothing immediately came to mind. I ran as fast as I could so as not aggravate the situation, and by the time I got to the office, I was completely out of breath. I waited a few minutes to get my breath back and then knocked at the office door and waited for an order to enter. When I was told to do so, I entered tentatively and lo and behold, Mr Flynn was standing there with the headmaster discussing a problem. I was taken aback, and still looking timid and nervous. Mr Flynn managed to calm my nerves by chatting to me about my brothers in Tamale.

After a while, when I was at ease with him, he began to ask me questions about the English lesson he had earlier conducted in our class. He told Mr Andoh that only those boys who answered his questions correctly in the class should be promoted to standard four and that he wanted to get their names from me. It seemed that my brothers who were in Tamale, especially Biz, must have impressed him; and he certainly must have noticed the close resemblance between Biz and myself (since all my father's children do bear some of his traits). Having been told that Biz and I were from the same mother, he gave me a full account of Biz's health and the progress of his work in his new school. After such detailed information about Biz, I was allowed to return to my school duties. But as I walked back, the conversation was still ringing in my ears and I could not believe that a school inspector could take such singular interest in a simpleton like me or in my brothers. For in those days, there was such an aura of reverence that was bestowed upon any European by the blacks, let alone a man of his calibre.[a] At that moment I was in cloud cuckoo

---

[a] Under the Colonial regime, the white man was so idolised that he was considered infallible. He was supposed to be knowledgeable in all things and could do no wrong. Indeed some of them, especially the District Commissioners, pretended to be so.

land and was only brought to reality when I got back to my compound and faced my school chores.

If Mr Flynn's instructions had been strictly followed to the letter, the boys who should have gone to the senior school with me were Tiisip, Dɛri, Suuribaariyɛ, Nibɛvuuri and Kpiikurɛ Nibaalu. However, before we could go home we took our final examinations. Both Kuupone Yirbɛkyũũ and my brother, Debomo, were among the top six in the class and if Mr Andoh was to use any criterion at all other than following Mr Flynn's instructions, it should have been the class tests, in which case Debomo, Gbari and Kuupone should have been among the six to be promoted to standard four. But it seems Mr Andoh had his own reasons for dropping Kuupone, who like me was also a wizard in arithmetic, and my brother Debomo. I was greatly incensed by this unfairness, since I was the victim of that by Mr Henkel, but there was hardly anything that my brothers and I could do about it.

When the school was sent on vacation, I could not help but tell my father the way Debomo was shabbily and unjustly treated by Mr Andoh. This occurred when my father was querying Debomo as to why he was not among the lot of us going to Tamale. My brothers confirmed my story and my father was livid about it. He could not believe that Mr Andoh, whom he took as his trusted friend, would do that to his own son.[a] Anyway there was nothing he could do about it either since the names of those going to the Middle School would by then have been posted to Tamale. The reason Mr Andoh dropped Kuupone and Debomo and replaced them with Kankpɔɔ War and Yaani, as I understood it at the time, was that if Yaani and Kankpɔɔ were to repeat a year, they would have been considered too old to go to the senior school the following year. Therefore, as Debomo and Kuupone were far younger than they were, they still stood the chance of going to Tamale the following year or even two years later. Thus in our year the school did not send its best boys to the senior school as it had done before.

Mr Andoh had some bright new ideas when he took over the school. He did not remain in the shadow of Mr Henkel who had stamped his fame on the school as well as on the district. He wanted

---

[a] When Dawson Andoh came to Lawra he soon heard about the powers of Kukpɛnibiɛ and as he and his wife had been trying to have a child without success, they went to the Kukpɛnibiɛ temple and prayed for a child. Not very long after the Andohs had twins. That is why my father felt he was ungrateful after all the help he gave him.

also to leave his mark large and clear so that he too could be remembered in the future. So he began to introduce his own ideas. For instance, during Mr Henkel's five years in Lawra, he had never presented the boys with any prizes except in sports where good athletes were given money as prizes. These prizes were normally presented by the DC or his wife, if he was married, on occasions such as the Empire Day celebrations or by the CCNTs on his visits when such events were usually held.

Athletes like Tiisip, Biz, Kankpɔɔ, Naamu Tɛgɛ, Diedɔŋ and many others collected prizes which I rather envied for I could not run for toffee. Mr Andoh, on the other hand, gave book prizes in addition to pupils who were good at their lessons as well as to those who were good at other school activities. This year, on the day we were to be sent on vacation, the pupils in standard three were the first to receive their prizes. Being the top boy in my class, I was presented with my prize, a book entitled *Dr Aggrey of Africa*. It was no surprise to me to be given that book since I had been given the nickname of "Dr Aggrey" by Mr Montia as far back as 1938, but it brought some jealousy among some the bigger boys who were my seniors in standard two. It must have been at Mr Montia's instigation that that particular book was given to me; and it was one I treasured all through my school life.

After the presentation of the prizes we were dismissed and everyone left for home. A fortnight or so later our brothers from Tamale returned to join us for the holidays. But prior to their arrival a grave incident occurred in the village. Although Mr Henkel was no longer in Lawra to interrupt our holidays if we did not keep the palace clean, the habit of getting up at dawn to sweep the entire surroundings of the palace stayed with us. So early on this particular morning, just before dawn, I got up and went down with some of my illiterate younger brothers to sweep the forecourt of the palace. We had hardly begun when I heard the roar of my father's voice bellowing out in such a panic, urging us to race upstairs immediately. No sooner had we done so than two horsemen, spears raised above their heads and with fierce and stern expressions on their faces, drew up to a halt at the very spot we had left. I was still panting for breath by my father's side when they came up and greeted him. My father was armed with his double-barrelled shot-gun and the adults in the palace were ready with their bows and arrows in case these were raiders coming to storm the palace by surprise. As it turned out, they were no other than the Zongo chief of Babile, Mahama Wala, and his deputy, Mɔɣtali Moshi, who had come to report a murder that had taken place within his area of jurisdiction. But my father was livid about the way they had approached the palace and had alarmed him and the entire family.

My father possessed a fetish, Ku'kpɛnibiɛ (meaning literally "I shall not dwell with an evil doer") which was well known in the southern parts of Ghana, especially in Ashanti and the Akan-speaking area, for its power to make people rich or to make them fertile and get more children. In this particular year a man from Koforidua, about twenty-four miles from the capital, Accra, had heard of this fetish and its great powers, so he travelled over five hundred miles to come to Birifu to acquire them.[a] He was a very frail old man accompanied by his robust adult son and their guide, Sidiki Wala, whom they had hired from Koforidua to guide them to Birifu; Sidiki's original home town, Wa, was only forty-five miles south of Birifu.

When they arrived, my father told them that one Kwame Nti at Kwapra, Kumasi, had acquired the fetish from him and by its rules he was the proper person they should consult. But this frail old man would not take no for an answer. Besides the Ashantis erroneously believed the fetish originated from my father and they preferred to have it from its originator rather than at second hand. They did not know that the fetish had first been acquired by Zugu Nũũ from Ŋmankuri Nũũ, both of these chiefs being in the Jirapa Division (now part of Jirapa-Lambusie District). So he and his gang daily pounded their way on foot from Babile to the palace, a distance of three miles in all, to try to persuade my father to let him acquire the fetish. This went on for over two weeks but my father would not change his mind. Indeed he was getting a little irritated at the way the old man was pestering him in this fashion. Sensing that my father was not going to relent, Sidiki schemed up a devilish plot with the aim of getting the frail old man on his own so that he could murder him and steal the money which he thought he had brought with him.

So he deceived the old man into believing that my father had asked for more money before he would allow him to acquire the fetish. When the old man sent his son back to the south to bring back more money, this wicked guide took his chance and told him that my father had asked them to go to the palace before dawn so that they could acquire the fetish very early at the first light of day before my

[a] This Ashanti man actually came from the Nkawkaw area where he had some cocoa farms but he presumably lived in Koforidua where he had a shop. Strictly speaking, this man was not an Ashanti but an Akan; in the north anybody from the south was termed an Ashanti.

father had to travel to Lawra for the day's administrative duties.[a] Being either a fool or too eager to acquire the fetish, the old man believed him and on the set day they got up before dawn and set off for the palace. When they reached the brow of the hill which forms the plateau on which part of Birifu stands, Sidiki walked a pace or two behind the old man, took out a cudgel made of iron, and stealthily struck him on his occiput and felled him. Not satisfied with this brutal and fatal blow, he took out his sabre and cut his throat like a beast.

As he did so the blood spurted out all over his clothes. He searched the body of the deceased, found the little money – a paltry fifty shillings or so–which he had on him and took it. He then found places to hide his loot and the murder weapons before anyone was up, especially the women, who normally leave their houses about five in the morning during this time of the year. He then ran back to the Zongo where he was lodging and raised a false alarm. He told the Zongo chief that he and the old man had been attacked on their way to the palace by some French Ivoirians, four men and a woman (French Lobis, as they were called at the time). So when the Zongo chief and his deputy reported the matter to my father, he immediately organised a search of the whole village in order to hunt down the killers.

The entire riverside was combed from Batan to Gũble. Luckily for my father, no one crossed the river that day after he had given orders to shoot at any Ivoirian in the area who attempted to resist arrest. He would otherwise have had more murders on his hands. While the hunt for the culprits went on, my father's assistant, Sakpi, was sent to report the murder to the District Commissioner, the Lawra Nũũ and of course the Police. With great foresight my father also asked that Sidiki be detained until the police arrived so he could narrate the story to them personally. Within a few hours the police were on the scene headed by Sgt. Mahama Grunshi and his General Police Constable (GP) who would take down written statements.[b] Dr Saunders, the

---

[a] The inhabitants of the Babile Zongo were mostly Muslims and the first call to prayer was usually at about four o'clock in the morning when the place was still dark. It was at this hour that Sidiki and his master set off for Birifu.

[b] The Gold Coast Police at that time comprised the illiterate class known as the the Escort Police armed with guns who did a lot of escorting jobs e.g. escorting the transport of money from one treasury to another; and the General Police constables (GP) who formed the literate class and whose minimum qualification was the height required by the Police Authority and the possession of a Standard VII certificate.

medical officer for the district, arrived to conduct a forensic examination of the place of the murder as well as a postmortem of the body. That day the schoolboys were involved in interpreting from English into vernacular and vice versa for my father and his investigators. By noon no person from the Ivory Coast had been found, but the police had a shrewd idea who the murderer was and the search was switched from the killers to one for weapons at the scene of the murder.

So after the searchers had been served with beer and given a few minutes rest, the hunt continued. By nightfall the murder weapons had been found as well as the stolen money. These were all hidden at different places beneath big laterite boulders that littered the whole area. Then when Sidiki's blood-stained clothes together with the murder weapons were found, he changed his statement to the police and told them that my father had ordered him and four others to murder the man so that he could use part of the body for the purposes of the fetish. From then on, the enquiry took a different turn. Five innocent people were pointed out as accomplices to the murder, one of whom was Sakpi, another a cousin, Zuun, the elder brother of Kɔb,[a] the sons of Ɔɔr.[b]

Since my father was heavily involved with the case, he was always at Lawra helping the police with their enquiries and trying to prove the innocence of his subjects as well as of himself. Sakpi and others were detained in the Lawra prison cells which also acted as the police cells. But they were later released and became crown witnesses. As a result I did not see much of my father during this particular holiday until it was time for us to return to school. This was the period of the Bɔɔr Dance and as he invariably played at these dances, he composed a song which showed his contempt for the way in which he and his people had been framed by a Wala man. He normally composed one or two new general tunes each year to be played at these dances, but one he would normally keep under his sleeve to be played in the Bɔɔr room at Bɔɔr Night during the interval between performances. This particular tune he kept for the occasion and the lyrics went like this:

---

[a] Kɔb was one of the Bɔɔr elders who recited the Black version of the Bagre Myth in *Une Recitation du Bagre* by J.R Goody and S.W.D.K. Gandah, Paris, 1981.

[b] Ɔɔr, a nephew of Gandah, was the father of both Kɔb and Zuun, the first of whom was falsely accused by Sidiki Wala as one of his accomplices.

1. Birfuɔr liɛba Waalɛ baar (repeat)
   Ba yel ka Bifuɔr liɛba Waalɛ baar
   Birfuɔr mũũ liɛba Waalɛ yaa
2. Ka Waalɛ ba tɛr tigan na (repeat)
   Ba yel ka Waalɛ ba tɛr tigan na
   Birfuɔr mũũ liɛb Waalɛ baar

This is translated literally as follows:

1. That Birfuɔr have (turned) become Waalɛ,
   They say the Birfuɔr have already become Waalɛ
   Birfuɔr have now become Waalɛ,
2. For Waalɛ have no earth shrine,
   They say the Waalɛ have no earth shrine,
   The Birfuɔr have already become Waalɛ.

After about one and half months at home, the six of us who were going to the Middle School had to leave for Wa to go with the other Lawra boys in a mammy lorry – the only part of the journey for which the Native Authority was prepared to pay our transportation. We left early because it took between ten and fourteen days to travel from Wa to Tamale on foot. I was very excited as I was going to a new school as well as escaping from the tyranny of my old one. Besides, I was also hoping to meet and become friends with the School Inspector who had been so kind to me on his last visit to Lawra. But this was a forlorn hope since he had already been relieved of his post by Mr Spafford, the resident inspector, who had returned from his four months tour of leave in Britain. We travelled to Wa and passed the night at the junior school. At dawn the next morning we set out on foot for Busa which was nine miles away. We arrived there at about 9 o'clock and the Busa Nũũ gave us some breakfast. His son, Adama Busa (B.K. Adama, former Minister of Defence in the Busia regime) joined us and after breakfast we set off again for Bulenga, which was a further twelve miles away. We arrived there between noon and 1pm, rested a while, had our lunch and then started off for our next destination, Dusie, which was a further eight miles away.

This last lap of our day's journey involved travelling through the bush where there was a lot of big game including lions and leopards. As I walked along this bush path, the heat of the scorching sun drained all my energy and I began to fall behind the rest of the group. I believe I was the youngest and besides was not that quick on my feet. When my brother, Biz, realised I had fallen behind and could not be seen, he became anxious and retraced his steps until he found me. He took the small bag in which I had wrapped my few clothes together with the pocket money which dad had given to each of us. The group ahead waited under the shade of a big tree, resting their feet until we caught up with them. They allowed us to stop and cool down before we all set out again. While we were resting, I noticed that my baggage had come loose and my pocket money was no longer in the place I put it. I asked Biz if he had taken it for safekeeping but he thought I suspected him of stealing my money. He was so enraged with me that he wanted to beat me up there and then. Were it not for the big boys, especially Adama Chansa and Bawa Chira, whom I had only got to know on the journey, he would have certainly done so. Nevertheless he refused to help carry my baggage for the rest of the journey. So Bawa Chira came to my aid and helped carry my things to Tamale. By dusk we had arrived at Dusie where we passed our second night.

After some days travelling through the bush, doing about thirty or forty miles a day and sleeping at villages such as Gbanwule, Ŋmanwule and so on on the way, we arrived at one village, Konkore, which lay at the foot of a scarp, a mountain range that extended miles eastwards across to Larabanga.[a] We passed the night there and as usual were given free meals just as the chiefs in the other villages had done throughout the journey so far. After dinner I was so tired and aching all over that I immediately fell asleep and gave some rest to the muscles in my legs and feet. The next morning, just before dawn, we were awakened by the big boys to get up and continue with the day's journey. Those of us who had never walked that way before had been warned not to look back or down as we climbed the scarp.

As we walked through this narrow valley which was lined with reeds and tall grasses, the fierce and icy wind of the harmattan hissed menacingly in our ears and beat against our bodies, bending down the tall grasses that were laden with the dew that drenched our thin clothes. Our frozen feet and hands made the climb much more difficult and one had to cling on for dear life lest one should fall down and land up many feet below. In desperation I clung on and did not allow myself to lose sight of the group in case I could not find my way if I was left behind. We were sheltered from the sun as we scaled

---

[a] These villages which I passed through were Gonja villages with Gonja names. Some of these could have been mis-spelt. [Larabanga is an old Muslim town with a Sudanese style mosque, situated on the Bole-Tamale road. Ed.]

this monstrous mountain but when we conquered it and reached the summit by about 9 a.m. the heat of the sun greeted us with some civility. I was more than glad to see the sun since my body could unfreeze itself by the heat of its glorious rays.

We descended the scarp on a gentle gradient and by about eleven o'clock that morning we arrived at the Gonja divisional town of Daboya–once famous for its salt–very thirsty and hungry. It was a shallow crossing over the river, the White Volta, at this time of the year, so we needed no boats to ferry us across. We bathed, paddled and swam in the river to cool ourselves from the burning sun, which earlier on had been a friend but had now become an enemy beating down on us with such intense fire over the last part of the day's journey. After about half an hour in the water we were all told to get out to proceed with the day's journey. Daboya was forty-one miles away from Tamale and we were determined to reach there the next day. Our aim was to cover another twenty-five miles that day and pass the night at the Dagomba town of Tolon which was sixteen miles from Tamale.

By between one and two o'clock that afternoon, we had arrived at a village called Gyɛrɛɣo-yili (meaning literally "a fool's settlement"). The villagers were not as hospitable as those we had met from Wa to Daboya and I was really taken aback when muddy water was actually sold to us. In Birifu, water was supposed to be God's gift and not to be sold to anyone. The Dagara adage that "if a child does not travel, he experiences nothing" rang true in this instance. For here for the first time I witnessed water being sold. After buying food and water to eat and drink we set off for our destination. The villages along the main road, which was now macadamised, were few and far between and the mirages on the road ahead did not help our cause or quench our thirst.[a] We persevered and by about nine in the evening we had arrived at Tolon. I am not sure whether we bought our own food or whether it was supplied by the chief. What I do know is that that night we had enough food and beer. And since I had lost my pocket money, I could not have paid for my own unless the other brothers had contributed to pay for my share of the cost.

---

[a] These mirages are very deceptive to inexperienced travellers. They make you feel as if there was a pool of water ahead but as soon as you approach the spot, they move themselves to another place in front of you. No wonder that animals chase after these mirages in order to quench their thirst and eventually fall and die of exhaustion.

That night, it was a full moon and a cloudless harmattan evening brought its biting cold wind; the moon was so clear and bright that a lost needle could have been found in the dust. The villagers were drumming and dancing in the moonlight and despite the cold wind the dancers were sweating profusely. Those who were tired of dancing or were simply spectators sat round the little bonfires that were scattered about the place. Tired as we were, some of the big boys who had travelled there several times went off with their girl friends. At that age sex meant nothing to me and even if it had, I would have been too tired to think about it.

I soon fell asleep only to be awakened the next morning before dawn to set off on the last lap of our journey. Between seven and eight o'clock we arrived at the daily market where we were greeted by women selling water and shouting "pii pii kom" (literally, "water for a nickel") as they rushed towards us jostling each other in competition for our custom. In those days ten West African nickels were equal to a penny and a calabash of water with porridge and pepper cost one nickel. As we arrived we formed into groups. There were six Gandah brothers plus our cousin, Diyuɔŋ Nitii, from Tugu. So the seven of us dashed straight to the stall where pito was being sold.

Pito in Tamale, especially that brewed by pure Dagomba brewers, differed markedly from that brewed in Birifu or in the Dagara area. In Birifu all the sediment is strained off but in Tamale the beer contained a lot and resembled porridge. Nevertheless we bought ourselves a pot or two to quench our thirst. That done, we bought some food to break our fast after which the three brothers and our cousin who knew the town well showed us round, until about four in the afternoon when we strolled to the school situated some three miles from the town. Although the school had not yet opened, we were accommodated and fed until it did so. However, to compensate for the free food we had to do general cleaning every morning and those wanting to visit the town did so after breakfast. Those of us who were new had to get hold of our basic uniforms including the gown that was supposed to be worn for evening meals. So we had to visit the town and buy the material to give to tailors to sew to measure.

The Tamale Government Middle Boarding School was opened in 1927 and took over from the former Government Trade School that had been opened in 1922 and where my uncle Miiru was trained as a carpenter. When the school was finally reopened, the headmaster, Mr D.A. Mahama, and all the teachers were present as the roll was called. The senior prefect, the compound prefects and the deputy compound prefects as well as the dining hall chairman and his deputy were appointed. Those who held posts the previous year were either promoted to a senior post or remained in their present one. When the appointment of these officers was complete, the newcomers were assigned to their compounds.

There were six of these in my first year and each compound comprised six dormitories or rooms which accommodated at most four boys each. I was assigned to compound four. I was lucky to have Adama Chansa as my compound prefect for I had got used to him when we had travelled from Wa. His assistant, Mumuni Kpaligu, was a Mamprusi from Gambaga (Nalerigu) School. In my compound there were a few Waala boys but I was the only Lawra boy. There was also Bapɛŋyiri Yelpoi (now the Jirapa Nũũ), but although from the Lawra District, he had attended junior school in Wa. My other brothers, Tiisip and Dɛri, were lucky to share compounds with other brothers who had been in the school the year before and who were already familiar with the place. On the other hand I was very glad to have in the same compound Bawa Chira who had befriended me during our long walk to school. Apart from the compound prefects and their deputies, we also had table and room captains. The room captain was responsible for seeing that no noise was made when the lights went out and that the cleaning of the section of the compound and its surrounds was apportioned out among the room members. He was also responsible for seeing that the lawn allotted to the room was kept cut and not allowed to become overgrown. My room captain was Natɔɣma Sakɔɣu who was a good athlete but wicked and oppressive to me.

The table captain with his assistant was responsible for appointing dining hall curators to dish out the food and to lay the tables before meal times; these appointments he made weekly. He was also responsible for seeing that no one made any noise while eating was in progress; for talking was prohibited in the dining hall as it was considered to be bad manners. That accounts for the fact that I am no good in conversing at meals. In Tamale, unlike the Lawra school, there were three dining hall curators at a time for each compound, two in charge of the bowls and one for spoons. These bowls were made of aluminium and had been designed for prisons all over the country. Each bowl and spoon was given a number and assigned to a particular boy. These numbers were then allocated to each compound in ascending order of magnitude.

Consequently compound one had the lower number while compound six had the highest. There were six tables placed along the length of the hall in a row with spaces in between, and three tables across the breadth of the hall. Each row of tables across the hall corresponded to a compound. This meant that each compound was seated laterally on three tables. About half an hour before meal time, the cooks brought the cooked food in large basins which they placed on the compound tables. The curators went in about fifteen minutes later to lay the table. It was the responsibility of the curators of the bowls to dish out the food on to each boy's bowl and place it at his sitting place. The curator of spoons was responsible for laying out the spoons on the table for each boy as well as for filling the water jugs with water and supplying the aluminium tumblers (which had also been numbered). All these chores had to be carried out by the curators before the drum was sounded for the dining hall call. Woe betide the curator, whether he was new or old, who put the wrong bowl or spoon at the wrong place. After the meals these curators were responsible for the washing up before the next roll call. If one erred in these matters, one's table captain could ask the boy to repeat his task the following week. It was usual for the smaller boys to be made curators of spoons whilst the bigger boys became the curators of bowls. However the terms "big" and "small" are relative in that this depended on the compound and the range of boys in it. For instance in compound four I was a curator of spoons whilst in compound five Biz, Gyub and Dɛri who were far older than me did the same work. On the other hand Tiisip and Nana were curators of bowls in compound six.

My table captain was one Fuseini Daramani, a Gonja, from Salaga School. This young man who was in his last year at school was a tyrant and scared me stiff; indeed I feared him more than my compound prefect and his deputy. In whatever way I cleaned his spoon he still found fault with it. However with such wicked table captains, still the curators of spoons knew how to deal with them. They would use sand or glass paper to polish the spoon until one could see oneself in it. In doing so they would sharpen the edges of the spoon with the sand-paper so that it would cut their lips or tongue. There were even worse tricks which some dare-devils used to punish their table captains, or any other big boy who dared bully them.

I was more than tempted to use one of these methods on Fuseini but did not have the heart to do so. In fact my school pen-pal when I was in Lawra was Bakari Kanantrope (later called Kanan Bak and now deceased), who became my best friend when I came to the senior school and he noticed that this tyrant was bullying me for no reason at all.[a] Bakari, who was also a Gonja, came from a village called Kanantrope in the Bole District. In the Gonja, Dagomba and Mamprusi areas many boys took their village and town names as their surnames. Coming from the same Gonja District, he had words with this Fuseini to ask him to go easy on me but his plea met with deaf ears. I was glad to see the back of him after enduring his tyranny for one year, for that was his last year in school.

---

[a] Bakari Kanantrope, after leaving standard seven, trained as an artist and became Mr Gomez's assistant at the school. He changed his name to Kanan Bak, which is the reverse and abridged form of his name in school. Although a big boy in the school and holding a post, he laundered and ironed my clothes every Saturday.

CHAPTER TEN

AT COLLEGE AND EVEN EARLIER at school, I was eager to promote myself in further education. I heard of a Correspondence College, Bennet College in Sheffield, in the UK. While at college I could afford to pay for a course by instalments and so I wrote to Sheffield for their prospectus. When this arrived, I enrolled for the matriculation course, the forerunner of the General Certificate of Education (GCE). I also bought some text books on maths such as algebra and geometry as well as some literature books such as ones on prosody, syntax, etc. As Latin was a compulsory subject for a matriculation course and exam, I bought textbooks on Cicero and other Latin authors on the syllabus at the time. The Teacher Training College did not teach maths to matriculation standard, especially geometry and algebra, nor did they teach foreign languages such as Latin or French. I approached my friend Miss Gladstone whom I thought would be only too pleased to help me. But like Queen Victoria, the lady was not amused.

After her literature lesson with us, she went and complained to T.C. Anan, the senior housemaster, that he should vet the books bought by the students from abroad as some of us were ordering useless books, citing me as a typical example. T.C. Anan called me to his office and told me what he had been advised to do but by then I had ordered all the books I wanted to buy from abroad anyway. I was waiting for the first lessons which Bennet College had advised they had despatched but they never arrived before I left college. I was not sure if the course had arrived and the college refused to hand it over to me.

My brother Biz and I were posted to the Lawra primary school where I was to teach class two and he, class one. During my teaching practice, a few months previously, I found out that my present class had not covered much of their first year's syllabus. I decided to start them from the beginning on the same syllabus as Biz but at a much faster pace than he would follow. After two months when they had covered enough ground to cope, I introduced them to their class syllabus. By the time the school inspector came round to Lawra, the majority of the pupils in the class were no longer timid in answering questions, but were lively and alert. The inspector was none other than Col. Wentworth who had seen me struggling in desperation with the very class a few months ago. He now found a different attitude in both teacher and pupils alike. He could not believe what he saw and visited my class at different lesson periods while he was in Lawra to assure himself that it was not a rehearsed lesson I had arranged and for which the children had shown such exuberance. On the eve of his departure, he met the school staff and I was surprised to hear him lavish so much praise on my performance and the progress of the class over the past few months.

Preparations for the Empire Day celebrations on May 24 were always a busy time for teachers and pupils alike and 1947 was no exception. As soon as it reopened, the school was engaged in preparing pupils for plays and recitations in order to entertain the chief of Lawra and his people. When this day arrived, the school marched to the town to the tune of their percussion band and formed a parade on the football ground where a temporary flagstaff had been constructed. The Union Jack was unfolded to the music of the Police bugle that sounded the Last Post whilst the DC took the salute. There was the usual march past by the school to the accompaniment of the percussion music and followed by the contingent of the Lawra police force and that of the prison warders. After the ritual we sang "God save the King" and the school then stood at ease; they listened to the DC reading the Empire Day message from King George VI. This was usually sent through the Governor of the Gold Coast to all the district stations in the country. After hearing the message and that of the Governor awarding the school children a public holiday, which invariably happened on each Empire Day, the children were dismissed to prepare to entertain the crowd with the school revue. After that the people dispersed to return for the afternoon session when the sports competition took place. It was at these events that those children who were good in sports often earned a bit of pocket money for themselves.

Every year, round about September when the groundnuts and the maize have been harvested, the people of Lawra and its surrounding villages perform their yearly festival of K'ɔbinɛ. The word *K'ɔbinɛ* is short for the phrase *kuɔr binɛ* which means the "drum dance" as opposed to xylophone dances. This dance is performed to the rhythm of the gourd drums which have been tuned to various pitches, high and low. Because it is performed when all the farming has been completed, it is sometimes misunderstood by foreigners to be a harvest festival. It takes place on every market day in the market place. Each group of dancers from a settlement visits the market on four successive market days before it is abandoned for the sɛbri and binɛ dances. The sɛbri is danced at the compound of the chief or of some other leader in the parish.

In Lawra there would sometimes be over six groups dancing the K'ɔbinɛ in the market square, from Lawra town itself, Tuori, Yikpɛ̃ɛ̃, Tolibri, Gbier, Dikpɛ and one or two from across the Volta, each coming when all harvesting and ridging had been finished. The Lawra market falls every six days. As they do not all start at the same time, the festival could last over two months. During this period the school children were allowed to go to town on every market day to witness the dance in the afternoon from about three to six in the evening. In 1947 all the teachers except the headmaster and the art teacher, one Sawley Sakara from Kusawgu in the Gonja district, hailed from the Lawra District and were especially interested to take part in the K'ɔbinɛ dance. Kuunũũ-i-ŋmin (Kuunayiŋmin), Biz and I normally joined the group from the Lawra town while Kpata from Gũũpɔr, a section of Yikpɛ̃ɛ̃, danced with the Yikpɛ̃ɛ̃ or the Dikpiɛlɛ group, whichever came to the market first.

It is at these dances that prospective couples choose their partners. A good dancer could have many admirers but was sure to choose at least one as his partner. There was one girl, Siŋmin, who hailed from Yikpɛ̃ɛ̃ but at that time was residing at the Lawra Nũũ's palace. She fancied me, and I her. At these dances, the women normally stood outside the circle of dance and as the men danced round, any girl or woman who fancied the man – or his steps – would join the dance circle behind or in front of him as he danced. So on each market day that we went to town, she was there waiting anxiously to see if I would turn up. But she had competition on her hands from the girls at the school. They were in their teens and one of them was to be my future wife. They competed with her for a place on either side of me. Of course as a teacher, I did not want or try to encourage these schoolgirls in any way. Some of them were perhaps just there for a laugh for I was nearer their age group than any of the other teachers in the school, and they tended to be very free with me and played practical jokes on me.

Nevertheless the girl I really cared for most at the time, although an illiterate, was Siŋmin, but she had been warned off when the chief learnt that she was paying too much attention to me and that I had invited her with my two sisters, who played cupid, to the school to have a drink. I later learnt from them that the girl had been promised to one of her maternal cousins in Nandom and the chief did not want her to disappoint her uncles. On the other hand, Katulɛ Sulley, who was to be my future wife, was telling her mates that I was to be her future husband and even spoke about it to her uncle, Kpata Sawley, and his wife. I did not believe what she was saying and took it as a teenage infatuation with her teacher until I had actually left the school.

Our weekly visits to the Lawra market were interrupted when we received the sad news that my uterine brother, Dɛn, had been struck dead by lightning. He died while harvesting groundnuts on my father's farm. As the group of people were stripping the roots under a tree, the lightning struck killing him outright while burning and numbing others in its path; among these was Volvuu, my father's eldest living son at the time (now dead). Biz and I left for home at the weekend to attend the funeral but unfortunately there was no funeral for him to be mourned publicly because the diviners believed that he was struck by lightning because of his evil deeds. Death by lightening was seldom mourned and the victim was assumed to have committed a crime against the gods. Since there was no mourning we returned to school on the Sunday evening to prepare our lessons for the next day.

In order to increase literacy in Lawra, the headmaster, Dawson Andoh, suggested to the teachers that we should give some of our spare time in the evenings to teach the unfortunate people of the town who could neither read nor write. All the teachers volunteered and we started night classes at the community centre in the town where initially a lot of enthusiasts enrolled. We tried to group them into those who could speak English and those who could not and into those who knew their ABC and those who did not have a clue. I took a class of about four or five, who, due to their Koranic training, could be considered literate but not in the English or in the western style. Two of my students had been employed in 1936 by the entomologist, Dr Morris, as "fly boys" and were responsible for catching tsetse flies at their breeding places. Dr Morris was in charge of the tsetse fly eradication campaign in the north under Dr Saunders and was stationed in Lawra.

From my past experience, I wanted to start them at the very beginning and take them through at their own pace. Two of them, Tanko (now an Alhaji) and Bukari, responded diligently. By the end of the year they had covered a vast ground and could read English text books. As far as maths or should I say arithmetic was concerned, they mastered that subject very quickly and were very good at it as soon as they learnt the concepts of division, multiplication, addition and subtraction. I later understood they pursued their studies on their own and were promoted to the highest positions in their Department. In fact Bukari confessed to me in the Lawra Nũũ's palace, during one of my visits back to Ghana in 1975, that it was through me he was able to sit for the 'Ordinary' level of the General Certificate of Education. I told him I could not take the credit for that since it was he who persevered to attain that position.

During the course of the year, the school decided to go to Wa to play a football match against the school there. The Headmaster, Dawson Andoh, had heard I had produced and staged Shakespeare plays while I was at the College and told me of his desire for the school to produce something on similar lines so that we could stage it if and when we visited Wa for the match. This would make it a memorable weekend for the townsfolk as well. I told him I was in agreement provided he could convince the other teachers to take part. That would be difficult for me since I was the most junior teacher in the school. As it turned out all of them agreed to our suggestion. The headmaster had a copy of "The Shoemaker's Holiday" and wanted us to act that play. But since I had the complete works of Shakespeare in my library, I suggested that we include in our production "Julius Caesar". As soon as the school inspector had come and gone, we set about auditioning the teachers and some of the boys in the upper classes. I was cast for the role of Casca in "Julius Caesar" and for the Prologue and Epilogue of the "Pied Piper of Hamlyn". It was decided that only pupils in standards one to three would go to Wa to watch except for those in the lower classes who were taking part in the dramas that were to be performed in the vernacular.

I had also developed a music group with my class and it was suggested I could pick the best of these to go along as well. As the time came nearer there were still some people who had not yet learned their lines by heart, including some of the teachers. I became very worried about the success of our venture. As a result we began to spend more time both in the mornings and evenings doing rehearsals but still there was very little progress made. In the end we used the afternoon and games periods as well. I breathed a sigh of relief when some weeks prior to our departure most people started to be confident with their lines. When the time arrived, we set off to Wa and put up at the Wa Primary Boarding School, which was headed by Mr D.A. Mahama, our former headmaster in the Middle School in Tamale.

The football match was scheduled to be played on the Saturday afternoon and the plays to be performed the next day at 5 p.m. So on the Sunday afternoon we again marched from the school to the town; for just like the Lawra school, the Wa one was situated about two miles from the centre. At about five we performed our plays in the open air before the Wa Nũũ, Koray, and his people, until about nine in the evening when the show came to a close. We left for Lawra that same night; and a week later we repeated the same show to the Lawra Nũũ and his people.

In November of 1947 Prince Philip was to be married to Princess Elizabeth (later Queen Elizabeth II). To celebrate the occasion, the school was as usual called upon to provide entertainment. A parade was also to be held in the town. So in the morning the school with its percussion band marched to town to join the police and the prison warders in the march past to celebrate the wedding and in the afternoon we repeated the plays which had been performed at Wa. All this was warmly appreciated.

About the same time, there was a case of an alleged murder in Tugu when the suspect escaped across the river Volta to Zambɔ in the Ivory Coast where he stayed with his kinsfolk. Through negotiations with the French authorities he was brought back to the British territory for questioning. Before he could be cautioned and charged with the crime an interpreter was needed to translate his side of the story from the vernacular into English and vice versa, so the police constable could take down his statement. It was possible the headmaster had been approached for one his staff to do the interpretation, since the constable was a southerner and did not understand the local language. The headmaster approached me and I agreed to help out.

It turned out that the nephew of the accused had visited him at Zambɔ and when he was returning, the accused gave him some baskets of grain as a present to take home. As the nephew could not carry all by himself, the accused asked his wife to help him to carry them home. When they arrived at Tugu, the nephew refused to let his uncle's wife return and they slept together as man and wife and she became pregnant. Although a nephew can marry an uncle's widow, he could not do so while the uncle was still living. His uncle sent several messages for his wife to return but had no response from him or from the wife. When he himself came from Zambɔ to Tugu he found that his wife was pregnant. Despite this, he was still interested in his wife and wanted to take her back home; for by custom the child would lawfully have been his when it was born. But the nephew refused to give up the woman. A struggle ensued between him and his nephew in which the wife joined in on the side of the nephew. On the spur of the moment the uncle stabbed his nephew to death and in a panic ran back across the river to his home town. In his statement he said he thought he was going to be killed by the two of them, hence his reaction.

Most police constables of the Gold Coast Police Force were either "General Police" whose minimum qualification was the attainment of the standard seven certificate, or else belonged to the illiterate class, the "Escort Police", who were given the nickname "khaki police" because of the uniform, or else *buka buka*, a Hausa phrase meaning the "beaters" to describe the lavish way the truncheon was used by them. The standard of English of most GPs was not that high. So this accused was lucky to have me to interpret his statement properly for the GP to take down. When all the investigations on the case were complete, his docket was sent to Tamale so a case could be prepared against him.

In those days there was only one Police Commissioner and probably an Assistant, always expatriates, in the whole of the Northern Territories. It was he who had to prosecute at the preliminary hearings in the magistrate's court. This was held in the DC's court presided over by the DC before an accused was committed for trial at the assizes. A few months later this Police Commissioner or the Assistant came to Lawra to indict the accused. At this preliminary hearing, which took place on a Saturday, I was called upon as a crown witness only to identify the statement of the accused which I had earlier interpreted from the vernacular into English and vice versa; and that it was the true copy that was in the docket. After reading through the document carefully I answered in the affirmative. The hearing was only a formality and took only a few minutes when he was formally indicted to stand trial at the Assizes, after which I returned to the school to carry on with my normal work.

There was to be the general census in the Gold Coast early in 1948 which should have taken place in 1941 but was postponed because of the Second World War. Almost all the educated people, especially the teachers who were on vacation at the time, were recruited to carry out this census. Biz and I were recruited as enumerators; Biz was to carry out the enumeration of the people of Birifu with Gyub as his supervisor whilst I was to cover the village of Tugu with Diedɔŋ as my supervisor. The chiefs in each village or town were asked to alert the people in the parish to stay at home when they were to be visited that morning, and not to leave for their farms, to fetch firewood or to herd the cattle.

My father had always kept an eagle eye on the safety of his children, especially those of us he had sent to school. As I was going outside his domain to an area whose people were distrusted by those of Birifu, he was afraid to let me travel alone to Tugu in case I might be poisoned through the drinking of beer (pito), unless some older person from the house accompanied me on my travels. Although I was now an adult my father still considered me a child and despite the fact that the Tugu Nũũ, Tambaa, was my brother-in-law and could take good care of me and protect me from those with evil eye or bad intentions, he still worried about my safety. He instructed his trusted nephew, Dɛrpur, to accompany me every day to Tugu so I could do my job. Before dawn, Dɛrpur would get up to saddle a horse for me to mount and another for himself and we would set off so as to be in Tugu by dawn. Since this was my first experience of riding a horse by myself, not only was I terrified but within a week I felt the soreness on my backside. However I had almost completed the census count for Tugu area when I received a message to call on the DC in Lawra.

When I was at college I complained to the Principal, Mr K.J. Dickens, of my poor eyesight and was sent down to the hospital in town to consult the medical officer even though he was not an eye specialist. After testing my eyes, he suggested I did not need spectacles at the time. He advised me to do some exercises by rotating my eyes round and round in order to strengthen the roots at the back. I followed his routine and never had any further trouble with them until I left the college. Although the war had ended over two years previously, there were still many shortages of ordinary necessities in the cities, and more so in out-stations such as Lawra. Necessities like kerosene (paraffin), candles and sugar were non-existent in Lawra as there were no big shops. The only small shop in the whole of Lawra town was built and opened by Kwesi Dam in 1936 but it invariably ran out of stock. We depended on the itinerant Yoruba traders to fill in the economic vacuum. They travelled to Kumasi to bring back these items to the district if they could find them to buy and get the transport to bring them back.

To be a good teacher, one had to prepare one's lecture notes for the next day's teaching in order to deliver the lesson effectively to the class. Headteachers were supposed to see that each teacher prepared his or her lecture notes daily; but as our headteacher was himself not complying with the rules, he found it difficult to enforce them. Any time there was no paraffin or candles in town, I had to bind some straw together and make a torch of that. My house boy, Zuuri A-ia, would then hold the torch above my writing table while I wrote my notes for the next day's teaching. In doing so my eyesight deteriorated. Then one day, when Mr Carman, the Acting Principal and Acting Head of Education in the Region, acting for Col. Wentworth, came round to inspect our school and to examine his final year students on teaching practice, I told him of my plight. He promised to check my records at the College and to let me know the outcome.

I did not hear from him until the schools went on vacation and I was in the field doing the census enumeration. But maybe he left the final decision to be made for Col. Wentworth who was shortly to return to his permanent post from his leave overseas. While I was in the field, a message came from the DC asking me to leave the enumeration of the census and to report to him the next day in his office at Lawra. I thought this must be in connection with the census. The next day I got up early and after breakfast was on my way to Lawra. When I got there, it was only to be told that the Principal of the College had arranged for me to visit Kumasi and see one Doctor Hupenbauer, the only eye specialist for the provinces of Ashanti and the Northern Territories, and possibly for the entire Gold Coast. The DC instructed his clerk to issue me with a travel warrant so that I could travel by the Government mail-lorry which came to the District once a week on Friday afternoons. Luckily there was a Government Transport lorry leaving for Kumasi the following day and the DC's clerk issued me with a transport waybill so I could catch it the next day at Babile, the junction road to Birifu. The driver was instructed to look for me and pick me up at the junction.

I returned home late in the afternoon and informed my father about my unexpected journey to Kumasi. I had visited there in 1943 as a schoolboy and had not been back since but was not daunted by that. I knew I would be looked after well if I asked for the houses of my father's friend, Kwame Nti. The next day my father took me down to some of his demigods, poured libations to them and asked them to take care of and guide me through a peaceful journey to and from Kumasi. After the pacification ceremony, I went down to Babile and within half an hour the mail-lorry pulled up.

After picking up some fares to line his own pocket, the driver set off with all of us aboard for Wa and Bole. In those days, if there were no breakdowns on the way, it took three days for the Government transport lorry to travel from Lawra to Kumasi, a journey of 365 miles.

The first night was passed at Bole, where we lodged in the transport yard which was on the outskirts of the town. The second night was passed in the lorry park at Wenchi as Wenchi had no transport yard. On the third day, instead of going straight to Kumasi, we had to divert to Sunyani, so that the driver could deliver and pick up the mail on the way. So we did not get to Kumasi until late in the evening of the third day.

Kwame had two houses in Kumasi and luckily for me the driver knew where one of them was and took me there as it was only about 440 yards from the transport yard. I was also lucky to meet one of his wives whom he had brought with him on several visits to Birifu. As soon as she saw me, she rushed down from upstairs into the courtyard to embrace me with the phrase *Ohene ba ni-oo! aatuu...* which I took to mean "here is the chief's son! You are welcome...". Among the Ashantis, as in most parts of Ghana, when a visitor arrives at a place, he is first given a drink of some sort before he or she would be introduced to everyone. The visitor is then welcomed with a further drink and the purpose of the visit is demanded. So when she had taken my luggage upstairs, she first brought me a cup of cold water and then a bottle of schnapps, which we managed to empty between us and some of the residents who followed her upstairs. When we had finished, everyone present shook my hand and she asked me the purpose of my visit to Kumasi. When I told her I had come down to consult the eye specialist at the hospital, she told me it was only a stone's throw from the house and that her nephew would take me there on Monday. She also told me that her husband was at the village and would probably be in town the next day but that if he did not come to town, she would take me to see him after my visit to the doctor.

As we had arrived on Saturday, I spent the next day looking round this beautiful city, window shopping and making sure I could retrace my steps to the house. At that time there was some tension in the air. Political uneasiness was brewing in the cities in the south and Kumasi was no exception to that turmoil. I did not wander very far away from the house but just walked around the surrounding area. Kwame did not visit town that Sunday but my hostess showed me how to get to the hospital and within ten minutes I was at its gates. Holding my letter of introduction from the principal to the specialist, I was ushered into his consulting room. Mr Hupenbauer did not prescribe any spectacles for me but gave me some eye drops to use and some daily exercises to perform.

After lunch on my return from the hospital, my hostess and I visited the village of Kwapra. This was situated five miles from Kumasi on the Wenchi-Kumasi road through a settlement called Kununum, and then two miles into the forest by footpath. We got on a truck that plied between Kumasi and Kununum, and then went by foot to Kwapra so that I could greet her husband and let him know of my presence in town. At the village, my father was greatly revered because of the fetish, Kunkpɛnibiɛ, which Kwame and his brother Kojo had acquired from him. I was lavishly entertained with many bottles of various kinds of spirits, mostly schnapps or gin which the Ashantis adored most at that time. My hostess and I returned to Kumasi at dusk.

The next day I walked to the Government Transport Yard Office to confirm my return booking. As ill-luck would have it, I was told there was no seat for my return on that week's mail-lorry because all the places had been fully booked. One day, while I was at the transport yard, I met my headmaster who was as surprised to see me as I was to see him. He had gone to his home town, Cape Coast, for the school holidays and was then returning to Lawra for the reopening of the school. He was lucky to get a seat on the next lorry bound for Lawra, but because my warrant was an open one, I could not be accommodated. I told him why I was in town and that if I failed to get a confirmed booking for the following week I would be at least two weeks late in arriving and if he did not see me at the opening day in school, he should know that I was still in Kumasi.

The next day he left with the Kumasi-Sunyani-Lawra mail lorry for Lawra. I visited the transport yard daily to see if I could get a booking on any of their cargo trucks instead of waiting a week for the mail lorry. On one of these visits to the Transport Yard I was lucky to meet one of my father's friends, who was at the yard; my father had so many Government Transport drivers as his friends. He was surprised to see me there and wondered what I was doing in Kumasi. I told him of my plight and he said he was loading his lorry to travel to Lawra by the direct route via Wenchi instead of through Sunyani. He told the booking clerk that he would take me on his lorry and the clerk agreed immediately since I had been a thorn in his flesh. So I was immediately booked to travel by this truck. I was told to go home and get ready and be at the yard the day after next before nine in the morning. The following day I returned to Kwapra and bade farewell to Opanyin Kwame Nti. Then on the day of my departure I arrived at the transport yard on time so as not to miss the truck. We moved out of the transport yard at nine precisely but did not leave the municipality until around eleven because the driver was collecting extra fares as his perks. As this was not a mail lorry we did not have to stop at each district unless there was need to do so. We were able to reach our destination much quicker than ordinarily.

I arrived at Lawra at about nine o'clock in the evening on the same day that the school was to be opened. It was bright evening with a full moon shining in the sky with all the stars and their twinkling lights surrounding it, and with the shooting stars occasionally going from north to north-east or south to south-west. As I alighted from the vehicle, I saw my headteacher also in town for he had come to town to say hello to his Yoruba girl friend who normally prepared his meals. Indeed the girl friend had also been a good family friend to the Gandah family. So I went and told him I had just arrived and would be seeing him the next day to ask for some time off, at least a week, so I could go home and collect my things which I had left behind in Birifu, since these were in sixes and sevens. He seemed to have understood what I was saying.

CHAPTER ELEVEN

I STAYED IN TOWN WITH my cousin, Diyuɔŋ Nitii, and the next morning I went up to the school to see the headteacher to ask for a few days off so I could go home and gather my things that needed to be cleaned and ironed. To my surprise, the headteacher refused to allow me time off. He argued that since my class was a new one, it was inadvisable I should miss a period with them. I tried to counter his argument by telling him that as the pupils were beginners, it mattered very little if they were without a teacher, provided they completed the syllabus and understood and grasped what they were taught within the year. I quoted the experience I had with the previous year's class and went on to stress the fact that had it not been for the driver who helped me, I would not have been at the school for at least another week. The children would have been without a teacher for at least a week or two. But Dawson would not see the logic in my reasoning, nor I his.

Mr Andoh told me that since I was an employee of the Native Authority, he could not grant me any sick leave and that I had to seek leave of absence from the Lawra Nũũ, J.A. Karbo. I did not foresee any problems with that and therefore returned to town to see the Lawra Nũũ; however, before I got there, Mr Andoh had taken his bicycle and rode ahead to town to acquaint the Lawra Nũũ with his side of the story and of his decision. I believe Mr Andoh's refusal to allow me the few days' leave was due to his personal grudge and vendetta against me during the close of the previous year. This was because I had had the courage of my convictions to oppose him in front of one or two of the school children. He therefore thought I had humiliated him in front of these pupils. But on the contrary, it was he who tried to humiliate me before these children because he felt I was once his pupil and must accept every thing he said without question.

I had left my bicycle in Birifu before I went to Kumasi and on my return came straight to Lawra. So I had to walk about a mile and a half back to town through the bush path. When I arrived the Lawra Nũũ was already down from his palace and was sitting by the Native Authority Offices. I went up to seek audience with him. After explaining to him why I wanted the sick leave, the Lawra Nũũ repeated word for word what Mr Andoh had told me earlier at the school, which was hardly surprising. After giving the chief my counter arguments, he told me he could not grant me the leave of absence against the advice of Dawson and the only person who could do that, was the DC, one Mr T.A. Meade. And that, as he too was away on trek to Nandom and would not be back in the office until three o'clock that afternoon, I should wait for his return. I waited in town from morning until three o'clock in the afternoon when I went back to see the Lawra Nũũ, that being the time he expected the DC back. I was told the DC had not returned. At that moment, Mr Dasobri, the interpreter to the DC, whom he seldom left behind on his treks, rode from the DC's office to the chief and informed him that the DC would not be returning to Lawra that day.

The chief was then in a quandary. Would he now grant me the leave I asked for against the best advice of the headteacher, or refuse me what it was necessary for me to have? He came to the conclusion that he would allow me to go home and I should get my things ready in the mean time. He would see the DC immediately on his return. If the DC refused to sanction the leave, then he would send a message to me by one of the Native Authority Police men on the Babile market day which was to fall two days later. I could then return to see the DC myself and negotiate my leave. If however I did not hear from him I should take it that the DC had approved the leave. Some members of the NA Police were normally assigned to visit the bigger markets in order to keep the peace and to help the toll collectors with the collection of the market tolls. I went home and on the Babile market day, I asked my father for permission to go to the market and enquire from the duty constables if there was any message for me from the Lawra Nũũ. I was told there was no such message and as a result I took it for granted that the DC had approved my leave. So I stayed at home for the rest of the week collecting my things together and getting ready to return to school.

Confrontation with the District Commissioner

AFTER MY LEAVE I RETURNED to Lawra and went straight to the Native Authority Office to report to the Lawra Nũũ that I was returning for duty. The reception I got from the Lawra Nũũ was very lukewarm and I took it that he had probably got other matters on his mind when he told me to report to the school. I was all the more surprised when

I got to the school and the headmaster told me that T.A. Meade wanted to have a word with me. I thought this would be about the remuneration for my census work. When I got to his office, however, and was ushered to see him, Mr Meade went red in the face on seeing me and told me that he understood from both the Lawra Nũũ and the headmaster that I had absented myself from duty without permission. I told him I did not take any French leave and tried to explain my side of the story and how the error came about, but he gave a deaf ear to what I was telling him. What made me really angry was when he told me whether I thought the Lawra Nũũ or the headmaster would tell a lie about a small boy like me. On hearing that I lost my temper and retorted very angrily and asked him whether he thought because I was small, I was capable of telling lies.

At that moment, I could feel the blood pumping through my head and the bile in my spleen rising to my mouth emitting some taste as bitter as quinine. I did not want to enter into any further altercation with him for fear of being violent or rude through no fault of mine. Without further ado, I told him I would not answer anymore of his questions verbally and any further questions should be put to me in writing, an advice Colonel Wentworth gave at College. On that note, I then burst out of his office without waiting a moment to hear his response. I could see the surprised faces of his junior workers whose room adjoined his. I was not known for my tantrums and had always been considered a quiet lad. My reaction was probably the first time he had been told by a black man when to get off his hobby horse. And certainly not by such a small boy of twenty-one as he thought of me, for these colonial administrators expected us to be obsequious to them. I rode back to the school and reported to the headmaster without letting him know the encounter I had had with Mr Meade nor what plans I had in mind. But what surprised me most was that neither the Lawra Nũũ nor the headmaster showed any signs they were aware of the situation or that they had reported me to the District Commissioner. I therefore waited until I actually had the written query from the DC six days later.

When I reported for duty I noticed the school was still doing general cleaning and that no classes had been started. This went to disprove the headmaster's argument that my pupils would fall behind with their class work if I had a week off. By the weekend the DC's messenger brought me a short query of less than three lines, asking me to explain why I had absented myself from duty without prior permission. I spent the entire weekend drafting my reply instead of preparing my lecture notes. After that confrontation with the DC, I had made up my mind to resign from the teaching service. In the end my letter was written in a similar vein as that of Dr Johnstone's letter to the Earl of Chichester: rude, sarcastic, but pertinent. This was to compensate for the DC's rudeness to me in his office as I hated to be called a liar. I had had enough time to cool down and to answer his query rationally.

On the Monday morning, when all the teachers and pupils assembled on the parade ground for the six o'clock roll call, I absented myself to complete my rejoinder to the query. I stayed behind in my quarters making a duplicate of my reply which also embodied my resignation from teaching. At eight thirty when the roll was called again for classes, I absented myself from the parade, still putting the finishing touches to my letter that filled about five sides of a foolscap paper. When I finished, I rode to the DC's office to hand it in. I gave this personally to Mr Meade and told him to go and take my class as I had resigned. I returned to the school, took my class register together with my lecture notebook which had been issued to me for the year, and dumped these on the headmaster's table in his class. He refused to accept them and when he saw the fierce and angry look in my face, he did not dare to thrust them back to me. It was there and then I told him I had resigned and that he could take my class in addition to his. I later bade farewell to the other teachers and left for home, leaving behind my things which my cousins from Birifu would come the following day to collect. When I resigned from the teaching job for which I had trained and really enjoyed doing, I despised all those persons who I thought wrongly or rightly had caused my resignation: the Lawra Nũũ, but most of all Mr Andoh and Tom Meade. For a long time I did not even want to set eyes on any of them since I felt they had shattered my life.

The next day when my cousins went to collect my things from the school, Mr Andoh refused to let them take my writing table. This was the table I had made at the teacher training college for my carpentry practical exams and which he now claimed did not belong to me. I was livid when my cousins returned without the table and with that insolent news. I immediately went up to my father to ask for permission to travel to Lawra and reclaim my table. Seeing the anger in my facial expression and knowing the sort of person I was in upholding my rights and principles, my father refused to let me go lest I should cause trouble there. Indeed he was still coming to terms with my sudden resignation and did not want me to add another to his worries. He told me that if I wanted a table, he would commission Kofi Nsiah, the station carpenter at the Babile Agricultural Station, to make me one. But I felt it was not the same thing having something made for you and having your own article made by yourself. I was therefore bent on getting my own table back even though Kofi Nsiah's handicraft would have been much better than mine as carpentry was his trade. I thought it over for a while hoping my father would forget and would one day allow me to visit Lawra. But any time I thought he had forgotten and went to ask for permission to visit Lawra on the pretext that I was going to post a letter, my father saw through me and would ask me to send one of my younger brothers instead. He suspected what would happen if he allowed me to go.

Two days prior to my resignation, I had sent a message to my father about my intention. I told him that after my resignation I would like to run a transport business, keep a retail shop or just act as his personal secretary. I was hardly at home for more than a week when Tom Meade arrived from Lawra and drove straight to the rest house. Seeing his car racing past, my father with Gyub and others followed him there to welcome him and to provide some eggs, a fowl and yams for his evening meal. I refused to go because I did not want to set my eyes on or speak to him. It was just before dusk when Mr Meade came to the village and it was nine in the evening that my father returned from the rest house.

My father told me that I was the subject of their discussion and that Mr Meade had asked him to persuade me to return to Lawra and resume my teaching post by rescinding my letter of resignation. My father told him that he could not force me to return to my job even though if he ordered me to, I would obey him. But since it was he, Tom Meade, who did not believe me and forced me to resign, he himself should come to apologise to me in the first instance. If the DC did so, then with his powers of persuasion and his pressure as a parent, I would return to teaching. But Tom Meade was too proud to come the next day and apologise. It was no wonder since that was the nature of all the DCs at the time; they acted as if they could do anything by divine right. I later learnt that there was pressure from Tamale and that Mr Meade was blamed for my resignation, and especially by Mr Wentworth.

Towards the end of February, 1948, I had arranged with one of my father's friends, an employee of the Government Transport Department, to teach me how to drive. Before I left, I asked my father permission to go to Nandom and bid my brothers, Nana and Dɛri, farewell. To this my father readily agreed, forgetting that I could get off in Lawra and go to the school to confront the headteacher about my table. That was just what I intended to do. Although I was carrying perishable food like pork, which my father had given me for the Nandom Nũũ, Imoru, and his father, I decided to pass the night at Lawra in order to go to the school and claim my table. When I got down from the lorry, I left my things in my cousin's room, borrowed his bicycle and rode off to the school.

When I got there, all the teachers, including the headteacher, were supervising the children's manual work. The school had moved completely from the old site to a new one just a few yards up the hill towards Yaatuuri. The sight of Mr Andoh immediately made my blood boil and my pulse raced rapidly up and down. I could feel a lump in my throat as I approached them, my heart still pounding heavily with anger and frenzy. I walked straight up to him demanding my table. When he saw I was trembling with rage in this fit of temper, he thought I was going to strike him instantly and ran off to the side of C.K. Bini so he would shield him. I followed as he ran from one teacher to the next for protection from this raging bull. At last one of the newly qualified teachers, Mr Salifu Dakura, told me where the table was. I went up to that classroom and brought the table on to the path. As I did so, Mr Andoh had the audacity to ask Mr C.K. Bini to help him take the table from me. But Mr Bini told him that since the table belonged to me, I had every right to take it away. At that juncture Mr Andoh turned round and told me that I could take my table away for after all there were no tables in the palace in Birifu, knowing full well that he had been served on tables there before. This was the unkindest insult of all that he could throw back at me and I swore in my heart to give him a good hiding for this insolence that night on his way to town.

I took the table down to one of the teachers, Mr Sawley Sakara, who was using the old Lawra compound as his quarters. I knew the headteacher would go to the town that day and I was determined to ambush him between the school and the town and beat the hell out of him for his insolence in a place where there would be no witnesses. But he was too clever for me. He came down from his quarters about to go to town, and when he perceived me at Mr Sakara's, he foresaw instantly what my devilish intentions were, and immediately turned back. I waited in the school until about nine that evening and when I found he had given up the idea of visiting the town, I retraced my steps. The next day I caught the earliest available transport to Nandom, where I was the guest of the Nandom Nũũ and his family. I lodged with my brothers, Nana and Dɛri, in their quarters, although the chief and his family supplied the foodstuff and the refreshment. The following day, after bidding farewell to them all, I left Nandom for Birifu and by the evening I was at home with my father. Two days later my father's friend came to take me for my training.

This particular driver usually carried freight for the Government Departments to the outstations in the north. So when we left on February 28, 1948, we passed the night at Bole, then left for Wenchi the next morning, arriving there at dusk. The next day, March 1, at about 9.30 in the morning, we were about to set off for Kumasi but first had to call at the Police Station for their usual check up. There was an unusual amount of movement among the police there, but no one except the authorities knew what this was all about. Our truck was delayed at the station for nearly an hour or more, not realising it had been commandeered to carry a contingent of armed police to Kumasi.

As we were fully loaded, we did not have to stop on the road for fare-paying passengers. Besides, were we not fully loaded, I doubt if the police who had a mission to carry out in Kumasi would have allowed the driver to stop anywhere on the road. We got to Kumasi at about four thirty in the afternoon. As we passed through the lorry park, Kejetia, all hell broke lose. I could see policemen with long truncheons hitting people indiscriminately on their heads and bodies. People were bleeding profusely and their assailants gave them no mercy whatsoever. My blood ran cold in seeing such brutality being administered by human beings on human beings. Everyone was running away from their assailants as they were pursued by these so-called law-enforcing officers.

Our truck moved slowly round the roundabout as we made our way westwards towards the Central Police Station opposite the Central Prison. There the policemen alighted and the driver drove to the transport yard to report his return. He brought me back in town to the house of Kwame Nti in Odum where I had stayed a month or two earlier. This time my hostess had her younger brother staying with her as he had come home either on holidays from his school or perhaps the school was closed down because of the troubles that spread like wildfire through all the southern cities. So the room I had been given on my first visit was now occupied by him and the sitting room was quickly turned into a bedroom for me for the night.

After the normal greetings, I was told why there had been a great influx of police and soldiers in town. As a result of this uprising there was a lot of looting in all corners of the city, and the soldiers and police were called in, especially from the Northern Territories, supposedly to keep the peace. The looting and rioting was in response to Dr Kwame Nkrumah's appeal for "Positive Action" and civil disobedience to the colonial regime. All the regions except the Northern Territories responded to Dr Nkrumah's appeal. The North was scarcely involved so it was no wonder that, when they were arrested, all the leaders of the United Gold Coast Convention (UGCC) were sent to different parts of that region; Nkrumah and a few others were sent to Lawra. I believe it was in response to this disturbance that the Watson Commission was set up. When we arrived, a curfew had been imposed from dawn till dusk and anyone found loitering in the streets outside these hours was ordered to be shot on sight. The next morning after breakfast, Akosua my hostess, her brother and I left for Kwapra to greet Opanyin Kwame Nti and to let him know of my presence in town. I was again entertained as lavishly as I had been a month or so earlier. Due to the curfew, we returned to town very early in order not to get caught.

During that week I witnessed a great deal of looting going on around me. Shops belonging to Syrians and Lebanese were the main targets but their owners defended themselves with rifles, pistols and shot guns from above their houses. The looting was not confined to those shops but other foreign stores, such as those owned by the British, French and Swiss, were also attacked. Many who stole from the Syrian or the Lebanese shops were shot at by them, but there was also the police and the army, who were armed to the teeth and manned by British officers, patrolling the streets in their lorries. Detachments of troops from the Gambia, Sierra Leone and Nigeria which formed the West African Frontier Force were flown in. Their orders, which they obeyed to the letter, were to shoot and kill, at least in Kumasi where I witnessed it. It was believed rightly or wrongly by the Colonial Office and Governor Alan Burns that the Ghanaian soldiers might not turn their guns on their own kith and kin if ordered to do so. So other regiments were flown in. Towards the middle of the week Opanyin Kwame Nti with his entourage visited the city from Kwapra. For Kwame Nti often travelled like a chief, although most of his retinue were more like parasites than sincere followers. Indeed some of them were involved in the looting and brought their loot back to hide at the house of their leader. On this particular visit, Kwame decided to pay a visit to the Odumhene, the chief of Odum, a section of the Kumasi Town Council in which his house was situated. The

Odumhene was a relation to whom he wanted to introduce me.

After we had consumed a few bottles of spirits, we set off on foot to the chief's house. I was wearing a pair of locally made sandals to match my attire, the smock. When we got to the palace, the Odumhene was sitting in his court awaiting us. As we entered, the rest of the party removed their sandals, lowered their cloths to the chest in accordance with the Ashanti protocol, and knelt down to greet him. I failed to do the same as I was unfamiliar with their custom but saluted as I would to my dad at home. I received a very dirty look from the chief, at which time one of Kwame's disciples, Adjei, nudged me, telling me in broken Birfuɔlu to remove my sandals. I was presumably forgiven partly because I did not know the Ashanti custom and partly because I was a guest of his relation. I would otherwise have paid a heavy penalty for failing to comply with traditional rules. After spending a while with the chief, we obtained leave to return home for lunch but hardly had we left the precincts of the palace than the double was sounded on the police bugle. This heralded that there was looting and rioting taking place in the vicinity. As soon as Kwame and his party heard the sound, they vanished into neighbouring houses where the gates were quickly shut behind them. I was left stranded in the street as the police and army lorries rolled by shooting into the crowds indiscriminately at anyone they saw panicking or they suspected of taking part in the looting.

Putting my thinking cap on, I knew if I ran I would be a target and would immediately be shot down as one of the looters. I walked leisurely and calmly as the lorries drove past me. Unfortunately, the street cleaner, who was cleaning the gutter by the United Africa Company (UAC) Central Stores, was not that lucky, for he was mistakenly shot dead as one of the looters. Perhaps it could have been a stray bullet that hit him. From the Central Stores to where I lived was only about four hundred yards, so when the contingent of soldiers and police had driven past, I increased my pace and hurried home and never showed my face again for the rest of the day. When the streets were clear and calm, Kwame and his entourage returned, and wondered how I had managed to get home safely. I told them of my narrow escape from death and they thought I had been protected by my father's fetish, the Kunkpɛnibiɛ, mispronounced by the Ashantis as "Kankanmia".

The looting and rioting continued for weeks. Abena Serwah returned to the village that day to stay with her husband for awhile. I was asked to move to Ashanti Newtown to house number ME 101, called the "Kankanmia House" where I was to live with one of Kwame's nephews, Mr Manful. It was there I first met the young Krobo Edusei, who was later to become one of Dr Nkrumah's ministers. He was then working for the *Ashanti Pioneer* newspaper in Odum.

As Manful did not have many rooms available since most had been let out, Krobo had to sleep on the verandah at nights and went to work during the day. During this upheaval, Krobo became one of the leaders of the youths in Ashanti Newtown and Odum where he worked and was very well known to them. He led the youth and taunted the army and the police by night and day, barricading the streets with heavy objects to prevent their patrol vehicles passing quickly from one point of trouble to the next. It was this role of leadership during the riots that heralded the beginning of his political recognition which occurred after the state of emergency came to an end. He was elected into the first Legislative Assembly in 1951 and was appointed a Ministerial Secretary to the Ministry of Transport and Communications under Mr J.A. Braimah as the minister.

One weekend when I paid a visit to Kwapra with Mr Manful, I was fortunate to meet the brother-in-law of Kwadzo, the younger brother of Kwame Nti, Mr Owusu Ansah. Owusu was a businessman in Obuasi, a mining town, in the Adansi District of Ashanti. I was introduced to him as an exteacher who had been sent by his father to learn to drive so that a lorry could be bought for him to run his own transport. Owusu told me that he had about four cars that were used as taxis and promised he could assign one of his drivers solely to teach me and that within a month or less I could sit for and obtain my driving licence for a fee of ten pounds. As an addendum, he said he would not take a penny from me until I had sat and passed my driving licence. I told him I would think about it for I wanted to let the driver who had brought me from home know about the offer so he could advise me as to what to do. When I saw and spoke to the driver, he said his training would take at least four years but at the end of it I would be a reasonably good mechanic capable of repairing my own vehicle if it broke down on the road. But if however, I wanted a quick training then Owusu's offer was a good one and I should take it and he would not be offended.

Two or three weeks later, Owusu returned to Kwapra and by this time I had already made up my mind to go with him. A verbal contract was witnessed by two of his brothers-in-law, Kwame and Kwadzo, in the presence of many people in the village, including the Kwaprahene. A bottle of schnapps was opened to seal the deal. The following day I travelled with Owusu to Obuasi. He had already guessed I would accept his offer and had therefore rented a room for me in the Zongo. Owusu had a large retail shop belonging to the Obuasi Trading Company (OTC), as well as a small shop run by one of his wives. For a month I went to the large shop and spent the time sitting in the front doing nothing but watching people play the game of drafts (a game I had been very good at during my college days) or taking part myself when there was an available contestant. I soon became a good competitor in the game and very few people could beat me at it in the entire town.

In the centre of the market at Obuasi was a big hall, the "Obuasi Cloth Hall", where seamstresses took up their trade during the day but which was used at night for dances and other shows. One day Owusu decided to run a dance there. He hired the entire hall giving him the absolute right to sell drinks during the dance. He invited me to help in the bar on that occasion. and when he noticed how well I served there he wondered where I had learnt the trade. I told him I had not learnt it from anyone. The following day he suggested I help his wife at the little shop, especially when she went home to prepare both lunch and the evening meals for the family. From then on, every day I went to assist his wife in the running of that shop and as time went on that became my sole responsibility.

Later in the year Owusu opened a drinking bar which he named "The Gentleman's Drinking Bar" and put me in absolute charge of it. Although a very small shop, my daily turnover usually grossed hundreds of pounds. The shop not only sold drinks but we also added sidelines such as cutlasses for which cocoa farmers came from the villages and bought by the dozen or even by the case, a case comprising about forty dozen. One day there was to be a dance at Akrokeri, the traditional headquarters of the Adansi state. Realising how well I had done at the last dance, Owusu asked me to go with him and help run the bar. We loaded one of his taxicabs with cases of drink. It had rained very heavily that day and the roads were very muddy and treacherous He decided to turn back when the rain was still pelting down. On our return he made up his mind to store all the drinks in my shop and asked me to stay in the shop that night in case it was burgled. For in Obuasi at that time, there was not a night a burglar or two was not found in some part of the town. So I passed the night at the shop acting as a watchman and the night was still young when I heard a burglar being chased nearby.

The next morning I returned to my room at the Zongo to have my bath and to change into clean clothes. When I got there, what did I find but that my room had been broken into and burgled. The burglar must have been aware that the room was unoccupied that night and the only persons who knew of this were Owusu himself, his girl-friend and one Frafra boy who lived next door to me. When I reported the burglary to Owusu he implored me not to go to the police and said that all my stolen clothes would be replaced. I had no reason to disbelieve what he told me but this turned out to be nothing but an empty promise. The only clothes I now had left were those I had been wearing on the previous day, except for my Bɔɔr bottle which is supposed to be carried on one's person all the time as the symbol of the second graders in the Bɔɔr hierarchy.

When Owusu realised that I was making money for him, he did not want to lose me and so failed to honour his part of our deal by letting his drivers instruct me in driving. Months passed and I had not yet sat behind the wheel of a car. I realised he was only using me for free labour. One day, I went up to him and asked when I was going to start my driving lessons, for the month in which he had promised to have me taught driving had long passed. He was displeased with my frankness but told me that it was a busy season (the cocoa season) and all his drivers were taking fare-paying passengers and goods. However he promised there and then to put me in the charge of his senior and most experienced driver to instruct me. At the same time he denied having said he would get me to pass my driving licence at a fee of ten pounds but that I would be taught to be able to drive. He asked one of his drivers to pick me up every afternoon when he was not busy and give me half an hour's lesson.

I scarcely had two lessons when this driver met with a near fatal accident. The car was a complete write-off and the driver was lucky to be alive. He was in hospital for months. Instead of assigning another driver to instruct me, Owusu was happy to let the affair to rest like that. Some months passed and Owusu had not authorised any of his drivers to give me further lessons while my regular tutor was still in hospital. I was livid about the whole affair and had to beard the lion in his den the second time. So I went and confronted him and told him that he should either fulfil his part of the bargain or take me back to Kumasi. He immediately called one of his drivers to give me some driving lessons.

On the first day that this driver took me out, it had rained very heavily and the roads were atrocious. However instead of driving on tarred streets in the town, he took me on a muddy road. As we crossed a bridge, the mud was so thick that the car started to skid towards the edge and the thought that we were going to fall into the river terrified us both. He panicked as I did, got hold of the steering wheel and managed to bring the car clear across the bridge. As soon as he brought the car to a stop, he turned to me and gave me a slap across my face, momentarily blinding me as my eyes watered. I was very angry but managed to control myself until after the lesson. When we returned to the taxi rank and before he could get out of the car, I held him by the throat and told him never again to hit me across my face. If ever he did that, I would skin him alive. Shaken by my threat, he went straight and reported to Owusu that he did not want to give me any more lessons as I had threatened to beat him up. Owusu told him this attitude was against my whole nature and the driver confessed that he had hit me across the face so I threatened to retaliate if he ever did that again. It was then Owusu told him that he should know I was an ex-teacher and he should not have hit me.

While in Obuasi I tried to get some activity going after I had shut my shop in the evenings. The only thing I could think of was to join a choir. A schoolboy who befriended me so I could help him with his home-work was a choirboy at a Roman Catholic church in the town. When he learnt I was interested in joining a choir, he told his choir master that I was interested in singing but was not a Catholic. The choir master told him that if I wanted I could come for a week's trial and if I liked it, I could join the choir. As it turned out I remained in the choir, and this man and myself became good friends. He was a good organist and I wanted to learn how to play the organ from him. It turned out he was studying for the intermediate BA of the London University degree in music by correspondence course. He could read the staff notation by heart without understanding the complete theory behind it. He found my college lecture notes on the theory of music very elaborate and adequate. He even found these were better than his correspondence course lecture notes. There was therefore a strong bond between us. I went to his house on Sunday afternoons to learn to play the organ while he learnt the theory of music from me. However, I could only illustrate the theory with solfa notation since I knew very little of the staff notation nor could I read it beyond the middle C. This man found my notes useful to him and since I was no longer teaching music in school I gave them to him for his university course. This showed the high standard that was set at the Training College in some of the subjects taught to the students, the college being the first of its kind to be built in the Gold Coast.

CHAPTER TWELVE

AT OBUASI I BEGAN PLANNING how to run the family business. I communicated my ideas to Tiisip who was then stationed in Birifu as an Agricultural Instructor with the Lawra Native Authority. I later communicated with Debomo who resigned his position as Foreman from the Native Authority service during the course of the year. He then worked in Wa under an expatriate Foreman of Works in the Public Works Department where he was employed as time-keeper. Even as a time-keeper, his earnings more than quadrupled what they were as Native Authority District foreman. My ideas or daydreams were not confined to the running of the family transport which I hoped to start as soon as I passed my driving test. They also included the opening of a family shop in Birifu because of the experience I had gained in Obuasi. In addition Tiisip, Debomo and Biz decided to include in this wide plan the installation of a grinding mill in the village as well as a sewing machine. All of these ideas or daydreams eventuality developed into reality within a year.

When I was leaving for the south, I implored my brothers not to disclose my whereabouts to any person outside the immediate family circle. This was because there was a ruling that no employer in the south or the north should wittingly employ a trained teacher from the north who resigned from the teaching service. Not that I was interested or intended to seek work in either the public or the private sector other than running a transport business, but I did not want any other person to know my whereabouts. You may recall that while a teacher I translated from the vernacular into English for the police in Lawra and vice versa in the murder case in Tugu. Consequently, I would be wanted as one of the crown witnesses in this case when it came before the Assizes.

This year the Assizes in the north was to be held in Tamale and all the cases in the various districts were to be brought there. As I was to be a crown witness for the murder hearing, and since no one knew of my whereabouts except my family, the police authorities in Lawra were frantic to locate me in order to subpoena me on time for the hearing. It must have taken great persuasion to make Tiisip release my address to the Lawra police. They in turn contacted the police in

Obuasi who traced me and subpoenaed me to attend the Assizes in Tamale. One evening while I was selling drinks in my bar, Sub-Inspector Ababio, who had previously visited the bar on several occasions, told me I was wanted by the police in Tamale. I was alarmed at hearing that and was immediately anxious to know what crime I had committed since I had left that town two years before. He soon put me at ease when he told me I was only wanted as a crown witness in connection with a murder case. As he was in the company of my boss, Mr Ansah, the latter promised to release me as soon as the Inspector had finished with the paper work.

Some days later, when the travel papers were all prepared, the sub-inspector came back with Owusu and handed me the warrants both for my train and road travel to Kumasi and Tamale. The next day, I travelled from Obuasi to Kumasi by train. On arrival, after leaving my luggage at my usual lodgings, I went to the transport yard and gave my warrant to the clerk so my seat could be reserved for my journey on the following Monday. There was no delay this time in my connection for Tamale. It took three days to arrive there in those days as the roads were in very bad condition and really very dangerous, especially during the heavy rains. At Tamale, the next morning I went straight to the police station to report to them. But I was too early as the other witnesses and the assessors from Lawra had not arrived. Besides, the Assizes was not opening until the beginning of the following week. Towards the end of the week, the others too arrived and were lodged in the same house, that of Kofi Kpɛb who was the chief cook at the Residency. The wife of my brother, Dɛri, the grandson of Dede and the chief steward at the Residency, was also staying in the house. I was soon made at home as she provided me with meals and water to have a bath. On his arrival, the police constable from Lawra, was very pleased to see me. For he was not sure whether or not I would be traced.

The Assizes opened on the Monday of the following week under the auspices of the Puisne Judge from Kumasi, Mr K.A. Korsah, who some years later became Chief Justice of Ghana. When all the medieval rites of pomp and circumstance that normally preceded the openings of these Assizes were over, and the judge fully robed, he came into the court room. Here as we stood, another short medieval ritual took place before the judge took his seat and every one in the court sat down. As the case in which I was to appear as a witness had been listed as the penultimate one, I reported to the court every day and listened to all the cases that preceded mine for the two weeks of the

Assizes. These cases ranged from bestiality and burglary, to murder.

When our case was called, C.K. Bini, J.K. Nitori, and Ar-iɔn Paga, a Native Authority sanitary overseer, appeared as assessors and Dasobri as court interpreter for this case. These assessors act as jurymen and are chosen from the area where the crime had been committed. They are usually literate or semi-literate depending on the number of available candidates. When our case was called and after both the defence and prosecution lawyers had made their opening speeches, I was the first witness called upon to testify that the statement of the accused that had been handed to me was the authentic one. After perusing the contents of the statement, I confirmed its authenticity. The judge asked me to step down as my testimony was only a formality and the defence did not want to cross-examine my statement. At the end of that week, after the Assizes, I was reimbursed for my out-of-pocket expenses and returned to Obuasi some days later. Prior to that I visited the Teacher Training College to see my brother, Gyub, who was then on his third and fourth year course. The Tamale Teacher Training College was the first two-year college of its kind to open in the Gold Coast. At the time you first had to train for your Certificate B and after serving some time in the field, teachers were selected and recalled to train for their Certificate A. Places were at first limited to two students. So A. Karbo and E.A. Mahama were recalled after a year in the field and Mumuni Bawumia and Gyub were recalled in 1948.

I got back to Obuasi and resumed my normal job at the "Gentleman's Drinking Bar", as my shop was called. In July, Owusu had a telegram from Kwame Nti to come up with me to Kumasi to meet my father who had arrived in town and was asking of me. One morning, when I was about to open the shop, Owusu pulled up in one of his taxis and told me we were travelling to Kumasi. I thought we were going to buy some goods for his shops but as we were about to get into town, he told me that my father was ill and had been brought to Kumasi for treatment. He probably thought that if he had told me the full message in Obuasi, I would have packed bag and baggage and left, thus risking the possibility of losing me for ever. Or perhaps he did not want to alarm me with the bad news until we came into town and nearer our destination. Whatever the reason, I was taken aback by the sudden news and very much worried because I had left my father in bounding health and vigour when I went to the south. When we got to Odum where my father was accommodated, Kwame and his entourage were already there with my father and his retinue which comprised Tiisip, Sakpi and two of my father's wives, Waal' Pɔɔsũũn (Naa Pelpuo's widow from Charkpong) and Lora. Tiisip had been given permission by the Native Authority to accompany my father to Kumasi in order to act as his interpreter.

When Owusu and I entered the room, I saluted my father as I usually did and stood at the side not realising that he had almost lost his eyesight. I was then told by Lora, his young wife, that he could not see me where I stood. I drew closer to him and he started to feel me to make sure I was really the person. I had always been in awe of my father and felt shy to speak to him unless it was in response to a question or to some statement he made. Owusu was welcomed with a bottle of schnapps according to the custom. He was surprised that when offered a glass of the drink, I accepted it. During my whole stay in Obuasi, he had never seen any alcohol pass my lips. What he failed to realise was that I had a strong will that enabled me to resist any temptation or do anything I did not want to do. I suppose it was this strong will that endeared me to my father. In any case, I stayed behind with him whilst Owusu returned to Obuasi.

When all the visitors had gone, I was told that Dr Hupenbauer, who had examined my eyes earlier that year, had refused to attend to my father. However, knowing what I know today from my own experience, Dr Hupenbauer did not perhaps refuse to treat my father intentionally. His sight could have been affected either by glaucoma or cataract. As medical advance and its availability were non-existent at that time in Ghana, it would have been beyond the realms of possibility to get treatment for him. Even today the treatment for cataract or glaucoma is not widely available. When Dr Hupenbauer refused to treat my father, Kwame Nti approached the elder Dr Asafu-Adjaye to examine him. The doctor called at the house that evening. If he could have treated him, I am sure he would have done so; but his blunt refusal brought suspicion to the minds of Kwame and members of his entourage who believed that had it not been for the fact that Dr Hupenbauer was a government practitioner and had refused treatment, Dr Asafu-Adjaye would not have declined to accept him as his patient. Whatever was the reason it was a great blow to us and to my father particularly.

Following this disappointment, Kwame Nti set out the next day to look for other paramedics. Within a few days, a man was brought to the house, whom I assumed was not fully qualified in the medical profession. Although he claimed he could cure my father's eyesight within a matter of weeks, I had very grave doubts since two eminent doctors had already decided there was nothing they could do for him. Apart from his incredible claim, he had asked for an advance fee, in double figures, before he could even start his treatment. I pulled my brother, Tiisip, aside as he was keeping my father's purse and told him of my distrust and scepticism. We then challenged him about his demand and he told us the money was only an advance to buy the necessary drugs to treat my father. As an addendum, he said that these drugs were only available in Abijan in the French Colony of the Ivory Coast. Reluctantly, we gave in and paid him the money only because my father was eager to have his treatment. After he got the money we never saw him again for two weeks when he turned up with one or two bottles of medication. This he injected into my father and then asked for more money. But this time, despite my father's eagerness to have the second advance paid, we refused to fork out further sums until the treatment had progressed enough to warrant any payment. That was the last we ever saw of him even though he promised to call back with further treatment.

After a week in the town, Kwame decided to move us to the village of Kwapra, where we were to be accommodated in one of his many houses. My father and his two wives occupied one wing of the house where Kwame Nti lived, while Tiisip and I slept in the sitting room of the wing occupied by Kwame and one of his wives, Abena, christened Florence, who was a former pupil teacher. As former teachers both Florence and I shared a common interest, the love of singing. I had previously met Florence's parents in Birifu when they visited my father in 1945 to fulfil their promise to the Kunkpɛnibiɛ shrine. This was when I had dislocated my wrist and had not returned to college. Because of our common interests, Florence and I took to each other like ducks to water.

In the evenings we would practice songs from a copy of her Oxford University Songbook. However, Kwame did not like my intrusion into his marital life as he felt I was preventing his wife retiring early to bed with him. As time went by, he began to moan and grumble about it in Asante which I hardly understood. Being a young bachelor, I did not realise that my innocent association with his wife was the cause of such friction and irritation. Oblivious to what was going on, we continued every night to practice our singing. But his dirty looks and undertones, and his sudden change of attitude towards me, made me suspect I had wronged him in some way or other. I did not realise he wrongly suspected me of courting his young wife—a thing our father forbade his children to do.

About the same time, Debomo had resigned from the Native Authority Services because he could not work in harmony with the District Station foreman, ZiS Nũũ, a Dagomba; he had been transferred to Lawra from Tamale and was occupying my father's house in Lawra. After his resignation, Debomo came down to Kumasi to see the condition of my father and to inform him of his action. Since Debomo also loved singing, he and Florence would sing the treble part while I sang the alto. Sometimes we practised late into the night which did not please Kwame one bit. His anger increased and he began taking it out on almost every member of my father's retinue. At first, we assumed it was drunkenness, since he was in drunken stupor most of the time. However, it was only when I spoke to Florence that she told me that her husband was jealous because he thought I was courting her and whatever she said, he would not believe her. We therefore decided to call a halt to our singing practice in order not to aggravate the situation and a few days later Debomo returned to the north where he was later employed by the PWD in Wa.

At this time, one of Kwame's nephews, Appiah, had a fitter's shop at Suame with several apprentices under him. I decided to make use of my time to learn from him a bit of car mechanics, as I was not sure how long my father would be staying at the village. After asking my father's permission, I went daily with this young man to Suame and tried to pick up whatever he taught his apprentices. In addition to that Appiah gave me a few driving lessons with the trucks he had repaired when he was testing their reliability, even though he himself had no driving licence. In those days to sit for one's driving licence, one had to pass a literacy test. One day he decided that we should go together and try sitting the reading test. These tests were normally held at the Police Motor Traffic Unit (MTU) under the auspices of the expatriate officer, the Commissioner-in-charge. The test involved reading the highway code and answering questions about it. The applicants were first of all screened by a General Police (GP) constable a week prior to the test. This was in order that any person not sufficiently literate or proficient in reading did not appear before the Commissioner. For most of the illiterate applicants tried to learn the entire highway code by rote, especially those who did not know their A from B. When eventually they appeared before the examiner most of them recited the passages by heart without understanding what they were reading and this practice irritated him.

There was often a long queue for these screening tests so one had to be there very early in the morning to be sure of being screened. On the Monday morning, Appiah and I got up very early, and by seven o'clock we were at the offices of the MTU, long before the constable on duty had arrived. It was not until about ten o'clock before the constable opened the little window to his office and started his screening. There were about six candidates ahead of us in the queue and only two of them passed the screening. That meant he still needed to screen at least another eight or more for the officer to examine the following week. When it came to my turn, the constable refused to allow me to read to him partly because of the dirty fitters' clothes I wore and partly, and more to the point, because of the facial marks on my face which gave me away as a northerner.

In those days northerners were supposed to be filthy and illiterate, only fit to be hewers of wood and carriers of water and lavatory pans. We were thus given the derogatory name of *pepe* or *ta ni* by the Akan-speaking people of the south, the latter phrase meaning "the smelly one". This constable therefore thought I was smelly and illiterate, and refused even to allow me to read to him because he felt I would be wasting the time of his expatriate boss as well as that of other applicants. He kept asking me in broken English "so you too sabe book?" Not wishing to disappoint him of his illusions or take all the fun from him, with my tongue in my cheek, I also replied in broken English, at which I was not very good, saying, "I go try massa", meaning "I shall try master". He told me to be off and not to waste the time of others. At that moment, Appiah, who was behind me, told him I was an ex-teacher and that I was learning fitting from him.

This ignorant constable did not believe what he heard and still insisted I leave my place. I stood my ground until the other applicants supported Appiah's assertion. Hoping to find some grounds for failing me, he changed the text which the others were reading and produced a very fat volume from under the counter. He opened a page and gave it to me to read. As I read, he opened his mouth wide and listened intently, not wanting me to stop until I had finished the entire page. It was then I asked him if I should continue over the next page or if he was satisfied with my literacy. At that moment he felt stupid and asked me why I had not told him I was so highly educated. I said he never gave me the chance and would not even listen to what the other applicants were telling him. As an addendum, I told him he only discriminated against me because I was a northerner and because of my appearance. Appearances, I reminded him, are deceptive since "all is not gold that glitters" and with that I had the last laugh. Apart from the fact that I was more educated than he, I was not in the habit of being arrogant or of bragging until I was forced into a situation to do so. He apologised for his impetuosity and told the others whom he had already screened that it would be in their best interest if my name was placed first to appear before his boss the following week. That if I read first and did well, it would put his superior officer in a better frame of mind and mood and he would deal leniently with the rest.

The following week, true to his word, I was the first to be called. When I entered, the officer gave me the Highway code to read. As with the constable, I read two pages of the code before he stopped me. With the type of applicants he had been dealing with, he probably thought I had learnt the entire highway code in parrot fashion. He grilled me on the comprehension of the contents and the demonstrations of the signals of the code with the hope that I might falter if I were not sufficiently literate. He did not waste much time with the rest of the applicants who followed after me and I shuddered to think if that was a good or a bad portent. The following week I went back to the offices of the MTU to find out whether or not I had passed my literacy test and at the same time to have some passport-size photographs taken if I had, so these could be affixed to my application forms, stamped and signed by the examining officer. It usually took a month before one's application was approved and only then could the person take his application form to the Government Transport Yard for a date to be fixed for the driving test. The administration of the actual driving test was under the auspices of the chief engineer of the Government Transport Department who was the testing officer, and there was often a waiting list of some six months or more between passing the literacy test and sitting the actual test.

While we were still in Kwapra, Kwame continued to bring quack medicine men for the treatment of my father. My father was keen to try any person who professed to be a medicine man and was capable of restoring his eyesight. He thought the people he was dealing with down the south were as honest as he was. One day, a malam, a Moslem priest, was brought along from the Zongo in Kumasi and told my father he could cure him spiritually so that he would be able to see and even thread a needle. However, he wanted an amount of four hundred pounds paid in advance and in cash before he started treatment. Once again we could detect a trap and insisted the treatment took place before any money was paid to him.

After hours of negotiating with him, the malam saw he would probably be exposed if he was a fake, and refused to agree to our suggestion. That again was the last we saw of him. After about a month or so in Kwapra, Kwame was getting on the nerves of every member of my father's retinue and began to pick quarrels and swear at every one of us, especially when he was in a drunken stupor. My father felt we had overstayed the welcome of our host and decided it was time we returned home. So we packed and left for Birifu. When we arrived at Wenchi, one of his friends, who had also acquired the same shrine, entreated him to stay a few weeks there in order that he too could find some medicine men who might be able to bring back his eyesight. After two weeks in Wenchi my father decided to return home, having stayed away for over two and half months. Besides, the cash he had brought down was running out while the number of his retinue increased daily. His driver friend, Donkor, picked us up from Wenchi for the return journey and we arrived home on an August evening to the great delight of the entire family.

I mentioned in an earlier chapter that when I was a teacher, Katulɛ Sulley had told her uncle, Kpata Sawley, a colleague of mine, that I was to be the man in her life when she grew up. However, her aunt, her father's elder sister, did not approve of her choice of a future husband. The reason was that being a literate it would be hard for me to get farmers to farm on the in-law's farm if she married into the Gandah family.[28] Besides, the aunt would prefer Katulɛ to marry into her uncle's parish rather than marry into a family in Birifu. Being her father's elder sister, her aunt had greater control over her than her father. She therefore tried to discourage her from the idea of ever thinking of marrying me and I feared it was a forlorn hope on the part of Katulɛ. Little did I know how resolute she was about this and did not realise that when I resigned from teaching, she also discontinued with her education.

A few days after arriving home with my father, I decided to visit Lawra to see my friends and my cousin, Nitii. Just as I was about to set off on my return journey, Katulɛ's father and the father of one of my former pupils stopped me at the Zongo to greet me. They were just leaving Kwesi Dam's beer bar,[29] and after exchanging the formal greetings, Sulley told me that his daughter, Katulɛ, was being courted by all the educated young men in town but she had rejected everyone's hand in marriage. He said she had told him that she would marry no one except the son of the chief of Birifu who was her former teacher but who had left for the south. "The next time I wrote to him, I should tell him to come home and take her away from the "hawks" who were hovering all around her." It was then that his friend told him that I was the teacher who had resigned and left for the south. He told me to send for my betrothed, otherwise the young men in town would snap her up if I delayed further. Since it was getting to the Kɔbinɛ festival, if I did not do so, she could be snatched away during the dance by any of her admirers and I would lose her.[30] I am sure Sulley knew who I was but was only pretending, tactfully telling me to come for Katulɛ and not wishing to appear as if he was pushing his daughter on to me. Whatever his motive, when I got home I told my other brothers of the strange conversation between my would-be father-in-law and myself. And the next day my brother, Kpaari, was sent to go and collect Katulɛ while we ordered pots of pito to await her arrival.

Prior to this event, my father's wife, the widow of the late Naa Pelpuo of Wa, was eager to arrange a wife for me as soon as I had left college and was posted to teach in Lawra. She had already done this for Biz in 1944 while he was a pupil teacher, I therefore warned her in front of my father that neither she nor any woman in the house should arrange any girl for me to marry. I told her I would find my own girl only when I was ready. When Kpaari returned from Lawra with Katulɛ (Kat), my father was immediately informed of her presence. Both my father and Sakpi knew Kat's father very well, for Sulley was the grandson of the first Lawra Nũũ before Nũũ Bini. My father approved this match. As this was a prelude to the actual marriage, which I call the engagement period, Kat had to return to her parents before she came to us permanently. For the girl is never one's wife until the bridewealth is paid. In addition it was getting close to the time of the Kɔbinɛ dance and knowing how much she loved dancing, we decided after a month to let her return to Lawra to take part in both the Kɔbinɛ and the Sɛbri dances while I returned to the south to continue with my training.

As my driving lessons were getting nowhere with Owusu Ansah in Obuasi, I decided to find another person to train me. When Mr Donkor drove us to Birifu, I asked him if he would be willing to train me as a driver and he agreed. About November 1948, Mr Donkor and his wife visited our house to greet my father and to see how he was getting on. I told him I was about to return to the south and asked whether his offer still stood. He said it did and asked me to meet him at Babile on the next market day. I told my father I would be returning to the south and asked his permission to leave. After getting his blessings and some pocket money, I left for the market and by three in the afternoon, Donkor came from Hamile en route for Kumasi.[31] I took off with him, arriving at Kumasi two days later. In Kumasi Donkor had two flats, one at Sabon Zongo and another at Odum.[32] He lived at the former with his family while I went to stay at the Odum flat. After about a month, I went to Obuasi to collect the rest of my luggage.

At Donkor's I encountered the same situation as I did at Obuasi; I was not being trained in what I came for.[33] While at Kumasi I met and was introduced to an old boy of the Lawra Primary School, one Tang Yakubu from Eremon. We became good friends, or so I thought at the time, and I usually visited him at his work place and stayed till closing time. Tang was an employee of a Middle Easterner, probably a Syrian or a Lebanese, the proprietor of the Ashanti Mineral Waters Company. As the name suggested, this company manufactured all sorts of soft drinks which were distributed to wholesalers and retailers in town and all over Ashanti. Tang did most of the retail distribution of the mineral waters in town.

There was a beer bar on the ground floor of the two-storey building where Donkor had rented his flat, which opened onto the main street. I occasionally went down to this bar in the afternoon to have some soft drinks or to listen to the music that was blaring away all day. A Sanitary Overseer of the Kumasi Town Council (KTC) was also a regular visitor. At that time Nkrumah had broken away from the United Gold Coast Convention (UGCC) of which he was the first Secretary to form his own party, the Convention Peoples Party (CPP). One day this man started talking politics, denouncing the leaders of the UGCC as imperialist stooges. This was the era of Ghanaian nationalism, and the idea of having more than one party was repulsive; to the fanatic, Dr Kwame Nkrumah could do no wrong. He was being deified and any bad word said against him was blasphemous to many of his followers.

Instead of keeping my big mouth shut during this argument, I retorted by saying it was Nkrumah who was a renegade for leaving the party which had brought him from abroad to become the General Secretary. I was at that time a sympathiser of the UGCC though not a paid-up member. An altercation ensued between us and, but for the barman, it would have turned very rough as he became nastier and nastier. One morning, Tang, who was on his way to work, passed by my lodgings so we could go together to his work place. As we crossed the Kumasi/Accra railway line that traversed the Zongo, I needed to empty my bladder. I went over to one of the railway embankments to do so. To my amazement my political adversary was there. Was this a coincidence or had he kept an eagle eye on me? As he saw me he told his labourers to round up everybody who was there urinating and creating a mess. He got the revenge he had promised. We were herded off, almost thirty of us, to the Zongo Police Station where we were charged with breaking a bye-law of the KTC. As I could not go along with Tang to his work, I returned home and told Donkor about my encounter. He advised that when the case came up, I should plead guilty and offer an explanation. The following week, all those arrested pleaded guilty but I did so with explanation. I told the magistrate that my bladder was full and the nearest lavatory was about a quarter of a mile away, so the only place I could free myself without wetting my clothes and myself was in the ditch by the railway line where I was hidden and flanked by both sides of the tall embankments. The magistrate then turned to this adversary of mine and asked what he expected me to do if the lavatory was so far away? He allowed me to go free while the others who had pleaded guilty were fined five shillings each. That was a feather in my cap and I had the last laugh. It was not long before I left the area and this man and I never set eyes on each other again.

As time went on, Tang persuaded me to move in with him to House No. OI 94 in Ashanti New Town. From then on I went with him every day to the factory and we drove round together to make his deliveries. When the deliveries were done early, we would drive to the Ridge, the residential area for the expatriates, where he would give me some driving lessons. In that way I at least got some driving practice and that encouraged me to stay with him. It was about July 1949 when I received a message of the death of Debomo's first wife, Lariba. Lariba was one of Lige Berry's younger sisters and a cousin of ours on the distaff side of the family. I did not have enough money on me at the time and I could not go to the Post Office to withdraw any further cash. The maximum of cash allowable on demand from any Post Office at that time was only three pounds, and no further withdrawal was permitted until after a fortnight. Any withdrawal of an amount greater than three pounds had to be sanctioned by the Post Office Bank in Accra. As it was imperative I should go to the funeral, I went to the Wa-Kumasi lorry station to book my seat which cost one pound ten shillings at that time and which was to be payable at my destination. When I arrived at Babile, I borrowed some money from the Chief of the Zongo to pay the driver and went home to get money from my father to reimburse him. When I got home, all the main funeral rites had taken place. This was done so quickly partly because the couple were young and partly because of Debomo's work to which he had to return.

CHAPTER THIRTEEN

I STAYED IN THE HOUSE while Tiisip, Biz and I decided to put our long awaited plan into action. As my father's health was failing daily, we felt it was our duty to uphold the good name of the family. We took over the running of the house as all the illiterate elders and brothers looked upon us as their wise leaders. Sakpi, who was the Linguist, attended all the Native Authority matters in Lawra on behalf of the chief and reported back to us.[34] Similarly, he consulted us on the running of the village. Katulɛ had now returned to the house as my wife and not very long after the bridewealth was sent to her parents. Bɔɔr, one of my cousins, became my best man (dikyiinɛ). It was his responsibility to deliver the bridewealth. But as the practice in Lawra differs slightly from that in Birifu, he had to solicit the help of our clansfolk, the Birgbɔlɛ of Tovuɔr, in Lawra.

While at home during this farming season, a few months after the bridewealth was paid, I received a message from my in-laws, asking for the next set of marital duties to be performed; they asked for some farmers to hoe their land. All the headmen of Birifu were asked to send some volunteers to accompany me and hoe on my in-laws' land. To my surprise I had sixty-eight volunteers from the village. On the eve of the day itself, the farmers called at the palace to get their instructions since most of them did not know from which part of Lawra my wife came. They were told to pass the night at Tolibri, a couple of miles from Lawra town so that they could all travel in a group at dawn. About four o'clock in the morning, they left under the leadership of my senior brother, Gyiripuɔ, together with my younger brother, Kpaari, who was the only person from the family known to my in-laws.[35] Indeed Kpaari was often referred to as Kat's husband by her relations in Lawra.

When they reached Kulbɔɔnuɔr, a parish behind the Lawra market, a little before dawn, and blew their horns and wooden whistles to herald their arrival, the people of the parish heard the noise and mistook them for invaders. They ran out of their houses into the compound farms to hide. Later they returned and welcomed the party to the house when they realised later what was happening. The farmers were divided into groups and taken to the farms. By noon they had finished all the farm land belonging to Sulley and were then sent to the fields of his brothers and cousins who had their own separate farms. At about one in the afternoon, Tiisip and I went to see how our people were getting on with the hoeing. When we arrived Gyiripuɔ told us that they had not yet been served with pito but only with millet flour and water, a practice alien to the Birifu people. We were rather unhappy, but we had to accept what was being done as Sulley was nowhere about for me to register my protest. By five in the evening, Tiisip and I went back to the house to see whether the farmers had finished and returned to the house to be entertained, only to find they were still farming. It was not until dusk, and only after I had expressed my displeasure, that the farmers were allowed to come back to the house for food and refreshment. We went back with the farmers to see how the entertainment went. After one or two calabashes of pito, Tiisip and I asked permission to go, leaving the farmers under Gyiripuɔ's charge. Since most of them had travelled on their bicycles to Lawra, these were able to return home to Birifu by ten in the evening. This was the first and the last time that my in-laws asked me to provide farmers; for they were overwhelmed by the number and the work they had done.

I stayed in the house until about mid-August when we took the decision to buy a truck for the running of the family transport business. The 'Austin A' commercial truck stood the roads better than any other similar vehicle at the time. Prior to this decision, I had consulted with my driver friends and transport owners about the truck they favoured most and the majority preferred this model. With so much time on my hands, I went round all the firms in Kumasi who were importing and trading in vehicles in order to compare prices. In fact the Austin commercial was the most costly, but on my recommendation, we decided to buy that. So on one August evening, we gathered the brothers and the elders in the house, put our ideas to them and they all agreed it was a very good idea. I assured them that within a year I could recoup the capital that was to be invested in the project. That evening we counted out a sum of £700 which I had estimated was what a five-ton Austin vehicle would cost at the controlled price. Little did I know it was not easy to get one at that price without being placed on a six months' waiting list. The next day, Tiisip and Biz took this amount, all of which was in coins dating back to the reign of Queen Victoria, to the Post Office at Lawra in order to buy some money orders. I stayed in the house for another week so that the money order advice would be received by the Postmaster at the Kumasi Central Post Office. The Postmaster at Lawra, Mr Croffie, who was a family friend, was sworn to secrecy and asked not to divulge our plan until I had brought the vehicle back to Lawra. We did not want our surprise to be discovered.

After waiting the extra week at home, I left for Kumasi with the money orders, arriving there three days later. I took my money orders to the Post Office the following day and was advised that my advice for the money had arrived, but was told that it would be best if I went to the Barclays Bank (DCO), which was situated across the street to arrange with the manager for my money to be transferred there. At that time it was a mammoth task to cash a postal order or a money order in Kumasi or any of the big towns in the south. One had to get a witness to countersign the order; and this witness had to be not just any friend, but one of the many licensed letter writers who usually lined up along the length of the verandah of the entire building, waiting to do such services and charging a fee. So by the time this letter writer had finished countersigning my many money orders, I had spent some five pounds on him and had passed the entire morning in making arrangements at the bank. The money was eventually transferred at about four o'clock in the afternoon. Mũũbɛkpi Bini was our guest and that morning he accompanied me to the Post Office where he heard and saw what took place. By the time I returned home he had informed Tang Yakubu what had happened and so it was hardly possible to keep it secret from him.

Having banked the money at Barclays, my next preoccupation was to approach the main dealer for the Austin vehicles in town. I went to SCOA, the sole agents for the Gold Coast and asked the Sales Manager who also was the chief engineer if I could get a five-ton vehicle to buy for cash.[36] I was told that there was a waiting list that extended over six months. As I did not want to wait that long, Tang informed me he knew a Middle Easterner who bought and sold Austin vehicles but at a small percentage over the controlled prices. When we approached him, he told me he could supply me with one but not before two weeks time and at an extra one hundred pounds above the price charged by SCOA. The next morning I went to his office and we both went to the bank where he was paid in full. After the two weeks had elapsed and he had not supplied me with the vehicle, I became very worried. I began to wonder if I had lost all the family money and would be unable to explain how it had happened. However, three days later when I went to his office he had taken delivery of the truck. In the evening Tang and I went to take it over and he drove us home and parked it in the street. There was a watchman who was guarding cars and trucks on a building site which had been let out as a parking space because the owner was not ready to build on it yet. We entered into negotiations and offered to pay him two shillings per night for his services. Every morning when we got up, Tang took me along the country lanes in the chassis to give me some driving lessons while I negotiated for the building of its body with one of the body-builders in Suame.

By the time the vehicle was built and licensed, I had spent a total of £830 which included the cost of a comprehensive insurance that was effected with the branch of the Guardian Royal Exchange (GRE), Kumasi. Before the building of the body was complete, Tang had been begging me to become my driver. As he had never driven any vehicle over the capacity of fifteen hundred weight, I hesitated at first to employ him. But by the time the vehicle was licensed I had decided to give him a trial period and see how he got on. Our first trip was to Tamale and the load had been sub-contracted to us by his former immediate boss. The load to be conveyed comprised some iron rods for the Public Works Department (PWD) in Tamale. The total laden weight for my vehicle was three tons; but the weight of the freight was seventeen. This meant I was illegally carrying a load of more than five times the laden weight. Luckily, I was not challenged by the police on the route to Tamale, simply because it was a Government load that was being conveyed on my vehicle.

We had hardly covered a distance of twenty-two miles when the vehicle began to give us trouble. The timing in the engine went wrong and it began to boil over. By the time we had travelled thirty-two miles from Kumasi, all the water-hoses connecting the engine and the radiator together with the spares I was carrying, had all been used up and were burst. All the sparking plugs had also been damaged due to the water pouring into them. The vehicle lacked any power to scale the treacherous, mammoth Mampong scarp. The driver, Tang Yakubu, returned to Kumasi to bring the electrician who had done all the electrical work on the vehicle, both at the SCOA where he was employed and at his home for the additional work I wanted done. The mate and I passed the night in the vehicle by the road side in this thick Ashanti forest. The next morning before dawn, the driver and the electrician arrived and by seven o'clock he had adjusted the timing of the engine and we set off again on our long and arduous journey. We moved very slowly stopping every few miles to replenish our water tank any time it was empty until we arrived at Yeji. Luckily for us, it was still the rainy season and there was water in abundance lying along on both sides of the road. From Yeji, the condition of the engine became worse than ever as we crawled along stopping after every couple of miles either to burn out the accumulated carbon on the sparking plugs so as to clean them or to refill the radiator with water.

As a result, we had hardly travelled twenty-four miles from Salaga in about four hours when the hoses burst again and the water filled the cavity of the sparking plugs. The engine began to cough and stall and the vehicle stopped immediately almost in the middle of the road. With the help of the few passengers, we managed to park the vehicle as near to the roadside as possible without going too near to the edge. To do so, would have let it sink into the muddy side of the road. We were about half a mile from a blind corner of the road. While the driver and his mate were busy burning off and cleaning the sparking plugs some yards away behind the truck, because of the cool weather we could hear the boom of an approaching vehicle some miles away. I ran to slow down this vehicle before it negotiated the bend. I had scarcely covered a distance of a quarter of a mile when this vehicle came round the bend, rushing towards me at a terrific speed. I waved at the driver to slow down. But as I did so, he must have applied the brakes of his vehicle abruptly. With the muddy condition of the road, the lorry skidded and leapt into the air with its back wheels hardly touching the ground, careering from one side of the road to the other whilst the front wheels rose in the air looking like the trunk of an angry bull elephant charging at its assailant and coming ferociously towards me. I ran for dear life still flagging it down. The passengers in this vehicle were flung out on both sides of the road like chickens escaping from their cage. As it reared towards me I turned and ran faster for my life not knowing when I passed my own truck only to hear the crash behind me. As I turned round I found it had crashed just one hundred yards away from my own vehicle. I was shaking like a leaf but after a few minutes I composed myself.

The human injuries from this accident were indeed very great and no doubt there must have been some fatalities. Instead of the driver helping to care for his wounded passengers, he was rather eager to shift the blame on to my driver. He ran to him demanding the keys to my vehicle until the police arrived. I could not see how my driver was to blame for this accident since every precaution to avoid the accident was taken and yet he tried to blame it on him. When I saw them struggling with each other, I was so enraged with his attitude that I went up to him and tried to dissuade him from his folly. For there was no way he could take the key of my lorry since the accident was due to his speeding too fast and had nothing to do with us. A businessman who was travelling with him agreed with me that we had done all we could to avert the accident and that it was his fault for speeding. He himself had cautioned the driver to slow down because of the treacherous condition of the road.

Seeing that we had a witness who had travelled on his truck, and knowing he would be implicated if he insisted that we wait for the police to come from Salaga, he desisted in his futile act. Besides I was not going to wait so many hours for him to travel to Salaga and bring back the police. There was no guarantee that he would find transport going that way and to return with the police on that same day since at the outstations they had no vehicles of their own and depended on commercial ones. As we started to move our lorry, this businessman decided to travel back with us to Tamale. I had thought that since the area where the accident took place was under the jurisdiction of the Dagomba district, the police in Tamale would have been responsible for the accident. When we arrived in Tamale we drove straight to the police station and reported the accident to the duty orderly who was at the desk and this businessman coroborated our story. But we were told that it was outside their jurisdiction and that we could report the matter to the Salaga police on our way back to Kumasi.

After we had finished with the police we drove round to the PWD yard next door to unload our heavy freight. This certainly was not our day; for although there was still enough time to unload the truck, the stores clerk was trying to elicit some bribe from my driver before the truck could be unloaded. He told him that it was a half day and that the truck would not be unloaded until Monday at the earliest. When my driver tried to explain to him that the load was too heavy for the truck to be laden with it until Monday, he became very offensive and aggressive because he felt Tang was lightly built and he could beat him up quite easily if there was a fight. As I was not prepared to stand aside and let my driver be bullied unreasonably, I went up to the storekeeper and asked why he was not prepared to let the labourers unload the truck. He told me that they had closed. I told him there was still at least an hour left before closing time and that by then, the lorry could easily have been unloaded. Besides his foreman had told me there was still time to unload the vehicle. At this juncture, he used some swear words at me that caused my anger to race up to a higher pitch. I hardly realised that I had raised my hand to try to hit him on the chin with an undercut. He dodged my ferocious swing and then screamed "so you sabe an undercut"? I went for him a second time but he began to back off towards his office. At that juncture the foreman of the labourers, a fellow northerner, took me aside and tried to pacify me. He told me not to worry and that they would unload the truck for me. After they had done so, I gave the headman a few pounds as a tip and told him not to give a penny to the storekeeper since he was trying to solicit a bribe from me before doing his duty. My driver had never seen me so angry nor had he seen me use any violence on anybody but as I was provoked to the extreme I was prepared to retaliate. After the truck was unloaded we drove back to town and parked at the lorry park.

In town, we found out that being the feast day which marks the end of the fast of Ramadan, many students from the Teacher Training College and pupils from the Middle School had come down to town to enjoy the holiday. As Gyub was in his fourth year at the college, I guessed where he would be with some of his college mates. Tang and I went to House No. D1, a pito bar where as students we used to go to carouse and revel every Sunday. There we met Gyub and I told him of the existence of the Gandah Transport. After drinking a calabash or two of the pito, I went with him to the lorry park and showed him the new truck. All that day I had lost my appetite because of the accident and also being upset at the PWD yard. After a day or two in Tamale, we left for Kumasi, stopping at the Salaga Police Station to report the accident that had taken place two days previously.

I was surprised that the police in Salaga thought we were at fault. If they had measured the distance from where the driver started applying the brakes of his vehicle to where it stopped, they would have realised that my driver was never at fault. But no doubt the other driver must have oiled the palms of those investigating officers and talked his way out of it. But since we were not at the scene when they arrived in order to give our side of the story, we were charged with the offence. From the insinuations of the investigating constable he was expecting us too to bribe him. This was truly against the grain of my ethical beliefs and I preferred to be charged so I could explain myself in court. In Ghana in those days, people were ill-advised to plead guilty with explanation whenever they were charged with a crime whether one was guilty or not. This I found odd but had to conform with the convention. Although I was the owner of the vehicle, it was my driver who was charged with the offence and we were told we would be notified of the hearing date. My driver would have preferred I gave a bribe and had the charges dropped. He felt his driving licence would be endorsed if he was found guilty but could not convince me to change my beliefs.

In Kumasi we went to the Kumasi-Wa lorry station to solicit some load and passengers for our next trip home. While we were looking for the load, Gyiripuɔ was sent down to me in Kumasi so I could get some equipment for our grinding machine that was to be installed in the village. I was also to look for a miller who would be prepared to stay in the village and train someone to run the mill. My driver's mate recommended a friend of his whom I decided to employ. However, I knew within my heart that he would not stay in the job for long because he was used to city life that was quite different from the village life of Birifu. As soon as we had sufficient load and passengers, we left for Birifu. The road from Kumasi to Wenchi was not too bad but that from Wenchi to the river at Bamboi was atrocious and my driver had never driven on such surfaces before. Even experienced drivers found the going tough during the heavy rains. Sometimes while a vehicle was being steered, the driver would find himself suddenly and involuntarily facing the reverse side of the road. That is, if the driver was lucky. If he was not, he could find himself skidding into a ditch and causing fatal injuries. I told my driver, who had not been on that road since leaving the Primary School in Lawra, to drive very slowly and warily because of the mud. We ventured on until we got to the river without any serious mishap.

However, driving on to the pontoon was even more dangerous and my driver was just as petrified as I was. But as good luck would have it, we met his former boss who was also driving to Wa and beyond. Being an experienced driver, this driver offered to drive the vehicle on to the pontoon for us after he had taken his across. We waited until he returned and drove us on to the pontoon to be ferried across. From the river to Bole and northwards the ground was a bit firmer and so we were able to travel at a much faster speed than before. It was about four o'clock in the afternoon when we were about twenty-three miles from Wa and four miles from the village of Ga, and there was an acute curve a few yards ahead where the road was very sandy. As we approached the bend, I tried to warn the driver since he did not know the road very well. I had hardly finished my sentence warning him to slow down, when suddenly we skidded into a shallow gutter. We were very lucky that this was not a deep ditch, otherwise the consequences would have been very grave. One side of the body of the vehicle was slightly damaged as it was laden with a hundred bags of cement weighing in all five tons. I was relieved that the damage was only slight, for I would not have known what to tell the family had it been very serious. We got the truck back onto the road and proceeded to Birifu that same evening to surprise the family with our new vehicle, which I had proudly signposted on the front as "Gandah Transport".

That evening I presented the driver to Biz and Tiisip and we discussed what emoluments he was to receive. At that time drivers were paid five pounds per month and two shillings a day pocket money. I told them that that was the salary I had decided to pay him. The driver's mate was to receive thirty shillings a month and pocket money of a shilling a day. As for my own emoluments, I told them that I would pay myself the same salary of five pounds that Tiisip and Dɛri who were my classmates at school were receiving, plus the two shillings a day pocket money which my driver was to be paid. Were I greedy I could have demanded to pay myself as Biz since we were college mates and as teachers our pay was slightly higher. To this, Tiisip and Biz readily agreed. Although I was the proprietor of the business, my driver and myself were to earn the same salary because I did not want to pay myself more than my classmates. I also decided to employ a younger brother who could learn the ropes from the driver as a second mate. As Sunkuol was not sufficiently grown up to farm with the adults, I decided to take him as a second driver's mate even though he was one of the leading cowherds in the house. On hearing my choice, Nikara vehemently objected to my suggestion because he felt Sunkuol was developing into an expert xylophonist and could grow up to play like my father or even himself.[37] However, Nikara should have known better that once I make up my mind, especially when I sincerely believe what I am doing is right, it was difficult for anyone to dissuade me. In the end he lost the argument to the family and Sunkuol was allowed to follow me to Kumasi.

As I was on the road for most of the time, I decided that my wife should stay in Kumasi where she could keep an eye on my accommodation and prepare food for Sunkuol and myself any time we returned to town from our journeys. I was given fifty pounds towards a deposit for my accommodation in Kumasi. However, as the accommodation was not yet ready, I could not allow my wife to accompany me to Kumasi for the time being. My landlord had promised the accommodation would be ready within a month; it was not until six months later that he provided me with temporary accommodation. Tang had a child with his girl friend whose parents would only give the girl to him in marriage if this was conducted according to the Moslem rites. The girl's parents originally came from the Yoruba land in Nigeria but had settled in Kumasi where she was born. The marriage ritual was a costly business which was beyond the means of my driver. He approached me to see if we could help him with a loan of fifty pounds to meet the cost of the preliminaries. On one of our journeys home, I discussed this with Tiisip and Biz and we all agreed to lend him the money. However, by the time all the marriage customs had been settled, I had spent over one hundred pounds on him, which was never repaid before he left the service of the Gandah Transport. Meanwhile, Sunkuol and I were sharing accommodation with Tang and his wife until mine was ready.

About two or three months after the accident at Salaga, we at last received a writ summoning us to appear before the District Commissioner's court in Salaga to answer the charge in connection with the accident that had occurred on our first trip to Tamale. We canvassed for some load at the Tamale-Kumasi lorry station and left on our journey so I could be in Salaga on time to stand in for my driver during the hearing. When we arrived, I stayed while my driver went ahead to Tamale to arrange matters concerning his wedding. The senior relatives of his future in-laws resided in Tamale, which was where the marriage rites were to take place. Our case went well since as the result of my explanation, the District Commissioner found out there was no case for me to answer and I was allowed to go scot-free. It was about noon when the case was eventually called and by one o'clock I had found a truck that was bound for Tamale and hopped on to it. By the evening I had arrived in Tamale and joined my driver and the two mates. After meeting with the relatives of his fiancée and settling all matters that had to be done, we loaded our truck and left for Kumasi a couple of days later.

Within a matter of months of starting the Gandah Transport, I applied to the Lawra Confederacy Native Authority to be the sole contractor conveying goods such as cement, iron rods and building materials, that the Authority might purchase from the south and that needed to be transported to Lawra. At a gathering for their annual estimates to be held this time at Lambusie, as these meetings rotated each year from division to division, Gandah Transport was nominated by the Native Authority as its authorised transporter. I tried to arrange similar contracts in other districts of the north. Luckily in Bawku the District Administration, in collaboration with the Native Authority, had bought some six hundred animal-driven ploughs from John Holt of Kumasi which needed to be transported to Bawku as quickly as possible before the farming season began.[39] I met a school mate of mine, Adabri Frafra, who was the chief clerk to the Native Authority there and when he heard of my mission, he told me that the District Administration were in need of transport. He took me to see the District Commissioner, Mr Bailie. After a few words with me, and learning that I was a school mate of Adabri, Mr Bailie decided to give me the contract for the transportation of these ploughs and to pay me at the Government rate of sixpence per ton mile. As my truck was a five tonner, the maximum I could charge was two shillings and sixpence per mile. However, my first contract was to go to Tamale and convey the school children at the Tamale Middle School for their holidays in Lawra.

At that time, Colonel Wentworth was in charge of both the school and the Teacher Training College and was personally supervising the despatch of these children. When he saw my truck marked "Gandah Transport", he looked out for me. When he saw me, he invited me to his office where he introduced me to some of his junior officers, amongst whom was one Mr Bryant, the first white headmaster of the school since the time of Rev A.H. Candler. Bryant later became head of Education in the North and Principal of the College. He did not try to convince me to return to teaching in front of his colleagues but when we drove the children down to the Government Transport yard to collect our waybills, he followed me. He tried to convince me to return to the teaching field but without success. I told him it was too late since I was now running the family transport in which we had invested so much capital. In those days £800 was a lot of money. Anyway failing to convince me to return to teaching, Mr Wentworth returned to the Education Ridge a disappointed man while I conveyed the Lawra and Wa boys home for their holidays. It was a year later in 1950 that Bryant came to inspect the Birifu School and told me that Col. Wentworth had vowed to bring me back into the teaching service.

By Christmas of 1949, I had netted a profit of over £385 from the transport undertaking alone; this included neither the earnings from the village shop which I had opened nor those of the grinding mill. But more on those businesses later. During the Christmas holidays Gyub had returned from college to take over his old school with Biz and Dibaar Kuuyele teaching under him.[40] The majority of the educated brothers also came home for the Bɔɔr and the Christmas festivities. We decided to have a family meeting. There it was decided that all the family income be collected and kept in one place. As my father was fond of giving large sums of money for safe-keeping to any of his sons, nephews, cousins, who happened to be near him at the time, we decided to collect all these bits and pieces together and give it to a single person in the house to keep.

At that time there were no banks opened in the North except in Tamale. Even though I was running the transport business, all the income derived from it was kept in Birifu with one of my younger brothers, Nyimɛdire (Nyimɛ) who was the custodian of my cases and the keys to them. Gyub was suggested by me (which I have to this day regretted) to be the treasurer, as he and Biz were the only brothers stationed in the village at the time. Tiisip was posted to Sabuli in Jirapa and John Dɛri and Nana were stationed in Nandom and Samoa respectively. It thus made sense to suggest Gyub and the rest of the members of the family agreed. If I had suggested Biz, it might have seemed that I had nominated him because we were both of the same mother.

After my resignation from teaching and before I left for Kumasi, one Yahaya Imoru, known to the Walas as Babile Imoru, had bought about one hundred and ten bags of shelled groundnuts from my father for which he paid £385 in cash. I was sitting by my father at the time of the deal, so he handed the whole amount of the cash for me to keep. When I was leaving for the south, I gave this amount to Nyimɛ to be given to my dad if and when he asked for it. But he never asked for it so Nyimɛ handed me the money. In all, Gyub received from me the sum of £770 as the new treasurer. Other brothers and cousins brought down what cash they had been given to keep and this was counted in the presence of all and handed over to Gyub. The amount that was collected from all those who handed in the cash they had in their custody amounted to over two thousand pounds, apart from what my father had buried in his own room which at that time was not accessible to us.

CHAPTER FOURTEEN

THE UAC NO.1 STORE in Kumasi was managed by one Mr Nkansah, whose brother managed the UAC store in Tamale.[41] I became one of Mr Nkansah's best customers in Kumasi, especially for petrol and cement and other building materials. We had planned to build a permanent structure for the village shop and I bought these materials from him, paying cash to the tune of three to five hundred pounds a week. I was only allowed credit for my trip up north and back but was able to arrange credit with him when I opened the village shop, the goods of which I housed in temporary accommodation in one of the visitors' quarters which my father had built adjoining the palace. These quarters were built when chiefs moved from one town to the other for the District Commissioner's palaver. As soon as I got the counter erected, I obtained a licence to sell beer and wines in the village. I appointed Wanzam, one of the bright boys I had taught to read and write, as the shopkeeper. We advertised the opening of the shop by word of mouth to all the educated folks in Lawra and at the Babile Agricultural Station. I went to Kumasi and bought cases of beer, wine and liquor, pieces of cloth, soap and tins of kerosene, hoe blades and other such merchandise which I believed the villagers needed. The drinks were for the benefit of the educated class as very few people in the village would bother to buy beer instead of a pot of pito that can serve more than ten people at a cost of only a shilling or two at a time. When the shop opened, I stayed behind to show Wanzam the ropes while my driver and Sunkuol left for the south with the truck. We made a handsome profit in the shop during the first month. At the end of that time I went down with Wanzam to Kumasi and introduced him to Mr Nkansah, the manager of the UAC No.1 store.

As the shop was making a handsome profit, I felt it was time I allowed credit for the salaried clients, a mistake which I have since regretted. I allowed each a credit limit of not more than his or her monthly salary. On my next visit to the south for provisions and goods for the shop, and also for materials for the new building, I bought some note books which I used as passbooks. Each of my salaried brothers was issued with one, as well as some of the trusted customers. But instead of keeping to their credit limits I later found out that most of them abused the conditions under which these passbooks were issued to them. They took advantage of Wanzam not having gone to school and not having had a formal education, but much of that later. In addition to buying from UAC, Kumasi, I was also supplied with goods by both Peter Ghanem and Badhia Halaby of Wa each to the value of £600 in the form of building materials or cases of beer.[42] Towards the end of January and the beginning of February 1950, I had loaded my truck as usual with provisions, drinks, and building materials from UAC Kumasi and we travelled to Wenchi in order to solicit loads and passengers for the truck to go ahead to Birifu. I was to return to Kumasi to purchase extra petrol for the conveying of sand and stones for the building work at home. The truck was always used to cart sand and stones from the river or from the culverts and bridges near Jirapa for the making of cement blocks and mortar for building.

On our way to Wenchi from Kumasi, I felt some tears running uncontrollably down my cheeks without any logical reason but which I assumed at that time to be caused by the cold harmattan wind blowing into my eyes. Nevertheless this continued until we got to Wenchi. There I retired immediately and soon fell asleep, hoping that by the next morning I would be alright. The next day the tears continued to flow involuntarily and I thought something minuscule might perhaps have blown into my eyes during the night travel. I never thought it portended any mishap whatever. As soon as my truck was fully loaded, the driver and Sunkuol took off for Birifu and I returned to Kumasi with the tears still pouring down my cheeks. We arrived in Kumasi in the evening and the next day after breakfast, I went to UAC No.1 to buy petrol in an 8-gallon drum. When I returned to the house at about eleven in the morning to have an early lunch and to set off for Birifu, a telegram had been delivered by the post office messenger to my address awaiting my return from the shops.

As I read the sad news of my father's death, I did not realise I had collapsed into my chair. I must have swooned because of the shock of the news. I did not come round until about two o'clock in the afternoon when my lunch was ready and the table was laid. When I came to, I saw my brother, Zumɔka, who had signed on as recruit with the Gold Coast contingent of the West African Frontier Force (WAFF) not more than a week earlier. He was sitting there and must have thought I was asleep, so he did not want to disturb me. When I saw him, I told him the sad news and asked him to eat my lunch. I had lost all my appetite. When he had finished I asked him to return to the barracks and seek permission from his superiors so we could leave for the North that evening. He was lucky to have been training under a family friend, R.S.M. Timbilla, a cousin of Chief Dombo, and the father of Vida, now the wife of my brother Nũũbomo. I also told the two women the sad news and asked them to pack a few things and get ready for the journey that evening. At that time a new loading station, Wa Station No 2, had been opened by the Dagaar and Issala collectors.[43] I went straight to that station to book our passage home.

I was booked to travel by one of the drivers who regularly travelled to the north and knew my home-town well. He was also aware that I was a transport owner and as it was a convention not to charge lorry owners or their drivers, he was loathe to have me on his truck since I would occupy a free seat that would have earned him a fare. However, when he realised I was being accompanied by three fare-paying passengers, he gladly agreed to take us. I went with him to pick up the petrol from the store and passed to my address to pick up the two women and whatever little load they had managed to pack. We set off that evening for Birifu for my father's funeral. It was an eternity before we arrived there and indeed took us seven days. For this driver had failed to maintain his truck properly before setting out on this journey. We continually encountered breakdown upon breakdown by the roadside from Wenchi onwards. It took us two days to reach the river from Kumasi and from the river, another five days to reach Birifu.

At Tasiliman, twenty-five miles from the Volta and forty-six miles to Bole, the driver stopped so he could pick up some passengers and so the travelling passengers on the truck could buy some food by the roadside to eat. At this village I gave some money to Zumɔka so he and the women could buy food for themselves and for the little Yakubu of about one year old who was travelling with the mother. As I sat in the front of the truck filled with grief, I could hear my wife and her companion involved in a slanging match with some of the women traders selling the food. I got down and saw they were surrounded by the women hawkers and some men who threatened to beat them up. I was livid with my wife and Zumɔka and blamed them for entering into that squabble in the first instance. I told them that if they thought they were going home for fun, I would put them back on the next truck to return to Kumasi. I also ordered the women traders to clear away from the side of the truck and take their trade elsewhere since they were picking quarrels with the passengers. Having dealt with the women, I turned on the two young men who took the side of the hawkers instead of stopping the fight. I threatened to beat them up myself if they did not go away from our truck. I happened to know them personally for they acted as unlicensed "lorry collectors". Collectors are agents of the Motor Union who find passengers and freight for drivers for which they received a ten percent commission on each fare. Each village has such agents. I vowed to take revenge on them after the mourning by not recognising them as agents for any load or passengers I picked up at that village.

We eventually got to Birifu at about two o'clock in the afternoon, and my father had already been interred half an hour earlier. The funeral parlour was the only thing left still standing as the mourning continued. As soon as we arrived and paid our respects to the parlour and to the grave, the funeral directors (bɔɔ-uune) dismantled the parlour and the mourning came to an end a few minutes later. The drinks for the shop which I had sent ahead on my truck were used to entertain the chiefs and the distinguished guests who had come to mourn my father and the local brew was then used as a supplement and to entertain the common people as well. The family took the credit for the timely arrival of the beer as if this had been pre-planned but that was not the case.

As all the drinks had been used for the funeral of my father, the shop had to pay for the goods from the capital. However, there was no doubt that within a short space of time this loss could be recouped. With Debomo now stationed in Tumu, he and I decided to extend the retailing side of the business by opening another shop, as there was only one shop in that town, belonging to one Kwame Mabre, the station carpenter. The Tumu Native Authority had built a terrace of market stalls along the main street in the Zongo which they let out at fifteen shillings per stall per month. I rented two stalls, one of which I used as the shop and the other to store the goods in. About the middle of the year 1950, the Birifu shop having been very well stocked, I bought some goods for the opening of the new shop. While at Tumu, I applied to the District Commissioner, Major Dickie, for a Beer and Wine licence. Spirit licences were forbidden by law to traders in the north. No one could sell to northerners until 1951, when the Tolon Na fought for this stupid colonial law to be changed.[44] Major Dickie relieved DC Redhead who was to return on leave to the UK. The Tumu District Administration had money in the budget vote to hire private vehicles for construction work in the district. While I was in Tumu, he hired my truck for the carting of sand and stones for the construction work of the new station.[45]

The Tumu District had been opened immediately after the war and was now independently administered and no longer attached to Lawra. As a new Administrative District, there was much building work to be carried out by my brother. At that time the District Administrators hired private trucks at the flat rate of £5 a day for such work. My truck was hired at that rate and we spent some months in Tumu carting sand and stones or travelling to Wa to bring goods for the administration as well as the DC's personal provisions. On such journeys I charged sixpence per ton mile. The two months' stay gave me the chance to train one of my young nephews, Dɔbayizie, the son of Dɔɔr-iɛrɛ. Dɔbayizie was nicknamed Gɔlɔ because he was left handed. Because of his relation as a grandson to my father, he was also related to me not only as a nephew but as a father (uncle), according to the Birifu way of life. His father had that same dual relationship with my father. By the time we had finished our work with the district administration in Tumu, the total pay voucher for the work had come to nearly a thousand pounds. The District Commissioner decided that as he was going down to Kumasi I should sign all the p.v.s so that he could take them to the treasury in Kumasi and cash them for my driver who was going down to Kumasi at the same time. That also was a mistake I made, agreeing with Major Dickie. This amount was never accounted for by Tang although he told a lie that it was used for overhauling the engine.

I left Tumu with my driver for Lawra where I was to collect a chit from the Native Authority authorising Gandah Transport to cart 960 bags of cement from John Holt in Kumasi to Lawra. I gave this chit to my driver to give to the General Manager of John Holt. I instructed him that if the load was ready, he should sublet it to other transport owners in quest of freight. Although the engine of my truck did not require immediate overhauling, since he was to receive nearly a thousand pounds from Major Dickie in Kumasi I decided part of the cash should be used to overhaul the engine at the same time as he supervised the carting of the cement to Lawra by the other drivers. Tang and his mate, Sunkuol, left me in Birifu, so I could attend to the affairs of the village shop while they went to Kumasi.

At Birifu, I found out to my horror that everything was in a mess at the shop and I regretted having issued the passbooks to my senior brothers. Tiisip, Gyub and Biz each owed the shop over £400. I decided to withdraw their credit facilities and I told Wanzam not to give them any further credit. This created discontent between us. The only brother who kept to the rules of the credit facilities was John (Dɛri) who at that time was transferred to Birifu. He owed the shop not more than ten pounds. I was flabbergasted that they should each amass such a debt knowing full well they could hardly afford to repay it. I thought that as senior brothers, they should have known better than to accumulate such debts since the goods from the shop were bought with cash and not stones. They had all bought for themselves iron four-poster double beds which at that time cost £15 each at the UAC in Kumasi. Even though I was the one running the business and earning the money for the family, I was content with sleeping on a locally made wooden bed that cost only £3.10s.0d in Kumasi at that time. Besides, I paid cash for mine and from my own salary of £5.00. The bitterness increased and became a feud between them and me especially when I gave orders to Wanzam not to give them any further credit as the year went by.

Since my father died on February 8, 1950, the funeral rites should, according to tradition, have taken place a year later. But Nana, who was eager to become the chief of the village, wanted the funeral rites to be performed much earlier, and against all traditional rules. Nana was worried that one of the educated brothers might challenge him for the chieftaincy, especially Biz, Tiisip or even myself. During my father's illness, Biz and Tiisip, who were stationed in the village, effectively acted as the chief and were consulted on every matter of importance in the village by Sakpi, my father's linguist. When Tiisip was transferred to Sabule, in the Jirapa division, Biz, who was then the headteacher of the village school, became effectively the only person to whom all matters were taken. All the villagers and the headmen looked upon him for all sorts of advice and guidance. By this time Nana was not only envious of my ascendancy in running the family business affairs, but was also concerned that Sakpi, who was then acting as a regent, or Gaziere, our uncle, might contest him for the chieftaincy.

Immediately after the funeral, a family meeting was held with those brothers in regular employment so that people on compassionate leave could return to their stations. We all made it clear to Nana that none of us were interested in becoming the next chief of Birifu. At the same meeting, we also decided that the funeral rites should take place on February 8, 1951. Reluctantly, Nana had to agrcc. Hc had wanted an earlier date named for the installation so he could be made the chief and collect the chief's pay as well as his own salary as a dresser. At this time, reassured that none of the educated sons was interested in the chieftaincy, his jealousy or uneasiness was no longer directed against Biz or myself, but against Gaziere and Sakpi. It was rumoured that the two were soliciting the late Lawra Nũũ, J.A. Karbo, for one of them to be made the chief. However, Sakpi who was so faithful to his deceased master and uncle, poohpoohed the rumours and said he was not the least interested in becoming the next chief. He said that in 1935 when the Lawra school was opened, my father was asked by the DC which of his four school children he would like to succeed him. The idea was to replace illiterate chiefs in the Northern Territories with literate ones. He nominated Nana who was the eldest at that time. Sakpi who was present at these proceedings said he would not go against his uncle's wishes now that he was dead.

As the year drew nearer to a close and the date of the funeral rites drew on, I notified all my father's friends in Kumasi and elsewhere down south that his obsequies were taking place on February 8, 1951. Kwame Nti of Kwapra promised to bring a brass band to the village for the funeral rites. I was solely responsible for the running of the family business and I knew what drinks to provide for the important visitors who would be coming for the occasion. When the time drew nearer, I travelled to Kumasi and had a full load of cases of beer and wine on my truck despite the fact that Gyub refused to fund any purchases I had made. This was because I had questioned the way the shop in Birifu had been run by the educated lot incurring such large debts. Seeing I had to pay for the beer and wine on my return to Kumasi and knowing that if I allowed them a free hand, they would drink it all without paying a penny for them, I gave strict orders to Wanzam not to sell any more drinks on credit to any of them. So I instructed him to lock up the drinks in the store room and put a few at a time out on the shelf to be sold for cash. This met with a hostile reception from most of my senior brothers who felt I was taking the upper hand in everything connected with the family business.

On the eve of February 8, 1951, Kwame Nti and his entourage arrived with the brass band from Kumasi. I had informed all the clerks in Lawra that there would be a ball when the brass band arrived. On the second day of the funeral rites, February 9, many people arrived from Lawra and Babile for this dance and business was brisk. As most of the VIPs were known to me, I was busy distributing the drinks to them and left the shop in the hands of Wanzam with the strict instructions that no drinks should be sold on credit. It was then that Nana, whose account was in the red, wanted to buy more drinks on credit. Wanzam told him that I had given instructions to sell only on cash basis and anybody without cash must first consult me. Of course this angered Nana and he tried to bully Wanzam or use brute force to get what he wanted from the shop. Wanzam, however, refused to give in until he had seen me. He asked Dɔndulɛ to call me and tell me that he was having trouble with Nana at the shop. When I went over, Nana, almost in a drunken stupor, was fuming with anger and wanting to beat up the poor young man. I told him that Wanzam was only acting on my orders and if he wanted any drinks he would have to pay cash for them as any of us had to do. At that moment he tried to cause an affray in the shop and I warned him that if he did not desist, I would call the police constable who was in attendance and was standing nearby. That frightened him off and he left without any purchase. I requested the police to be in attendance although I did not foresee that my own brothers would wish to cause a disturbance at this particular time.

A few minutes later Gyub arrived wanting some bottles of beer on credit, although I had a few moments earlier refused to serve his errand boy who wanted the beer without cash. I told him that without the cash, I was not letting anybody have the drinks from the shop. Before the night ended, I had incensed three of my senior brothers, Nana, Biz and Gyub, by not allowing them to buy drinks on credit. The next day and the subsequent days I was sent to Coventry by the three of them and before the week was over, they had convinced the other brothers that I was trying to gain more influence in the family at their expense. I became the black sheep of the family as far as the educated lot were concerned and was not on speaking terms with most of them. But the elders in the house, and my illiterate brothers including my father's widows, still looked upon me as their guardian angel.

As I mentioned earlier, when I went to Tumu I put in an application for a beer and wine licence to Major Dickie, the DC in Tumu. The Officer in charge of the Police Station in Wa was asked to come and inspect the place and approve it if it met with the Act. At that time Tumu had no police post of its own and was therefore policed from Wa. This was approved but Major Dickie delayed the issue of the licence until he left for the UK on his tour of leave, even though I had paid the fee of five pounds into the Government Treasury at Wa. While on leave, Major Dickie was succeeded by a Mr Moor-Darling as the DC for Tumu and he took an immediate dislike to me, for no apparent reason that I can think of.[46] He tried to put so many hurdles in my way in order not to issue the beer and wine licence to me. My bar at Tumu was better furnished than the Gentleman's Drinking Bar in Obuasi which I had kept for Owusu Ansah, even though that was given a fuller licence which permitted the sale of spirits. Yet Mr Moor-Darling felt my bar was not well furnished and was too small to accommodate drinkers who might be drunk and needed a place to wait out the drunkenness before leaving for home. What I could not understand was that even the bar in Birifu was not as well furnished as the shop in Tumu and yet I had been issued with a licence for it. I did not know what exactly Mr Moor-Darling wanted me to do before he could issue me with the licence. I complied with his suggestions and built an extension to the bar before he reluctantly issued me with the licence. This was the era of British Colonialism, in which the words of our "civil masters", to use Nkrumah's political jargon, were always final.

Because I needed to train a shop assistant in Tumu to run the shop as Wanzam did in Birifu, I gave my driver a free hand with the running of the transport for the period I was at Tumu training Gɔlɔ. As mentioned earlier, when John Holt was ready with the consignment of cement for Lawra I gave my driver specific verbal instructions as to how to subcontract the transport of the cement to other drivers at a particular price. I followed this up with a written instruction in which I told Tang that the freight for each load of 100 bags of cement should be £20 and not a penny more, when I heard he had given the load to his former boss for a sum of £22 per 100 bags. I also instructed Gyub to pay these subcontractors the amount shown on their waybills if they were counter-signed by the Native Authority storekeeper. As the rainy season was a lean time for both freight and passenger services to the north, these loads were snapped up by eager transport owners. Within two weeks all the loads were delivered to the Lawra Native Authority stores after which they were paid from our private coffers. I submitted my bill for the cost of transport of over £550. At the end of the month the Lawra Nũũ authorised the payment and I was eventually paid. I collected this money and took it home all in coins in my little wooden box. At Babile I met a nephew, Suɔtah, on a bicycle returning to Birifu. I can still remember tying this box of coins on to the back carrier of the bicycle. Suɔtah rode with it in great difficulty from Babile to Birifu because of the weight. When Suɔtah and I finally got home with the money, Gyub, Wanzam and Dɔrpur helped us to count it and then handed it to Gyub, the treasurer.

As I could not run the two retail shops as well as the transport side of the business, and as I believed I could trust my driver, I allowed him to run the transport side of the business and to make weekly account to Gyub any time he went to the north with the vehicle. This left me free to concentrate on the running of the retail shop in Tumu. For one complete year, Tang was running the transport between Kumasi and Hamile without going to Birifu to account to Gyub. At least that was Gyub's side of the story when I was accused of running the transport and paying the proceeds into an account in a Kumasi bank—a bank account I never had. Any time I went to Wa to buy beer or provisions from either the Halabys or the Ghanems and met Tang there, he assured me he had been doing the accounts with Gyub in Birifu. During the dry season I took time off to visit Birifu to take part in the Bɔɔr Ceremony at Mal and also to organise the preparation for the performance of my father's funeral rites.[47] Biz' wife, nicknamed Pule, was being initiated into the Bɔɔr by her father, the headman for Mal and Ŋmangbil. During the Bɔɔr dance almost all the brothers who could afford to buy a present to shower on her did so, to show their appreciation that their wife was being initiated. It was one of the best Bɔɔr performances ever done in that section except one in which one of my father's young wives, Iɔnnuri, had been initiated in the late twenties or 1930. Then I could remember as a toddler, being carried on the shoulders by my mother's cousin to the festival. Immediately after the performance of the funeral rites for my father and the last performance of the Bɔɔr, I left Birifu almost for good. I hated the conduct and behaviour of my senior brothers, especially Gyub, Biz and Nana, and had I stayed behind I would have been tempted to commit a crime such as manslaughter or murder.

In the Birifu custom of marital relations, the direct sons of a father cannot marry their father's widows. Only the grandsons and brothers of the deceased can. However, in the Sissala area of Tumu and the Dagaa area of Jirapa, direct sons of the deceased can do so. They cannot, however, marry their real mother. Anyway, Gyub managed to convince Nana and others that since the Dagaa of Jirapa and the Sissalas of Tumu do it, there was no harm if they did the same. Every night they would invite some of the widows down, especially the younger ones, to give them drinks to make them drunk so they could fumble them and presumably take them to bed. Whether they succeeded in going thus far, I am not in a position to say, since I was not down there with them. I shunned their company because of their repulsive conduct. One night, during a drinking binge that went very far into the night, one of them attempted to try to go the whole way with one of the widows who had a teenage girl. I was fast asleep on the rooftop of the palace when I heard the yells and insults issuing from this woman, telling them that she would rather use a stick to penetrate herself if she had the urge for sex than yield to her own sons. At that moment I also got up on the rooftop and yelled down below at them, adding my own insults. I asked the elder of the house, Dɔɔriɛrɛ, what he was doing about the moral degradation that was happening in the house. He told me there was nothing he could do about it. But I need not have bothered for the tongue of that woman was much sharper than the razor of a barber, and she could have taken care of herself. By this time events were happening in the family which had been the gossip of the village and I did not want to be part of it, so I closed the village shop and left almost for good to Tumu to concentrate on the shop there.

However, before I left for Tumu, Gɔlɔ, whom I had earlier trained as the shopkeeper, also came over from Tumu for the performance of the Bɔɔr which was being performed by his maternal uncles. I was surprised to see him as he did not tell me he wanted to come for the Bɔɔr activities. While he was at home, Gyub and others managed to convince Gɔlɔ that on his return to Tumu, and as a grandson of my father, he had as much right to the family property as any of us. On his return, he squandered and made use of the funds of the shop while I was still in Birifu. They were very sure I would remain in the house until the last performance of the Bɔɔr was over before I returned. Gyub was the "Iago" and the demon of this plot and Gɔlɔ took him at his word. Had I still been staying with them down in the quarters, I would perhaps have known of the plot and would have stopped it. On the other hand if I had stayed down there, there could have been an unpleasant scene which would not have set a good example to the folks at home. When Gɔlɔ returned to Tumu, he found a way of upsetting Debomo, who chastised him. So Gɔlɔ took all the proceeds of the shop and escaped to Bolgatanga where I understood he bought some fowls and took them down to the south to retail.

After the Bɔɔr, I collected some of the building materials (iron rods) that had not been used and which I had bought on credit from the Ghanems and the Halabys and returned with them to Tumu. I was able to re-sell these to the Tumu Native Authority at a much reduced price in order to repay part of the cost to these traders at Wa. At Tumu, I found out that the shop was devoid of any goods without a penny in the till. It was then I asked Debomo what had happened to the shop and its proceeds. He told me that Gɔlɔ had sold most of the goods and absconded with the money to the south. I was in a dilemma since Gyub's demonic scheme had worked, although I was unaware of this plot until a year or so later.

Nevertheless, I had to make a decision. I had very little savings in my post office book. But Debomo and I decided that in order to continue with the shop in Tumu we should each contribute a certain amount to set it up. He could only raise £15 in cash, so I also added £15 from my savings and then rushed to Kumasi to buy some provisions. As the amount could hardly buy enough cases of drinks, I initially concentrated on the sale of provisions. In Kumasi I went to Edward Nasser and Company, dealers in provisions and beverages, and bought these at wholesale prices. These goods were snapped up in no time when I returned to Tumu and our capital doubled. Debomo was very pleased with the outcome. I went back to Edward Nasser and bought more provisions and within a few days returned to my shop. By the end of March 1951, the capital had increased from a mere £30 to £120. With this I felt I could now include in my list of merchandise the sale of beer. However, it was not feasible to travel to Kumasi and buy only a few cases of beer. Consequently I decided to approach the Ghanems and the Halabys in Wa to see if I could buy the drinks from them instead of going to Kumasi. With great persuasion, I managed to convince them I would pay in cash until I was able to repay the debt incurred by the family business. This family debt was over £600 and because my signature was on the invoices, I was held liable for it. I think they realised that if they did not help me, then the likelihood of their ever recouping the £600 was nil. In the end they consented to supply me with drinks from their stores at Wa.

The palace at Birifu.

DC Dyer-Ball and Nuonatuo, Chief Gandah II.

The Kobine dance, Lawra market place, 1950. The teacher Kunyamini Bini and an advisor to the chief.

Dancers paerforning during the Kobine festival.

CHAPTER FIFTEEN

WHEN GANDAH TRANSPORT WAS ESTABLISHED, I was given the sum of fifty pounds as deposit towards the rent of my accommodation in Kumasi. Although I paid this deposit to the landlord, Kuffuor, my accommodation was not made ready on time. Kuffuor collected deposits from prospective tenants and did not provide them with accommodation. When he did eventually supply the tenant with accommodation, the tenant had not used up all his deposit before he was kicked out. In adopting such tactics, Kuffuor managed to evict his old tenants on false grounds and then promise some new ones by getting fresh deposits of fifty pounds until he was able to complete building the ground floor. After completing the ground floor he started the building of the first floor. Those tenants on the ground floor whom he could evict by intimidation he did. Those others whom he could not, he issued summonses for them to appear before a magistrate's court. As Kuffuor knew I was away most of the time in the north and only visited Kumasi once a month, he issued a summons against me but the bailiffs could not serve me with the summons whilst I was in the north. On one of my visits to Kumasi, Kuffuor knew I was in town and consequently alerted the bailiffs. I was served with the summons and I stayed in Kumasi until the hearing date.

When the case was called, instead of the landlord appearing as the plaintiff, an old lady came in his place while he sat as a spectator. I appealed to the magistrate, who was a white colonial officer, that I did not know the plaintiff in the dock. I told him my landlord was a male and not a female and that I never set eyes on that lady in my life. But the old lady kept on insisting that she was the owner of the house and her brother was acting on her behalf. The magistrate seemed to be on the side of the landlord. I told him that the piece of paper in which I entered into contract with the man was in the north and that if I was allowed time, I could go and bring it back to prove that Kuffuor was my landlord and that he still owed me money from the deposit I paid and not the other way round. The case was adjourned and I was asked to pay ten pounds as costs. As we came out of the court and I walked down to take a taxi to Ashanti New Town, a young man who also lived on the other side of my street caught up with me. He immediately entered into conversation and told me he had listened to my case in court and that he would advise me to hire a barrister, otherwise I would not succeed. He said the magistrate was known to receive bribes from landlords and that when landlord and tenant cases came before him he was always biased in the landlord's favour. He told me he knew a good lawyer who would take up my case and took me to see the clerk to Victor Owusu who booked an appointment for me to see Victor at five o'clock that evening. I wondered whether that young man was discretely touting for him.[48]

In the evening I went to see Victor Owusu whom I had never met before. After listening to my case, he told me his fee was twenty-five pounds and if I agreed I should pay this amount to his clerk the following day so that a brief could be prepared on the case. The following morning I went to the office and the clerk prepared a docket for me. Had Kuffuor been an honest landlord, the deposit I paid to him would have covered thirty-three monthly payments of the rent of one pound ten shillings per month. This would have covered the period from 1950 to the end of 1952 and he would still have owed me ten shillings. I returned to the north and a month later when I came back for the hearing, Victor Owusu had travelled to Cape Coast for the hearing of another case without handing the brief for my case to another barrister to conduct the case for him. He only told a police prosecuting officer to apologise to the magistrate on his behalf. The case was again adjourned for a week and I had to pay another ten pounds cost. When case again came before this magistrate, Victor at last showed up in court. When the crookedness of the landlord was exposed, he began to be rude to the magistrate and I wondered whether the rumour that he was taking bribes was not in effect true. Otherwise he would not have tolerated the rot this old man was dishing out to him. In the end the costs awarded to me by the magistrate was only ten pounds. In the long run I lost since I had paid twenty pounds as costs for two adjournments and twenty-five pounds for legal fees.

Towards the end of April 1951, I went to Wa to buy some beer and provisions from Ghanem and Halaby and met Tang Yakubu. He was travelling with my little niece, Ziɛm, whom he said the family had betrothed to him. He also told me that my wife had given birth to a baby boy on Friday, March 2. I was delighted with the news and gave him five pounds out of my pocket to be given to my wife for her upkeep when he got to Kumasi and three pounds for her to buy some new clothes. I noticed he was not driving the Gandah Transport lorry but was travelling by another vehicle. I asked him what he had done with the truck and he told me the battery was flat and he was returning to Kumasi to buy a new one. I had no idea that Tang had fallen out with Gyub and others at home and had been sacked by them or had walked out on them. They had at last caught up with his swindles and falsehood and yet he still did not have the courage to tell me the truth. When Tang got to Kumasi, he did not give the eight pounds to my wife but spent it on his own wife who had also just given birth to a baby boy. Thinking that my wife was alright financially for the mean time, I returned to Tumu to carry on with my trading, biding my time to visit Kumasi when I had made sufficient profit to warrant the journey down there. On a day in May, one of my friends, Issifu Nyamekyɛ, a transport owner and a convert to Islam like myself, came to Tumu with his truck. In Kumasi we lived on opposite sides on the same street. When I saw him, I rushed out of my shop to greet him. But he refused my greetings and began chastising me that I was uncaring and not a true Moslem because I had left my wife and her newly born baby un-catered for. He told me my wife had been penniless and he had to lend her four pounds. I was dumbfounded and tried to explain to him about the amount I had sent by my driver, Tang Yakubu, but he would not believe me. As he was returning that day for Kumasi, I gave him the four pounds he purported to have given to my wife and a further four pounds for her.

It turned out that Issifu Nyamekyɛ had given my wife only two pounds but told the white lie in order to get more for her. I was in a terrible rage with my driver when Issifu told me this of ingratitude on his part and if Tang had been there at that very moment, I would have throttled him with my bare hands. I could hardly believe that, whatever my brothers had done to him at home, Tang, whom I trusted, would have tried to starve my wife and a newly born baby by refusing to hand over the money I gave for their upkeep. Nonetheless he had done so and I waited patiently until I got to Kumasi to confront him. Luckily, towards the end of May, he visited Tumu, driving a different truck, and had the audacity to visit my shop. The mere sight of him made me tremble with rage as a bilious taste came into my mouth. I asked him what he had done with the money I gave him for my wife. He told me a complete lie that he had used the money to buy a ram for the naming rites of my child in the Moslem way. I told him the money was not to be used for the naming of my child. Besides, the naming of a child in our custom took place after the child had attained three months if a male and four months if a female. I was ready to fight him there and then but was advised to watch my status in town. For in Tumu I was much revered, especially among the Zongo community. Tang had come to Tumu with the intention of passing the night and loading his truck the next day for Kumasi. But he could not stand my threats and returned instantly without even asking for a drink of water.

I decided to hand him over to the police when I got to Kumasi. But on hindsight, I should have reported the matter to the police at Wa where the money was paid to him. It turned out that the so-called naming ceremony had never taken place at all, for my child did not bear a Moslem name but only the name usually given by the Akans according to the day a child was born. In his case, it was Kofi, the boy Friday. Any naming ceremony that took place must have been for his child, who arrived a couple of months before mine. To save his face before my brother, Debomo, and other friends of mine in the Zongo, he told that big lie. With regards to Gandah Transport, Tang had made a fool of Gyub, the entire family and myself. He knew that both Gyub and I were pig-headed and as we were not on speaking terms, he played his treacherous tricks on us just as Iago did between Othello and Desdemona. He achieved his ultimate goal of swindling the Gandah Transport of its revenue. No doubt had Gyub listened to my request for both of us to confront Tang to know what he had done with the transport earnings, we could have unveiled his cunning schemes and perhaps averted much of the swindle. Nevertheless, running Gandah Transport without accounting to anyone for the past eighteen months, Tang had managed to save enough proceeds from the earnings to purchase a second-hand truck for himself. This was the truck which he had brought to Tumu and which I knew nothing about until many months later.

Between April and June, the turnover of the shop was at least £120 per month. This merited my going to Kumasi to buy goods at much lower prices than those prevailing in Wa as well as to see my new born baby for the first time. On my way to Kumasi in a friend's vehicle, Tang swept past us on his way to Kumasi in another vehicle. As his truck was smaller, it gathered more speed than the one in which I was travelling. He arrived in Kumasi long before I did. So we passed the night on the way because the vehicle had a breakdown in a village near Kumasi and arrived the next day at about one o'clock in the afternoon. On arrival on the previous day, Tang laid a complaint against me at the Asantehene's Police Station which was a few hundred yards from where we both lived.[49] He was advised to keep vigil and to report back as soon as I arrived in town. The driver of the vehicle I travelled with brought me to my door. Hardly had I arrived home than Tang went across to the Police Station and alerted them of my presence. My young wife handed me the baby whilst she fetched me a cup of cold water to drink. I had hardly finished drinking when a constable from the Asantehene's police force arrived at my door and told me I was wanted at their police station.

Without washing down or having anything solid to eat, I followed the constable. At the police station a sub-inspector interviewed me. He read out Tang's allegations that he obtained a contract from the Lawra Confederacy Local Authority but I had falsified the pay vouchers and collected the money. I tried to explain to the sub-inspector that they were false allegations and that the plaintiff was at that time my employee and doing the job under my instructions. Besides, the contract was given to Gandah Transport and the chit to John Holt was in their name. But the officer would not listen to my explanation and tried to make me admit to the crime so that we could share the money. I reiterated to him that the plaintiff was my employee and had been paid for doing the job when he was not driving the truck. Apart from that, I told him the money did not belong to me but to the family business and had been paid into the family chest. The amount of pressure that this police officer put on me was so great that I had a sneaking feeling that he had obtained a bribe from Tang; otherwise he would not have been so oblivious to my explanations. I was at this Police Station from about 3 p.m. to about 9 p.m. but he could not make me change my mind through any duress. Having failed to cower me into submission, he told me that the case was beyond his jurisdiction and that he would drive us down to Odum to the Central Police Station of the Gold Coast Police who were the appropriate people to deal with it.

When we arrived at the Central Police Station, the sub-Inspector of the Asantehene's police told his counterpart about the allegations made against me instead of allowing Tang to make his formal complaint. Without any further ado, I was told I would be locked up until the police in Lawra came to collect me since the offence had been committed there. I would have thought the correct procedure would have been for the police to dismiss the case and advise Tang to go to Lawra and make a fresh complaint against me. If his allegations were substantiated, then the Lawra police should issue a warrant for my arrest. On the contrary, I was immediately thrown into the police cell there and then without any statement being taken from me. That night Tang returned to the house playing the innocent, and alerted my wife that I had been detained at the police station and that she should prepare a meal and take it to the cells. Even though the night was far gone, she prepared some hot pepper and kenkey to bring it to me at the cells, with my one month old son strapped on her back. But Tang had an ulterior motive to get my wife out of the way. He knew his room keys opened my door and he knew that I always carried heavy cash when I travelled down south for purchases. By getting my wife out of the way, he could enter my room and steal the box of cash I had brought down. This was exactly what he did. The next morning when my wife brought breakfast, she informed me Tang had taken the box out from my room. I immediately asked her to call the duty orderly. When he came, I tried to tell him what had happened, but the constable informed me I could not make a complaint while I was still in the cells and and instantly shut the cell door behind him. There I was, now penniless in the cells, with wife and child outside having to be fed.

Inside the cell, I was behaving as if temporarily insane and all that I could think about was how to murder Tang as soon as I came out. It was a good thing that the Lawra police took a long time to investigate and reply to their counterparts in Kumasi. If I had been let out earlier, God knows what would have taken place. For the four days that I was held in the cells, I ate none of the food my wife brought and gave it to my fellow inmates. I hardly uttered a word to any of them other than constantly sighing heavily to myself, confined in that little cell which sometimes accommodated about four or five of us at a time. In fact the other inmates thought I had committed murder or a serious crime that I could not bear to talk about. While at this cell I actually witnessed some police brutality and I wondered whether I could have tolerated what was being meted out if I had been at the receiving end. During the second day of my stay, a teenager was brought into the cell and was followed later by the Sub-inspector. As he entered the cell, he shut the door behind him and started beating this teenager with his fists and stamping on every part of his body with his feet. I was really shocked that such a small boy could be treated so cruelly by a man old enought to have been his father and a supposed keeper of the peace as well. But there was nothing that any of us could do. Four days later a message came from the Lawra police saying they could find no truth of the allegations made against me. Whoever was making those statements should come to Lawra and make them there.

About 10am on the fourth day, I was summoned to appear before the Sub-inspector in the charge room. There and then he told me that he had heard from the Lawra Police and that according to them they could find no evidence connecting me with the alleged crime. He asked me to find someone in town who would bail me to the sum of £1,000; that the Lawra Police would want to meet both myself and the plaintiff in Lawra so the case could be investigated. I went to one of my father's friends, Mr Kwesi Dam, who was a manager of one of the UAC stores in Kumasi to see if he could stand bail for me. However Kwesi Dam declined to do so. I travelled to the village of Kwapra to Opanyin Kwame Nti, and he and his entourage returned with me to Kumasi and stood surety. When I was let out on the police bail, I thanked Kwame and after I saw them return to Kwapra, I went back into the police station to report Tang's theft committed in my room. I was told by the orderly on duty that the said theft took place outside their jurisdiction area. If I wanted the case to be taken up, I should go to the Zongo Police Station and report it there. Still wearing my dirty and dusty clothes in which I had arrived from the North, I hurried off to make my complaint. At the station while I was making this complaint to the duty orderly, a Detective Sergeant of the CID was standing by the counter listening. When I had finished, this young detective asked me if I was a northerner. To this I replied in the affirmative. He then asked me if Tang was a northerner too and I again answered in the affirmative. There and then he asked the orderly to assign the case to him. As we went outside the station, he immediately hailed down a taxi and we drove down to Ashanti New Town to OI 94 where Tang lived directly opposite my accommodation. He was absent but his wife was there. The detective collected the keys from her and asked her to take out whatever things she needed for the night and then locked his room. He told the wife to ask Tang to call at the Zongo Police station if and when he returned home and to ask for Sgt. Ayiriteh Gariba.

Meanwhile he took the keys to Tang's door and tried them on the doors of my room and they opened. Luckily the old lady who saw the box being taken from the room by Tang was sitting with my wife on the verandah. The door to my room opened on to the street and we both shared a common verandah. He tried my keys to Tang's door and they opened and shut. After that Sergeant Ayiriteh took another taxi and went with me and the old lady back to the station to take down our statements. While this was being done, Tang arrived with one Yakuu Karbo late that evening. Without any fuss, the sergeant gave Tang three good slaps on his cheeks, pushed him into one of the cells, stripped him naked, covered the floor with water and locked him in there for the night. I was then asked to go home and call back at the station the following day at about 9 a.m. By nine o'clock prompt the next morning, I was at the Zongo Police Station. By ten the sergeant came down from the office of the Assistant Superintendent of Police, whose office was on the first storey above, with a signed search warrant to search Tang's room. The cell was unlocked and after dressing Tang came out looking as if he had been locked up and starved for days. Mr Ayiriteh hailed a taxi and we went back to OI 94 where we alighted and he made Tang foot the taxi bill with his ill-gotten gains. It was the greatest mistake that Tang had made in still keeping the letter I had written to him from Tumu, instructing him in the method of discharging the contract. As we arrived at Ashanti New Town, the sergeant took out the key and unlocked Tang's door and when we had all entered, he began to search the room for the stolen money. But Tang was too wise to keep it in his room. Nevertheless the sergeant found one vital clue in my favour, the letter I had written to Tang. As soon as I saw my hand writing I told Ayiriteh Gariba that this letter would absolve me from the false allegations Tang had made against me. Tang reached forward to snatch the letter from the sergeant's hand and received another slap. After the search we took another taxi back to the station where he told the ASP that he was taking me back to the Central Police Station to acquaint the officers there of my innocence of Tang's false allegations. At the Central Police Station, when the Sub-inspector read my letter to Tang, he was not amused at all with him and warned him he would be charged for deceiving a public officer and wasting police time. The officer apologised to me for the false imprisonment and asked me to go to Lawra to clear my name and then return when they dealt with him too.

While Tang was making allegations against me in Kumasi, the family members who knew nothing of this had also made allegations against him in Lawra. Tang was supposed to have abducted one of my nieces and eloped to Kumasi without the knowledge of any of the family members, even the elders. When I returned home, I went to the police station to report and I met Batan, the direct brother of Ziɛm, and from him I gathered that the allegations might have been instigated by Gyub and the other educated brothers in Birifu. When the corporal in charge of the station asked me what I thought about the allegations, I told him that I could neither confirm nor deny them since I was at Tumu when Tang met me at Wa and told me that the girl had been given to him in marriage by the members of the family.

I therefore failed to see why they had not reported the case until two or three months later, nor did I see why Tang did not report his falsification claim to the police for nearly a year. The police, I believe, could not find any evidence against Tang and that case faded into oblivion, for I never heard anything more about it. But the girl, Ziɛm, was returned to the house and she later married Dɛr (Cooper) Nyuɔr, who was a teacher at Birifu at that time.

As for Tang's allegations against me, after taking my statement the police asked me to return to my station and carry on with my business while they looked into the matter. The next time I was in town, I should call in at the station to find out how far they had gone with the investigation. I had been to the Lawra police station on more than three occasions and on each one the constable prevaricated and I suspected that Tang had given him some money to oil his palm because of his failure to proceed with the case. I began to lose my patience and told him that either he charged me with the crime if the allegations were true or he should dismiss the case so that I could proceed with civil action against the plaintiff. The next time I was in Lawra and reported at the station, the corporal told me that he had spoken to the Lawra Nũũ and the chief had told him that since both Tang and I were his subjects, he would like to settle the dispute between us. I could not understand this, for since I resigned from the teaching field, I had never set eyes on the Lawra Nũũ. So I insisted on knowing if he was closing the docket on the case but he would not give me either a positive assurance or a negative one. Time went by and I did not hear from the Lawra Nũũ nor from the police constable on this matter before he was transferred from Lawra and I left for Britain some years later.

My case against him in Kumasi also faded into oblivion in the same way. For when I eventually got back to Kumasi and went to see Sgt Ayiriteh Gariba, Tang had gone to solicit the help of the chief of the Dagartis in Kumasi. Kobina Dagarti succeeded his father, the famous Kofi Dagarti, on his death. At that time most Dagara coming down south stayed in his house and even chiefs such as the Nandom Nũũ or the Lawra Nũũ did so when they passed through Kumasi. At that time Nuɔtiŋ Konkuu, my cousin and the daughter of the late Nandom Nũũ, Konkuu, was studying midwifery at the Midwifery School in Kumasi and usually spent her days-off at Kofi Dagarti's house in Ashanti New Town. She was at that time being courted by Ayiriteh to be his future wife. He was well known to Kobina and with his influence Kobina got Ayiriteh to drop the case against Tang. When

I returned to Kumasi, Ayiriteh told me that Kobina had approached him and told him that since both Tang and I were his subjects in Kumasi, the case should be withdrawn so that he, Kobina, could settle the matter between us. Tang had obviously managed to wangle his way out of trouble the second time. Neither the Lawra Nũũ nor Kobina called me before them to settle these cases. However, as I was not at all conversant with the criminal law of the Gold Coast at the time, I did not know if a private citizen could initiate criminal proceedings against another, as is the case in Britain today.

Not very long after Tang had left the employment of the Gandah Transport, chief S.D. Dombo bought a new 'Austin A' commercial – a five tonner truck. As soon as Tang heard of this he approached the chief to be the driver. The chief in turn asked me for a character reference. I told him what I thought of Tang and what he had done to Gandah Transport. What I was telling him might sound like sour grapes. If he did not believe what I said, he could employ him and find out for himself. Perhaps the chief was desperate for a driver to drive his truck or he did not believe me but he employed Tang and within a few months the chief's transport was off the road. The chief later claimed that Tang had replaced all the new parts of his new vehicle with old ones and sold his own to the other drivers. The chief's relations who accompanied Tang on the road knew very little or nothing at all about vehicle mechanics, and so he was able to destroy their vehicle and put it off the road. Anyway when the chief wanted to have him jailed Tang sought out the chief's landlord, Kofi Kpɛbi, head of the Dagara in Tamale, to intervene on his behalf. Kofi did so and Tang was again let off.

THE UNIVERSITY COLLEGE of the Gold Coast was opened as a college of London University in 1948 and by 1951 the Department of Extra-Mural Studies had extended its tentacles to the regions, with resident tutors and organisers in each of the five provinces. The first resident tutor for the Northern Territories of the Gold Coast with offices in Tamale was one Mr William Tordoff, with Mr Newlove Mamattah as the Organiser.[50] Before the beginning of the University academic year, Newlove Mamattah arrived in Tumu to form a branch of the People's Educational Association (PEA) and if possible to start an extra-mural class of the University here. Newlove lodged with Mr Boison, the DC's clerk, since they both hailed from Cape Coast.

In the afternoon of the next day, I managed to contact as many literates as possible and we met in the Native Administration court.

Here the PEA branch was formed and I was nominated as the Secretary and Mr Imoru Egala as the chairman.[51] As the group was a very small one, only a few officers of the association were appointed. After the formation of the association, Bill Tordoff arrived with Newlove to begin his extra-mural classes. Bill then addressed the group and told us that on his next visit he would form a class on animal husbandry, which would be run by his wife. The lectures took place every week and a day and date that suited both lecturer and the group were chosen.

The Dept of Extra-Mural Studies used to organise New Year and Easter schools in conjunction with the PEA. In December 1951, the New Year School was to be held in Cape Coast at Adisadel College.[52] Towards the end of the year, Newlove Mamattah came round to persuade some members of the group to attend. As I would anyway be going down to the south to purchase some provisions for my shop I decided to attend the school, which usually lasted a fortnight. It was the first New Year School among many I attended. When I got there I found that there were only two northerners attending, one Avanyiri, a school teacher from Navrongo, and myself, and we both joined the music appreciation group. When the school came to a close we all left for our various destinations.

Before I left for the New Year School, the Tumu Native Authority had awarded me a contract for roofing the school compounds with thatch. The Native Authority had bought the thatch from the villages and the only material I needed was fibre. A week after signing the contract, I left for the New Year School leaving the work in the hands of one Alidu Grunshi, a lorry collector and a member of my Gumbe Band. Alidu assured me he was a good thatcher and that as all was in good hands, I should go to the conference while he would take care of everything until my return. I was a fool to believe him. I was shocked when I returned and found the shoddy work he had done. Before I returned from the New Year School, Mr Egala the headmaster had gone to report the bad work to the DC, Major Dickie, and to register his protest at the bad workmanship. Indeed the old roofing was better and in sounder condition than the new one that had replaced it. Not only was the work badly done but the thatch had all been wasted. I had either to buy new bundles of thatch or go into the bush to cut them. As I had no capital left and as the balance of my contract money had been frozen by the DC, I had no alternative but to go and to cut the thatch myself.

I got up at dawn every day and went into the bush to collect the thatch without a sickle but only my bare hands. To be able to do so, I got hold of the bunch of the grass and tried to swivel it vigorously until it broke off from the bottom. Many days passed while I continued to fetch the thatch in this way. Then one day when I went to the bush and caught hold of a bunch of grass, it started to swivel round and I suddenly felt something slide from my hands. I heard a thud and a hiss about four paces away in front of me. I got up, looked towards where the hiss came from and lo and behold, I saw a short spotted, puffed snake about a foot in length with bulging eyes looking at me fiercely. It must have been very angry and frightened as well.

The moment I saw the snake, my heart began beating loudly in the deep cavity of my chest and I shook like a leaf. For some moments I stood shaking, momentarily pinned to the ground unable to move. How long for I couldn't say, but I kept my eye on this viper in case it sprang up at me. When I had sufficiently calmed down, I saw a sun-dried brick some feet away sideways and a little behind me. Slowly I retreated, taking a pace at a time, still keeping my eye on this dangerous creature until I was near enough to get hold of the brick. I edged forward again holding the broken brick firmly in my right hand until I was within easy reach of my prey. At that moment, a group of the late Tumu Koro's wives were approaching to go into the bush to fetch firewood. I signalled them with my left hand to stop. Taking a good aim, I let loose my missile with such ferocity that the stomach of the puffed snake burst open and it died instantly.

I beckoned the women to proceed on their way and when they came closer to the spot and saw the deadly creature, they told me that I was lucky not to be bitten for I would have died instantly from its poison. It is one of the most poisonous snakes in the area and because of the quick way it kills, it is given the nickname *ma bie ku pɔɔma* (literally "matrilineal relatives will not meet me alive"). That is how deadly this short little creature is. It was the last time I ever went to the bush to fetch thatch for the roofing. I did not even collect the thatch I had cut but returned home empty handed. How I managed to get enough thatch to complete the roofing of the school dormitories is still a wonder to me. However I did complete the roofing to the satisfaction of the DC and the Headteacher, Imoru Egala.

CHAPTER SIXTEEN

In 1951 when the new Legislative Assembly was formed with Dr Kwame Nkrumah as Leader of the House, the first thing he did was to make available one hundred scholarship places for artisans to train abroad. The application forms were received in Tumu and both Debomo and I applied. He applied to do building construction and I to train in carpentry or joinery. Debomo's application was sanctioned by the District Commissioner since he was working under him as the district station foreman. My application had no official backing. I later found out that of the 100 scholarships, only two persons from the entire north were successful, my brother, Debomo and another schoolmate from Kumbugu in the Dagbon area, who went abroad to learn pottery. It is not certain how many of these application forms were returned from the north to the offices of the Establishment Secretary in Accra. The Head of that Department at the time was my old friend, Col. Wentworth. By the time I returned from Cape Coast, Debomo was called to Accra en route to the U.K. To get himself some pocket money, he had gone into our shop and cleared the till of whatever cash he could lay his hands on. I also understood he collected all his furniture from Tumu and gave them to Gyub and others for a small sum which he used as his pocket money to spend on the way to the U.K. I was again left penniless when Debomo left for England and was in debt from the contract from which I had hoped to make some profit. The only capital I now had was the goods I had bought and brought from Kumasi. I sold these but the majority of my customers bought them on credit, in order to pay at the end of the month. Trade took a downhill turn from then on but I plodded on, not willing to succumb to defeat. Gradually trade started to pick up again and my head was above water.

The Local Government Act of 1951 was passed to supersede the old Native Authority Act of 1933, which established the Native Authorities in the north and later in the south. The Act of 1951 enabled the setting up of Local and District Councils in each of the Administrative District areas in the country. The elections to these councils were to be on a non-party basis but in the south they were fought in later years on a party-political basis. In the North, however, except possibly in Tamale, these council elections were fought on non-party basis. In the Tumu District there were to be six small Local Councils with one District Council whilst in the the Lawra District whose population at that time was nearly three times that of Tumu, there were to be four Local Councils with one District Council. This must have been the recommendation from the Northern Territories Territorial Council through the Chief Commissioner of the day and of course the members of the Council were all Paramount Chiefs or Presidents from the Districts. Consequently, these chiefs would not want to divide their areas into smaller units and most of them stuck to the old divisions of the Native Authority.

While in Tumu the devolution returned to the status quo prior to the implementation of the Native Authority Act of 1933, in the Lawra district, the divisional areas delineated after the 1933 Act were used as the Local Council areas. As a side observation, it was the selfishness of the divisional chiefs in the Lawra District attempting to hold on to their power and areas of jurisdiction that deprived them of the possibility of local development. Similarly, when the Traditional (Chiefs) Council was more recently being set up in the Upper West Region, the chiefs in Wa and Tumu were not that selfish and put up several names who were promoted to the paramountcy status whereas in the Lawra District they only promoted themselves from divisional to the paramount chiefs status when they could have promoted a few of their subchiefs who were of equal rank with them before the advent of the Native Authority system. I saw the harm they were doing to the district as a whole when I was last at home in 1991/2 and I discussed the seriousness of their omissions with my friend, A. Karbo, the present Lawra Nũũ. But less of this digression.

When I left Birifu for good to settle in Tumu, I tried to sever my relations with the family for two reasons. Firstly, I was treated by my educated brothers as the black sheep in the family even though the rest of the members of the family had great confidence in me; but if I had stayed behind I might have done something that would have spoiled the good name of the family. For instance, on one particular occasion, Gyub, Biz, and Nana, came upstairs and saw me coaching my younger brothers from the Tamale Secondary School in music. Jealous of their association with me, Gyub ordered that they leave my place and go down to their quarters and do some work. I was so incensed with his arrogance that I took my dad's unloaded double-barrelled gun and pointed it at them when they threatened to enter my quarters and remove them forcefully. They were so frightened that they quickly turned back and went down to their quarters. Luckily the gun was not loaded; but what would have happened had it been loaded and they carried out their threat? The devil would have been unchained.

Secondly, the illiterate brothers and nephews, especially those of my age group and below, normally gathered around me for some pito and were despised by these literate brothers, especially Biz, Gyub and Nana. Their company was shunned and any time they went down to their quarters, they were ordered to return to their chief upstairs, implying me. I found that if I remained in the house, I would be the cause of a great rift between them and my vindictive brothers. I decided to make a clean break and to have nothing to do with them at all except once in a while when I went home for local festivals. Indeed when Nuũnatuo Gandah was being enstooled as Gandah II and the Birifu Nũũ III, I did not bother to go home and help in the organisation of the ceremony. That was how great the bitterness between myself and most of my senior literate brothers had become.

The opening and closing times for beer and wine bars were between eight in the morning and eight at night, and more often than not trading stopped around six in the evening. At that time, Tumu town was not even as large either in population or area as the Naayile section of Birifu from where I originally hailed. Being an ex-teacher and still keen on my profession, I had enough time on my hands to do something beneficial for the community in which I was now living. First of all, I organised and formed a Gumbe Band among the Zongo community. The Tumu Koro, Luri Kanton II, had employed a driver from the south, nicknamed "Small Boy", to drive his car.[53] The Tumu Koro bought this car from Mr Amherst, the then CCNTs who was returning to the UK on leave prior to his retirement. Small Boy had learnt many songs from Gumbe bands in Kumasi. So he joined my group and taught them some of the tunes he had learnt in the south. The nights were occupied in entertaining the townfolk with our music and dancing. With my musical knowledge from the teacher training college days, I improved their singing ability by giving them exercises during the day and, as their conductor, made them sing in tempo. The band became very popular and very often we performed in front of the Tumu Koro's palace mostly on Tumu market days where a large crowd gathered. We were sometimes invited to villages such as Wallenbellia, Bugbellia and the surroundings. As time went on, I became very popular with the local people.

Not satisfied with the Gumbe band, I felt I could help to improve the literacy rate of the community by opening a night school and providing my services free in the extra time I had in the evenings. In those days, the Gold Coast Government was encouraging mass literacy and self-help, for which Robert Gardiner was brought back from Nigeria and appointed as Director of Social Services.[54] In the north this was spread through the Mass Education team headed by Mr Shirer, an American missionary in Tamale. At the outstations this actually was encouraged through the DCs. Mr Imoru Egala was a best friend, and then the headteacher of the Tumu Primary Boarding School. One day I went to his school and discussed my plans with him. Mr Egala was more than obliging. He issued me with an easel and blackboard with boxes of chalk and some slates. From that evening I began my evening classes, or night school as these classes were called. Later as the group progressed from chalk to pencils, Mr Egala again supplied me with some exercise books and pencils for my pupils, some of whom were men with wives. I was very grateful to Mr Egala for his assistance, for without it there would have been no night school at all. On that first night, my class numbered over sixty pupils, too big for one teacher to manage. But since most of them were teenagers and adults and very keen to learn, I had no trouble with them. I started with the three "r's" in the vernacular, even though I could not speak Tumuulu properly. Tumuulu is a dialect of Issaliŋ spoken by the Tumu people.[55] In addition I taught spoken English. After a few months, the class dropped to a manageable size with only the zealots still attending. I provided my own Tilley lamps which I used for the Gumbe practice when the moon was late in rising, and the pupils provided the paraffin by contributing to the cost; at that time a pint bottle of paraffin cost one shilling.

THERE WAS A small cleared area on the other side of the street opposite my shop that served as a lorry park but which was seldom used as such. There were very few commercial vehicles visiting Tumu regularly. I found the young boys were using their time in the afternoons to kick tennis balls about. It occurred to me to have a word with the DC to provide them with a football for their practice. One day, I went to his office and asked the clerk if I could see him. When I told Major Dickie of my scheme he was more than interested himself. He told me that if I got the park extended to the size of a football field, he would supply us with the football as well as the goal posts for which there was a vote in his budget. I consulted the pupils in the evening that day after our lessons and told them what Major Dickie said. They were very pleased and were willing to start work on the field as soon as possible provided they were given tools such as pick axes, spades and shovels. The DC had travelled on trek to one of the outstations. I waited until his return and went to have another audience with him in his office on the Monday morning. I told him the decision of the young lads and he promised to bring down the tools on the Sunday morning as well as allowing the use of the District tipper truck to cart the weeds, twigs and roots of shrubs that were to be cut down. On the Sunday, true to his word, he turned up in his car, followed by the tipper truck with the tools. By this time my pupils and I were already in the field working with whatever available tools were at our disposal. After the tools were unloaded, Major Dickie turned round followed by the tipper truck driver and drove off towards the Tumu Koro's palace. Within half an hour to about an hour, he returned with the Tumu Koro followed by the tipper truck with many able-bodied youths from the other side of the town. This surprised me for I had not expected help from the chief or the youth around his section.

As soon as they had alighted, everyone joined us in clearing the field of the roots and shrubs, then levelling the little mole hills and termite mounds that were scattered all over the place in order to put it in a condition suitable for playing football. Even Major Dickie and the chief joined in, and by ten or eleven when the sun was rising high we had completed clearing a large area capable of housing two football pitches. It was a day well spent. The DC had some goal posts made for us and also bought a football and some repair kit. At last we had provided a football pitch for the town and every day between five and six in the evening the young boys kicked the ball about. As I have never been good at playing soccer, I could not coach them other than telling them the rules. A young boy from Cape Coast, one Wobil, who was himself very keen at football, helped to organise them and look after the repair kit. He was employed by the District Administration as an assistant storekeeper and timekeeper.

In 1952 Local Government elections were to take place in the Northern Territories and in Tumu this took place about May. In the Tumu Local Council, there were to be nine members elected by popular vote and three nominated by the chiefs as traditional members, for the Act allowed two thirds of the councillors to be elected by popular vote and one third nominated from the traditional councils. So the Tumu Local Council comprised twelve members excluding the President, the Tumu Koro. There were two wards in Tumu town: the Zongo

Ward which I represented and the Tumu town ward which Issaka Kanton, a teacher under Mr Egala, represented. As the election approached, I thought I was standing unopposed. But the zongo chief decided to nominate his prospective son in-law to contest the election in the ward. Of course I never dreamt of losing but was pleased for it gave some realism to the elections rather than if one was being elected unopposed. There was not much canvassing to be done since the zongo was a more compact community than the town area. On the election day I was overwhelmingly elected to the Tumu Local Council.

After the elections, the Clerk of the Council sent out letters to all the councillors for attendance of the first meeting to elect members to the District Council. Every councillor was issued with the copy of the regulations of the Act by the DC. At this meeting the Tumu Koro presided as head of the council to elect officers such as the Chairman of the Council and to nominate and elect its members to the District Council. The composition of the District Council was to be on the same ratio as that of the Local Councils, that is, two thirds of the councillors being elected members and one third traditional ones. The Tumu Local Council therefore had to nominate two elected councillors and one traditional member to the District Council. But Mr Imoro Egala was elected as a traditional member of the Local Council. During the nominations, I had hoped Mr Egala would be elected with two other elected members to the District Council so that when it came to the elections into the District Council, he would strengthen its effectiveness since he was the most experienced literate in the District. He declined my nomination because as a traditional member, the Kwapun Pio (Chief of Kwapun) had already been nominated by the Tumu Koro as the traditional member and he did not want a contest. Issaka Kanton and I were nominated as the Council representatives on the District Council. These names were put to the vote and Issaka and I were voted into the District Council as the elected members.

A few weeks later letters were sent out by the Clerk of the District Council to all members summoning them to the first meeting of the Council. The agenda for this meeting was mainly to elect the chairman and the members of the Finance and Staff committee. The Tumu Koro, being the President of both the Local and the District Councils, presided over the opening after which members sat down to elect their chairman. Issaka Kanton was elected the District Council Chairman. The chief then left the hall and the Chairman took the chair for the election of the members of the Finance and Staff Committee. The members of the Finance and Staff Committee comprised George Nandzo Dimbie, Mumuni Dimbie, Bawa Wallenbellia, Issaka Kanton, Benin Duori and myself. After the elections of the Finance and Staff committee members, the meeting came to a close. However, the members of the committee also met immediately afterwards to elect the Chairman who was normally the chairman of the Council.

The preparation of the annual financial estimates used to be the prerogative of the chiefs of the old Native Authority with the guidance of the District Commissioners. With the inception of the Local Government system, the preparation of the annual estimates became the prerogative of the Finance and Staff Committee. In normal circumstances these estimates should have reached the Chief Commissioner's office for approval before April. But due to the late election of the councillors, these estimates were running far too late. Because of the late elections it was a matter of urgency that we prepared these estimates as soon as possible and presented them through the DCs to the Chief Commissioner. We immediately set to work on these estimates. But none of us had ever prepared annual estimates before and the District Commissioner, Mr Redhead, did not come down to the Council Offices to offer us any guidance as was done for the chiefs and people, so we were left to our own devices. We had worked on these estimates for just a week and were unable to balance the books. Our expenditure was far above our income but we did not want to cut down past regular expenditure and we were also loath to increase the old taxes such as the poll tax which we inherited from the old regime. I tried to introduce a cattle tax which had been collected in the Lawra Confederacy Native Authority for many years but never introduced in the Tumu district. My colleagues, especially the Chairman, Issaka Kanton, who were indigenous members of the place, objected vehemently to imposing a cattle tax. Not being a native of the place, I could hardly argue nor press my point too far. Anyway we continued with the estimates the following week trying to balance our books.

Then one mid-morning of the second week of our deliberations, the office messenger came into the committee room to announce the presence of a European who was outside wanting to speak to both Issaka and Nandzo for a few minutes. Bagyo Kanton, acting as both Clerk and Treasurer to the Council, went out to see who this European visitor was. He returned to inform us that it was Bryant, the Principal of the College and Head of the Education Department in the Northern Territories. We therefore moved a motion to suspend the meeting for the few minutes he requested so both teachers could go out to see what he wanted of them. The few minutes turned into more than hour. The rest of the committee members became very anxious as time was passing by. We decided to join them outside to find out what was happening. As we went out I saw Mr Bryant talking to Issaka and Nandzo. I recognized him immediately for I was introduced to him by Col. Wentworth in 1949 and later in 1950 when he came to inspect the Birifu school and to select Biz for his certificate A course, even though he did not recognize me at first. The rest of those present were his former students at the college. I greeted him and then introduced myself after which I wanted to know what the hold-up was all about. He told me that he had come to select one of them to return to the college to study for their Teacher's Certificate A and that he had decided to let them choose or toss between themselves who should go to the college first.

I had never agreed with the methods of selection of teachers back to the College for their third and fourth year studies even when I was a student there, and pointed the loop holes out to the Principal at the time. But Mr Bryant's method of selection was even worse and more crude than what Col. Wentworth tried to sell to us in our last year in college. I could not help but tell him that his method was so crude that it would create envy and enmity between two friends who had previously worked amicably together. Firstly, I told him that each of them would like to return to college before the other, given the chance. Once a student has left an educational institution for a longer period, his or her brain would cease to function as effectively as the one who was out for a shorter period. Evidently each of them would like to enter the college first in order to do well for their third and fourth year training. Secondly and more importantly, since he had in his office the records of their performance at College together with their field reports, it was rather stupid of him to ask them toss or choose between themselves. Finally, even though he, Bryant, did not believe in black magic, these two teachers did and could use that magic against each other. Of course in those colonial days, no white person would tolerate being criticised by a black person or be told what to do much less call his actions silly and stupid. However, my brush with T.A. Meade which led to my resignation from teaching made me question the arbitrary decisions of most District Commissioners. I did not however expect such a stupid decision from a person of his calibre, hence my outburst. I later learnt that he had gone and told DC Redhead that same day that I had been rude to him when he came to select his student for college, presumably thinking I was an employee under the DC who could put me on the carpet. Mr Redhead told him that we had been working on the estimates for the past fortnight without making any headway and he did not know what on earth possessed me to interfere with his job.

Bryant thought he had been given a weapon of attack with which to hit me. He told Mr Egala what had transpired between him and myself and then added that even DC Redhead had told him that I had been engaged on the preparation of simple annual estimates of the Council for the past fortnight and could not even balance them and yet I was trying to teach him how to do his job. Unfortunately, Mr Bryant did not have the courage to come and tell me this face to face so I could tell him what I thought of his bragging. For I would have told him that our failure to prepare simple estimates was not a thing he should be proud of, but rather be ashamed of himself since the majority of the members of the committee members were past students from his college. Besides, the curriculum of the college and that of the schools in the north were prepared by him and his colleagues. So if "they could not do simple estimates", as he put it, the fault lay with his education program that he had devised for the entire north but not with the committee members.

When the elections to the Legislative Assembly were being held in the south for members of Parliament of the Gold Coast in 1951, the North sent delegates to an electoral college from where nineteen of them were elected to occupy the allotted number of seats. Among the nineteen members of parliament that were elected were the Wa Nũũ, Koray, from Wa, Mr S.D. Dombo, the Duori Nũũ, from the Lawra district and Mr Alidu Kanton from the Tumu district. At the death of the Wa Nũũ, there was a vacancy left to be filled and each district was to send representatives to the electoral college for the election of a member for this single vacancy. For the Tumu District, George Nandzo, Issaka Kanton, Mumuni Dimbie and I were the delegates. I was also to attend a conference on Social Welfare organised by Mr Shirer, the Director of Mass Education in Tamale. When the time came DC Redhead was also going to Tamale and gave both George and me a lift. During the elections the vacancy was filled by a delegate from the Mamprusi district.

When the 1951 Legislative Assembly first opened, a few members from the North were selected to serve in Dr Nkrumah's first cabinet. Among these were J.A. Braimah, Kabakye Wura, as Minister for Transport and Communications, and J.H. Alhassani, Ministerial Secretary to the Ministry of Education. Mr Abavana, Mr Asumda Ayeebo and Ayana Imoru became ministerial secretaries initially, some of them later rising to ministerial and other higher position. Mr J.A. Braimah, the minister, was to visit all the districts in the north including Tumu. The District Council together with the chiefs arranged to meet him and to listen to what he had to tell us and for us to ask him questions on matters that we felt were affecting the efficacy of our work as councillors. At that time our council work was being interfered with by the DC, Mr Moor-Darling, who threatened to withhold all the Government grants to the council that came through his office if we did not agree with some of his suggestions. After the minister's speech, when it came to question time, I could not resist asking whether District Commissioners had the power to withhold government grants from the council at their own whim. He told me that they had no such power and the council could appeal straight to the Minister of Local Government. I was so glad that both the DC and the Clerk of Council were present to hear the minister's reply. As time went on, councillors began to realise their rights as councillors and resisted dictation by these autocratic DCs even though some of them could still not act independently as many of them, especially teachers, were answerable directly or indirectly to the DCs as far as their daily work was concerned. It meant that in Tumu I was the only independent voice whenever an injustice was done, for I could argue against them without fear of any reprisal being taken against me.

The District Council annual estimates were tossed between the Government Agents of Tumu and Wa on one hand and the Council on the other. The DCs were now called Government Agents (GAs) and the Chief Commissioners, Chief Regional Officers (CROs). At the same time the Lawra, Wa and Tumu Districts were grouped to form a larger group called the North-West District with a senior Government Agent in Wa. Moor-Darling at this time was stationed at Wa as the senior Government Agent with Major Dickie in Tumu. Up till about August, the annual estimates had not been passed and consequently taxes, especially new ones, could not be collected. Nevertheless the council employees had to be paid. There was no problem with employees whose salaries and wages were paid from Government grants but it was another matter where they were paid from council revenue. As there was no authority to collect taxes, these were not collected and we could not pay our employees such as sanitary and administrative officers and labourers.

In this predicament, the Government Agents thought they could force us to agree on what items to insert or to remove from our estimates. Mr T.A. Meade who was now in the CRO's office was going round from district to district to approve the estimates for each council and was due in Tumu about August to approve ours. To get these ready for his boss, Major Dickie had altered some of the entries of the items without consulting the full council or the members of the Finance and Staff Committee who had worked so hard to produce them. The only persons that Major Dickie consulted were Bagyo Kanton, the Clerk and Treasurer, and his brother, Issaka Kanton, the Chairman both of the Finance and Staff Committee and of the District Council. I was furious when the news came to me and I confronted Issaka Kanton to find out the veracity of this rumour. I told him in no uncertain terms that I intended to tell Tom Meade when he came to sign the Estimates that they were not done by the Council but by him, Issaka, and Major Dickie.

We have seen earlier how I devoted all my spare energy for the provision of voluntary social services to the community to such an extent that there came a time I became so penniless that I did not know where the next meal was coming from. Maybe that might have been the reason for my forming the Gumbe band to sing away my worries. Every night after saying my last prayers for the day, I lay down and wept, calling upon my father and his ancestors for help to get me out from this deep abyss of poverty. One day it dawned upon me that I should contact the DC, so I wrote to Mr Redhead laying bare my predicament. Instead of asking for a permanent job with his administration or applying to return to teaching, which my pride did not allow, I asked if I could be given some contract work to do. I told him I might be forced to return to the south to look for a job if he failed to offer me any work and so the voluntary social work I had started would go to waste. After two weeks when I did not hear from Mr Redhead, I decided to walk to his office and beard the lion in his den. I was ushered in by Mr Boison and when he saw me he called for his ledger which contained all the work to be done for that financial year. Mr Redhead told me there was no major constructional work to be done but that the Government had voted the sum of £600 for the building of a small dispensary in the town. He had spent £120 of that for the purchase of cement for the job leaving a balance of £480. He advised me to go and draw a plan that would meet the cost of building the dispensary, and bring back the plan to show him. At that moment I thought Allah had heard my prayers or that my father and his ancestors had listened to my cries.

I returned to my shop in a much brighter mood and immediately began to put pen to paper. Debomo had left behind with me some of his drawing tools such as the T-square and the large set-squares for making plans. By the next day I had finished with the plan showing in detail the ground plan, the front and elevations and the side sections. My school and college training did not go amiss. I then sat down to cost the entire work allowing myself a ten percent profit margin. By the fourth day when I was satisfied with what I had done I took it to Mr Redhead on the Friday morning, a bit apprehensive that he might reject it on the ground that the plan was too small for the amount voted for the job. On the contrary, after perusing the plan he thought it was too big for the money available and advised me to reduce the dimensions of the building, but I assured him I had done my calculations properly and that the money would suffice for the job. He told me to call on him on the Monday and if possible to start the work that day. At 9 a.m. prompt on Monday, I was at his office and there and then he offered me the contract. He offered me the use of the District Administration pick-up truck for three days to cart sand and pebbles and stones to the building site. This was a gratitude I did not expect. Maybe Mr Redhead did not have faith in my own estimates but was doing his damnedest to help me and who was I to refuse such an offer. Unfortunately, I did not sign any contract with the administration when Redhead offered me the construction work but I was aware of the standard set for cement mixtures. For concrete mixtures, the correct mixture was one part of cement to four parts of sand; for building mortar, the proportion was one to six and for making blocks the proportion was one to eight. However, in order to produce very strong building blocks, I used the proportion of 1:6 instead of 1:8.

After a couple of weeks when the work had reached floor level, Mr Redhead came one day to see how I was getting on. When he came and saw that the colour of my blocks were yellowish, he thought I had not used the right mixture of cement to sand. He tried to test the strength of these blocks that we had made by rubbing his thumb against one of them. Of course he bruised his thumb and it started to bleed. He selected one of the blocks and asked one of the labourers to pick up above his head and throw it hard on the concrete floor and hoping it would break into pieces. When the labourer did so, the block did not shatter into pieces as he had expected. That was the last time that Mr Redhead came to the site while we were at work but he did sometimes inspect the work after we had closed for the evening.

CHAPTER SEVENTEEN

I SUPPOSE DC REDHEAD was as anxious to see that the work was well done as I was to prove that I would not let him down for trusting me. As for the building work, I employed one of the District Administration's masons who had been laid off when Debomo left for the UK and six other labourers. I worked as the second mason or as the sixth labourer when this was necessary. If not supervised, Government labourers or wage earners tend to be very lazy, so I was always at the site working very hard with my workers just like one of them. Working along beside them did not give any of them the opportunity to idle about. Two of them could not keep up with the pace I had set and decided to resign. The building had almost reached window level, when the Government announced that it would double the minimum wage level of its labourers. The wages for labourers were then two shillings per day and seven shillings and sixpence to artisans. This amount was doubled and backdated to April 6. So the labour content of my contract was increased proportionately and the amount of £480 was nearly doubled to £960.

As I was getting nearer to the roofing level of the construction, I decided to collect forty percent of the contract money to go down to Kumasi and buy timber and roofing materials as well as paint for the finished work. It was not long before Mr Redhead left Tumu on leave to the UK. It was the last time I set eyes on him before coming to the UK myself for further studies. Major Dickie took over from Mr Redhead as the Government Agent in Tumu. He did not seem to be happy that I had been given the contract for this job. We disagreed about the work for this contract. I had myself hired a three-roomed section of a compound house for myself and my brother, Dɔdulɔ, whom I had brought back from Accra to help me run my business until I was able to bring my wife and child from Kumasi. At the same time Peter Ghanem had opened a shop in one of the Native Authority stalls and employed a southerner, an Ashanti, as his shopkeeper. We soon became friends and combined our expertise in cooking. In the north males were hardly taught how to pound fufu or to cook at all. When I returned from the day's work at the building site, I usually supervised the cooking of the stew whilst my friend, the Ashanti man, supervised the pounding of the fufu. Very soon I picked up the knack of pounding as well as turning over the fufu in the mortar without the fingers being hit by the pestle. As soon as the accommodation was ready, I went down to Kumasi and bought goods for my shop and a few bits and pieces of building materials to complete my contract and hand it over. Prior to my going to Kumasi, I had sub-contracted the roofing of the building to my uncle, Miiru, and his friend and workmate, Iddisa, who were employees of the District Council.

On my return from Kumasi with my wife and child, I found that my uncle and his colleague had done the roofing very badly. Their shoddy work gave ample ammunition to Major Dickie to shoot at me. He told me that he was not paying me another penny until the shoddy work on the roof was rectified, which was fair enough. I subcontracted this work again to one Ayiteh from Accra who was employed by the District Administration as a carpenter. He did a very good job by saving some of the material wasted by my uncle and his mate. When the contract was complete I handed the keys to the Major and demanded payment of the balance of my money. He refused to authorise the payment until six months had passed. If the building was still in perfect condition, he would then pay me the balance. At that time, the retention fee for Government contracts was ten percent and the period was three months. But Major Dickie had doubled the retention fee as well as the period. I told him what I thought of his idea and that he should jump off his hobby horse. Tom Meade of the Chief Regional Officer was visiting District Councils to approve their annual estimates and he was due in Tumu. Because Major Dickie and Issaka had altered some items of the estimates without reference to the Council or its Finance and Staff Committee, and because I threatened to tell Tom Meade that neither the members of the Council nor those of the Finance and Staff Committee were responsible for the estimates, the Government Agent tried to appease me by offering to pay the retention money immediately even though he had refused to sanction the payment only a month earlier. One morning Major Dickie asked his office messenger to call me to see him in his office. When I arrived, he told me he had instructed his clerk to prepare a voucher for the payment of my retention money and to write a covering letter authorising the Government Treasurer at Wa to pay the voucher so I could return to Tumu by Friday, the next day. He also got the district pick-up truck on a standby to take me to Wa and bring me back. I reminded him of what he told me about not paying me the money until six months had elapsed and told him I was not that desperate for the money.

I left Tumu with Adama, the driver, for Wa at about 4 p.m. We got there just after 6 p.m. and the Treasury offices had closed, so I had to pass the night. When I arrived at the offices the next day, I met the treasury clerk who was not unkown to me. By 11 a.m. everything had been completed and we were on the way back to Tumu. We got to Tumu some minutes before 2.00 p.m. before the office closed for the day. I saw the Major in the office and he told me he would be grateful if I joined him, Issaka and Bagyo on the Saturday morning to go over our estimates before the arrival of Tom Meade. It seemed that Dickie's sudden change of mind to pay the retention money earlier than he had threatened was intended to soft soap me into not rejecting the changes that he and Issaka had made in our annual estimates and to gain the support he needed. He wanted me to have a prior look at the changes that he and Issaka made. But he needn't have bothered, for no amount of soft soaping me would have made me change my mind.

On the Saturday morning, I had my breakfast early as usual. This was normally some cups of the Edward Nasser brand of coffee which I drank before having my bath.[56] The meeting was held in the court room since there was more room there than in Dickie's office. Some of the items that had been changed in a way I did not agree with were re-instated, as members of the Council or of the Finance and Staff Committee had approved. When we met Tom Meade the following Monday to consider the estimates, it seemed as if he had been briefed about my stand, or obstinacy as some people might call it. It also occurred to me that Tom Meade still remembered my confrontation with him in Lawra when I handed in my resignation letter. All through the discussion on the estimates, Tom Meade kept on asking me after each point of discussion if I agreed with the figures. But since I had already agreed with the points under discussion only a few days ago, I could hardly see the need for these questions. Besides, why was he not posing the same questions to Issaka, the chairman of both the Council and of the Finance and Staff Committee? After about one and half to two hours of deliberation, Mr Meade approved our estimates and later that day proceeded to Lawra.

During the early part of this year there descended on the French customs post of Leo a man who claimed to be a messenger of God (Nũũŋmin-le). Leo was an administrative district of the Upper Volta under the French colonial administration and was only 18 miles from

Tumu.[57] The Dagara believe God is everywhere but is not mortal and resides in the heavens or the skies. Consequently, they were loath to call this person God, although *wihɛ* in Issali means God. So the Dagara called him Nũũŋmin-le or Nũũŋmin-ble, meaning small God or little God. The fame of this man soon spread far and wide and pilgrims came in their droves through Tumu to Leo in lorries and on foot. Those who came in lorries had to obtain a "laissez passer" from the DC, issued by his clerk. Hearing of this demi-god, the Birifu Nũũ and his people decided to travel to Leo to see this god and obtain evidence of his powers. Being the President of the now defunct Native Authority and a member of the Northern Territories Territorial Council, the Lawra Nũũ was given a grant to buy a car for his transport. So the Birifu Nũũ, as chairman of the Lawra District Council, used the Lawra Nũũ's car for himself and three of his followers whilst about eighty of his subjects were packed like sardines into a big commercial truck which they had hired.

One July or August afternoon, as I sat in the verandah of my shop, I saw the Lawra Nũũ's car drive down and pull up in front of the shop. I immediately recognised Niɛrɛ, the driver, when he alighted followed by Wanzam, Nikara and Nuyaa. As soon as Wanzam saw me he rushed over and begged me not to take umbrage against my brother, the chief, who was at that time alighting from the car. But he needn't have bothered for my bark was worse than my bite and however I despised Nana, I would not have taken revenge for family feuds outside the family, much less in a strange town. I asked my wife to go with them to my quarters which was about two hundred yards away, whilst I locked up the shop. I followed and while he and his party were being entertained, Wanzam told me that a lorry load of the Birifu people was still to come, numbering between sixty to eighty. How was I to entertain such a large crowd? Since the Dagara can live on pito and less on solid food for days, it was not much of a problem to me but I still had to provide something for them to eat, however small.

Debomo's second wife, Hako, whom he had married in Tumu and left behind with the parents before leaving for the UK, was under my care. Luckily her mother had brewed pito for sale that day but it had not all been drunk. So I asked Hako to go and pay for all that was left unsold. My landlady too had brewed pito and had been unable to sell all her brew. I paid for the quantity that was left. As the pito in Tumu had no kick in it, I gave in addition one case of beer containing 48 quart bottles to lace the pito. Meanwhile I bought all the yams that were on sale in the market to be cooked for the visitors, pending their arrival. Obviously, my wife and Hako were very busy preparing food for the chief and his party and boiling the yams for those still to come on the commercial lorry. By nine in the evening the truck arrived and within seconds the entire courtyard of this compound house was engulfed with these pilgrims. The 48 bottles of the beer were opened and poured into these large pots of pito as a sort of cocktail, which is not exactly "snake bite", a mixture of stout and cider, but which I should call "cocktail à la Gandah" or "Gandah bite". As for my brother, he was lavishly entertained with bottles of cognac brandy which at that time cost fourteen shillings a bottle on the black market but which I could get from my Yoruba friends at twelve shillings. As soon as they had been entertained, they left for Leo at about 11 p.m. and probably returned in the early hours of the morning. We never saw them pass again.

When the Birifu Nũũ arrived, we did not exchange greetings or words, but I kept on entertaining him. Maybe he was ashamed of the way he and the other brothers had treated me in Birifu. Before leaving for Leo he addressed his people, telling them of his gratitude for the manner they had been received by me. But one part of his speech was especially pertinent and referred more to him than his people. This was when he said that if they have a relative at home whom they despise as the black sheep of the family, it is this very individual who will be their saviour in the bush (that is, in a foreign land). At that moment Wanzam and Nuyaa who stood behind him were making secret gestures at him that his address applied to him more than to any one else. It was he and his two other brothers whose actions drove me away from Birifu to settle in Tumu, and not the villagers. It seemed the reception I gave to my brother, Nana, and his people must have mellowed his attitude towards me. From then on, anytime I went to Birifu there was no longer that hostility between us. I understood when he returned home he was pouring lavish praises on me and how I did not even exchange a word with him but went on entertaining him and his people

Towards the end of the year, the Finance and Staff Committee were to provide posts for the new teachers who had just passed through the Teacher Training College and/or the Middle Schools, with the advice of the Education Department in Tamale. Hilla Limann (later Dr. Hilla Limann, President of Ghana), who had just completed his Certificate 'B' course, was one of those to be posted to his new school. He was scheduled to go to the Zini Day School. I understood from

Issaka Kanton that Hilla had objected to going there and was interested in the Gwollu Day School. I had met Hilla for the first time for a brief period of about half an hour as a pupil teacher, when he came into my shop one day and asked to be shown how to solve simultaneous equations with two unknowns. I explained it to him and told him he had been solving these equations in the Middle School even with three unknowns without realising they were simultaneous equations. From that day I never set eyes on him again until he left for college, qualified and returned to the district. It would have made no difference whether or not I was well acquainted with Hilla, my decision would still have been the same; that is, to insist that Hilla be posted to the school at Zini. If the Committee had agreed to Hilla's wishes, we would have set a precedent and it would have been very difficult for the Committee to effect any future posting. Any teacher who disliked the place where he was being posted would turn round and cite our decision as an example. Hilla eventually accepted the posting and went to Zini to teach under Bawol. Zini was only a few miles away from Gwollu which he could always visit any time he so wished. The idea of Issaka soliciting me to resist Hilla's refusal to be posted to Zini was perhaps to absolve himself of any blame from Hilla of having a hand in the posting.

I was the only non-Sissala in the Committee and the only one vaguely known to Hilla; by the year he was enrolled in the Lawra Primary Boarding School, I had already gone to the Tamale Middle Boarding School and by the time he went to the Middle School, I was at the Teacher Training College. The only time we met briefly, and only for half an hour, was when he was posted to Tumu as a pupil teacher and occasionally when he visited my shop with George Nandzo to buy provisions. The rest of the members of the Committee would have been his schoolmates in both the primary and the middle schools. But as the years went by Hilla and I became very good friends. In 1953 there was a vacancy in the Gwollu Local Council and Hilla was elected and from there was elected into the District Council. As George Nandzo had returned to the college for his Teachers' Certificate 'A' course, there was a vacancy on the Finance and Staff Committee. Hilla was elected from the District Council and we worked amicably together until he left for the UK in 1955.

The Extra-Mural Department of the University College, Legon, in conjunction with the Peoples' Educational Association held the New Year School at the Wesley College in Kumasi this year, during the Christmas period when educational institutions were usually vacant.

Apart from the general talks given by distinguished guest lecturers, which everybody at the school and visitors from the town attended, the students were divided into seminar groups of their choice. Each group followed a particular course for the duration of the time at the school. In Tumu I was able to convince Hilla and Bagyirɛ Daŋnikuu to attend the school with me. Luckily for me, my mate, Alidu Kanton, the sitting MP for the Tumu constituency, was returning to Accra for the penultimate session before the dissolution of the Legislative Assembly. Alidu offered to give his best pal, Nandzo, his brother, Issaka Kanton, and myself a lift in his car. I persuaded Alidu to give Hilla and Bagyirɛ a lift since this was their first time of attending an Easter School. With great reluctance he agreed to take both of them. His car was over the number of persons allowed by law but being an MP and with the MP label stuck on his car screen and the car being a private one, the police turned a blind eye to any offence and raised no problems. We arrived in Kumasi on the same day without any mishap. We parked the car in front of my door while I took them to a bar run by the ex-wife of Opanyin Kwame Nti, Akosua Sika. The bar was situated directly behind the house in which I lodged. After the entertainment Alidu and his pals drove off to their lodgings and I returned to my room.

When the day came for us to register at the school, I called for a taxi to take us to Wesley College, which was situated about one or two miles from my lodgings on the Kumasi-Yeji-Tamale road. At the college we were shown our dormitories where we showered and got ready for the evening meal. But prior to that, Dennis Austin, who had replaced Bill Tordoff as the Resident Tutor for the Northern Territories, was at the registration point to welcome us to the conference. After the meal, we gathered in the Assembly Room where David Kimble, the Director of the Department of Extra-Mural Studies, addressed us, outlining the programme and the duration of the course, after which we retired to bed. Before we did so we were each given some question papers for a quiz competition, which were to be completed within a certain date. It would seem that those persons who lived in the city were advantaged in that they knew where to search for the answers. I was in that privileged position for I knew some of the libraries to go to, including the British Council where I often got free literature on writers such as Thomas Hardy. Besides, I was a regular customer at many of the main bookshops in town such as the Basel Mission Bookshop or the Methodist Bookshop where I bought stationery for the Lawra and the Tumu District Councils. I was able to ask for the names of authors of books which I had never come across.

At this school we had as visiting guest speakers, people such as the late Sir Lennox Boyd who was then the Foreign Secretary. It was at this school that K.A. Korsah visited one of our evening functions as a guest with his wife and daughter. I believe Korsah was appointed to the Administrative service as a Puisne Judge in 1946 and rose up to become Chief Justice in later years. That evening, after the lecture and dinner, there was a revue and I took a seat in the front row and a few seats to the right of me were seated the judge and his family. He was flanked on either side by his wife and daughter. The programme of this revue included drama, recitals and dancing. Dennis Austin was the master of ceremonies and the next item on the program was to be a dance, to be participated in by a couple. Music was to be played and when it stopped the master of ceremonies would point to a person in the congregation and that person would get up and pick a partner to dance with. The music would then resume and the couple would dance to the tune that was played. So when the music played had stopped, Dennis immediately pointed to me. I was totally embarrassed and was still sitting there when Dennis started calling out my name to get up. At that moment, I heard the late Bagyirɛ's dirty laugh next to me; Bagyirɛ would laugh at anything whether it was funny or not. Whether his laugh meant I could not dance, I couldn't say; but little did he know that I had been taking lessons at the YMCA any time I was in town. I was determined to show him I could do so. I got up and the nearest female to me was Korsah's young daughter and I turned to her, bowed and stretched my hand as was the ballroom etiquette and asked her for a dance. I could not tell who was more embarrassed in this episode, the young lady or me. Anyway her parents egged her on to get up; and when she eventually did, we danced to the tune of a "high life".

The answers to the papers on the quiz returned by all the entrants were marked and returned during the course of the week. And lo! and behold, I scored the second highest mark in this competition. The person with the highest mark was an Assistant Education Officer stationed in Sunyani, Ashanti, now the Brong Ahafo region. Both Dennis and Newlove were proud that I came second and both came to congratulate me for my effort. On the eve of our departure, a dance was organised at Hotel de Kingsway where I usually practised my new steps when I was in town from the north. Both the resident band and the resident manager, Mr Hope, knew me very well and the prizes for this competition were to be presented there. As a prize winner I had to go whether I could dance or not. When my name was called,

Newlove came to my table with two or three of his friends and lifted me up high and escorted me to receive my prize of ten shillings.

Princess Elizabeth was proclaimed queen on the death of her father, King George VI, in 1952 and the Coronation was to take place on June 6, 1953. The Gold Coast was to send representatives to this Coronation. Some personalities were asked from all regions and all the Districts had to send representatives to attend. From the Lawra District, the Duori Nũũ and the Birifu Nũũ were among the chiefs that went. The Birifu Nũũ was then the Chairman of the District Council whilst the Duori Nũũ was a member of the Northern Territories Territorial Council. The Birifu Nũũ must however be very grateful to the late DC Dyer-Ball who was then the senior DC for the North-West District. I was in Birifu when he came to try to persuade Nana to take that opportunity and visit Britain. For apart from the grand ceremonial pageantry of the Coronation, his visit would also widen his outlook. Although Nana and I were no longer at loggerheads with each other, our relation as siblings was still very lukewarm. Nevertheless I added my voice encouraging him to take DC Dyer-Ball's advice and go. Whether or not my voice carried any weight is another matter. He eventually accepted the invitation and went as a member of the Gold Coast delegation. While in the UK Nana was lucky to have Jack Goody as a family friend who occupied him for much of his leisure time, with other activities when there were no official activities in progress. For instance he was able to get the BBC Overseas Service to allow Nana to record and broadcast the xylophone music which was played on the Radio ZOY, the national radio of the Gold Coast. When the Gold Coast delegation returned, it was by accident that I met Nana at my lodgings in Kumasi when I went down to purchase my merchandise for the shop. However he did not stay more than a day with me before they were provided with transport for the north.

In 1954 the New Year School was to be held at Holy Child College, Cape Coast. Whenever I attended these schools, I usually joined the seminar in which economic theory and applied economic problems were discussed. The seminar was under the tutorship of Walter Birmingham and one Kubinski who was a Polish economist at the University College, Legon. Other lecturers who gave us talks on Economics included Mrs Helen Kimble and Dr J. C. W. de Graft Johnson. It was at this seminar that Dr de Graft Johnson prepared a paper on how to finance the Volta River Project without depending on outside help and distributed it to all members of the seminar. I was the only northerner at the school but was able to meet an old friend, one Mr

Ofori, who was the Headmaster of the Tumu Primary Boarding School just for a short period. When Mr Ofori was in Tumu he knew the interest I took in wanting to go abroad to study. When we met at this school, he wanted to know how far my plans to go abroad had proceeded and whether I had got a school to go to. He informed me that his brother-in-law had an address of a college in the UK and he would get me the address before the school closed. Luckily for me, his brother-in-law who was a police constable, was stationed at Elmina, a suburb of Cape Coast. One day, Ofori went to Elmina during our afternoon recess, which was normally between 2 p.m. and 5 p.m., and got this address for me. This address helped one or two northern young men to secure their passport to travel abroad. Anyway I was very grateful to Ofori for this help.

During the New Year School in Kumasi in 1953 there was in attendance in that school an American Negro, a diplomat from Accra who was supposed to head the American Embassy. During one of our intervals for coffee, I approached him to find out the possibility of studying in the States. He took down my name and address and I returned to Tumu to continue with normal work. As time went on I forgot all about it until one day, an envelope came to me from the American Embassy in Accra. When I opened it I found an application form and a letter asking me to complete it and return it to them in Accra. I did so and posted it under a registered cover as I did not want to miss the chance. It took a long time before I heard from them in the form of a telegram requesting me to attend an interview at the scholarship secretariat in Accra. Luckily I was in Tumu when the telegram arrived, otherwise I could have missed the interview at the appointed date. I set out the next day for Kumasi where I took another truck for Accra. From here I went to the Teshi-Nungua busstop to get transport to my destination. When the bus finally arrived after a long wait, I jumped on it and was taken to Teshi, arriving there about six in the evening. The next day, I left Teshi-Nungua where I lodged with my brother, Zumɔka, who was in the army and driving an army officer. Not knowing Accra very well, I depended on taxis to take me to the Scholarship Secretariat for the interview and managed to arrive there on time. There were five young school boys and myself making a total of six who were called for this interview. We were not told how many scholarships were available for which the six of us were competing. Nevertheless I was so confident that I would be one of the successful ones when I found out that the five were still attending school. At my interview, I spent more time with the interviewers than any of the candidates that went before me. Among the interviewers, there was the American diplomat who had sent me the application form. But it seemed he was merely there as an observer and did not ask me a single question. However, there was one elderly man who grilled me about my resignation from teaching and whether I would make use of my training for the benefit of the country if I were successful and returned to the country. After the interview I was told I would be informed by letter of the outcome of the interview. A few months passed and a letter arrived informing me that I had been unsuccessful in my application for the scholarship.

As has been noted earlier, while I was a teacher at the Lawra Primary Boarding School there had been a few school girls who had a crush on me. One of these girls was Assibi (Margaret) Nitori, who grew up to be a very beautiful damsel. I had never set eyes on her again since my resignation from teaching. She was still a pupil at the school until she finished her Middle School education in 1953 or thereabouts. When I paid a visit home I learnt that she, her classmate, Mata-malam, and her dad had visited the village but that her father had left whilst the two girls passed the night at the palace. I did not trust my three lecherous brothers to stay with two beautiful, single damsels without molesting or interfering with them. I was aware that Gyub at that time lusted for Mata-mallam and pretended he was in love and wanted to marry her. But Mata-mallam would not have been the first virgin to be molested and later cast aside by Gyub. Anyway, the next day I rode down to Kuũnyukuũ in the company of my cousin, Ŋmin-yaa (nicknamed Tumtum by the Ashantis because of his very black complexion), to see Margaret at her home and find out if she had given in to any of the machinations of these devils. It was about 5 p.m. when we got there–about fifteen minutes ride from Birifu–and I found the mother and her stepmothers sowing some seeds in the compound farm. I stood at the road junction which was about fifty yards from their old house and asked my cousin, Tumtum, to go and call her if she was at home. A few minutes later Tumtum returned, followed by Margaret. On arrival, she greeted and without mincing words I got to the point. At that moment Tumtum discretely left us alone and went back to chat with the women on the farm. I told her I knew what happened at Birifu and I wanted to hear from her what she had planned for the future, whether or not she still loved me enough to marry. She confirmed her love for me after we had had a serious tête à tête and I forgave her for her indiscretion. A year or so later, Margaret and her mates had finished their Middle School education and were given scholarships by the Education Department to attend Holy Child College; Kanari and Mũũfaa were to do secondary education and Mata-mallam and Assibi a four-year Teacher Training course. The Lawra District Council had an extra-ordinary meeting to discuss among other things whether or not to accept the scholarships for these girls. The meeting was presided over by the District Commissioner, Mr Westland Adams. Luckily for me I was in Lawra that day and heard of the meeting. I decided to attend as an observer and see how the Lawra District Council conducted their business. When the matter of accepting the scholarship came up, there was hostile opposition to the acceptance of these scholarships, especially those for Mata-mallam and Assibi.

There came a point in the discussion when I felt I should give my views on the matter to one of the councillors at the meeting, to be put forward on behalf of these two girls. I was sitting behind Abayifaa Karbo who was one of the vocal speakers. I tapped him on the shoulder and whispered to him to see me outside the hall. The meeting was being held at the DC's court. Abayifaa listened to my views and we both went back into the hall. When he got up to speak, I thought he was going to relay the views on my behalf, but instead he asked the meeting if I could be allowed to express an independent view on the matter. And so I did, and eventually the scholarships were accepted and extended to Assibi and Mata-mallam. I wonder what would have been the outcome if any of the councillors had known I had a special interest in Assibi. Her parents did not know of my interest in their daughter even though I often drank pito at their house any time I was in Lawra. My interest at the time was nothing but honourable – to give each sex a fair educational opportunity. For what the majority was saying was that they were now mature women and would get pregnant before their course and thus waste the council's money. These girls were called to Tamale to be given group transport to travel to the south and also to collect their rail warrants to Accra and Cape Coast.

While in Tamale they were housed at their school dormitories but were allowed freedom to travel to town. At the same time Alidu Kanton who was then an MP was in Tamale with me, and Mata-mallam and Assibi were seen in our company during the day. Alidu and I were even seen collecting these girls at night to go for entertainment at our accommodation in the Mass Education Centre where we had been housed while attending a conference in town. News went back to her father that if he did not warn me, I would make his daughter pregnant in no time. Later when I was at Lawra, I was having a drink at Kwaku's bar when Nitori came in and I bought him a drink. In the course of our conversation he told me that he had learnt that his daughter had been associating with me in Tamale and he had been told to warn me off. I told him his daughter was in my company in Tamale and he should have no fears. If there was any hanky panky between his daughter and I, she would not be made pregnant. I added that I was even very careful with my wife when she was betrothed to me underage. I did not attempt anything, even when we slept together on the same bed and we didn't get a child until she was seventeen. Being inquisitive, I wanted to know where he got the rumour from. He told me it was Chief Dombo who alerted him. My desire for Margaret was for her to finish her teaching course before we married and started a family and not spoil her education on the way. For this I had argued in the council. My love for her intensified and our letter writing became more frequent. From the onset I was frank with my first wife and put her in the picture that Margaret would be the second wife when she had finished with her training. Although my late wife was pleased with the idea of my marrying a second wife, she was jealous that I might then cast her aside. Consequently when my letters were delivered by the post office messenger, she had them opened and read to her. One or two years passed when I received a letter from Margaret informing me of her holiday break for that year. I wrote back telling her that I would meet her in Lawra when she came home. When the time came I left my late wife in charge of the shop whilst I rode to Lawra on a friend's bicycle. On my arrival after a sixty-nine mile ride, as good luck would have it there was pito in her house, brewed by her step-mother, Pɔɔnyuo. I was entertained to a free pot of pito after which I bought one or two pots for our consumption. As the sun was setting fast, I decided to ask permission to travel the nine miles to Birifu. At that moment Margaret asked if I could give her a lift to her village to which I agreed. Riding sixty-nine miles from Tumu to Lawra did not tire me out at all. Her company actually enlivened the burden of the journey. As I rode off, with Maggie sitting on the bar of the cycle, she told me she had been posted to Birifu to do a fortnight's teaching practice beginning the following Monday. I dropped Maggie at Kuũnyukuũ before proceeding home and I anxiously waited for her arrival on the Sunday evening.

CHAPTER EIGHTEEN

WHEN MARGARET ARRIVED SUNDAY EVENING she was warmly welcomed by the family and the teachers and clerks that were there. The teachers at the school were Mr Dapaalu Nibɛ, the Headteacher and E.S. Dam his assistant. There was also Jɔvaa, the Agricultural Instructor for Birifu. These personnel occupied the quarters which my father had built for us when we became adults, while with my fiancée, Margaret, I occupied the same quarters below his as when we were teenagers. At this time, the Birifu Nũũ had become pally with me and had now occupied my father's quarters at the very top of the house. Every night, Nana would come down from his quarters as a peeping tom to peer through my bedroom window to see if we were playing some hanky panky so he could tease us the following morning. Nature did not give him that opportunity for Margaret was in her menstrual period all the time I was with her in Birifu. After bidding Maggie my final farewell in case she did not meet me in Kumasi, I left for the south that midweek on the Babile market day. I was still in Kumasi when Margaret and her mates came down. On the eve of their departure for Accra, Kanari, Mata-mallam and Mũũfaa were directed to my house and came to greet me and to bid me goodbye. Margaret was not with them and when I asked about her whereabouts, I was told she had gone to bid goodbye to her uncle at the Ridge where he worked as a steward. I expected her to call round when she returned to her lodgings but she never did. Anyway, the next morning, I went to the railway station where I met them together with some of their mates from other parts of the north and bade all of them bon voyage as the train moved off towards Accra. After purchasing all my merchandise, I returned to Tumu to equip my shop with them. Almost two months passed without a letter from Margaret to announce her safe arrival at her college. One day I returned to Birifu only to learn that Margaret had written to Jɔvaa announcing her arrival and thanking him and his mates for their company. At that moment extreme jealousy crept into my blood stream for no apparent reason. But before I could react, I had to return to Tumu to see if her letter was waiting for me there. However, there was no letter when I got Tumu.

I waited another fortnight and did not hear from her. I wrote her a very sarcastic letter and posted it before leaving for Lawra again. Within a week I was back and found a letter from Maggie waiting for me. In it she told me she was pregnant and was asking me to help her get rid of the pregnancy. It seemed the envelope had been tampered with but I did not accuse my wife of having done so for I had no reason to suspect her at that time. On reading the letter, I went immediately to the Post Office and sent a telegram telling her to ignore the contents of my sarcastic letter if and when she received it and to know I was on my way to her. As I got ready, I told my wife where I was going but this did not seem to surprise her, which went to confirm my suspicion that she had been opening my letters and having them read for her before resealing the envelope.

In the Gold Coast at that time, abortion was a criminal offence carrying a maximum sentence of about seven years with hard labour. Despite the outcome, I was bent on getting to Cape Coast to find a doctor that would get rid of her baby, even though I knew I was not the father. Holy Child was a Roman Catholic college and stricter than most schools of other denominations in the Gold Coast. The dispenser who was stationed at Tumu came from Cape Coast town. I therefore solicited his help to see if he could give me addresses to contact when I got to Cape Coast. Although willing, he was unfortunately unable to help. Within the next three days I set off for Cape Coast. I took a train to Takoradi, a town I know better than Cape Coast. After passing the night in a hotel, I took a truck the next morning to Cape Coast and a taxi to Holy Child College. At Holy Child, one of the girls, Emma Marinoni, came out to enquire whom I wanted to see. I told her I had come to see Kanari and company. She told me that Chief Dombo, who was an MP at that time, had come and collected the four girls to go to Accra for an early vacation. I was greatly disappointed at not being able to help Assibi at a time when she needed my help most and so I returned to Kumasi very dejected. In Kumasi I wrote to Maggie care of Chief Dombo expressing my sorrow at not being able to get to her on time to help her. I must stress that I knew very well that I was not the father of Maggie's baby but was prepared to accept the responsibility provided she admitted to me who the real father was. Despite this mishap, I was still passionately in love with Maggie but would not shoulder her troubles if she was not frank with me. The other reason I knew that I was not the father of Maggie's baby was that when I was in Obuasi, I had bought two books on sex education, "Approaching Womanhood" and "Approaching Manhood" from which I studied the subject intensively. I therefore knew when to have safe sex with a girl and when not to, that is, the danger period in a woman's menstrual cycle. But since Maggie was still in her menstrual period when I left Birifu, the probability of my being the father of her baby was zero. Anyway I received a reply to my letter from Maggie from Accra which stated that she did not want to set eyes on me again and that she had a better man who would take care of her. I was alarmed at this outburst in her letter. My endeavours to risk everything to save her were thrown back in my face.

I was given some building contract work in Lawra, Birifu and Eremon. My merchandise included some building materials and timber which I loaded on a lorry I had chartered to take home. At Wa I transferred my merchandise to another truck to be taken to my shop at Tumu while I proceeded to Birifu with the rest of the load. At Birifu I unloaded the materials and instructed the driver to deliver the material to Lawra and Eremon and to have the waybills countersigned before I could pay him. I was building a new quarters for Yaani Konkuu and a teachers' quarters for the Eremon school where my brother, Biz, was the head-teacher with Sugem Gyielɛ as his assistant. So Biz and Yaani countersigned the waybills and the driver returned to Birifu to collect his freight charge.

I stayed in Birifu for about a fortnight to recruit some labour and to have some building blocks made. I tried to find out if Maggie had stayed in the room I had left for her or if she had gone down to live in the teachers quarters while I was away. My late brother, Bekanuɔ (Dr H.B. Gandah), who was still in the primary school, served me any time I went home by running errands or making tea for me. When Maggie was there, he ran the errands for both of us. Consequently, when I was leaving for the south I told him to continue to run errands for her and instructed my senior sister, Kuupiirɛ, who was cooking for us, to cook for her until she left Birifu. While in Birifu, I asked Bekanuɔ if Maggie had stayed in my apartment while I was away and when he hesitated to tell me the truth, his hesitation said it all. One day I was down with the teachers in their quarters when Nitori sent a message by his son to ask me to see him in his home. After entertaining his son with a large pot of pito, I rode off with him to Kuũnyukuũ accompanied by Jɔvaa.

When we arrived, we went upstairs to the roof into his little hut, and were welcomed with a pot of pito. After we had emptied the pot, the father came in and threw this bombshell at me. According to his daughter, I was responsible for her pregnancy. I was dumbfounded and sat there for a few moments. I then asked him to call his daughter. When she was called into the room, I asked the father to repeat what he had just told me in front of front of his daughter. As he did so I fixed my gaze on Maggie to see her reaction but she could not even look into my face. At that moment I told the father that since this was a matter for his daughter and me to settle, I could not deny or confirm her story until we had discussed it between ourselves. As Jɔvaa and I rode off to Lawra, I was on the horns of dilemma since I was still ardently in love with Maggie. Was I to cover up her shame and admit to something I had no hand in or tell him the truth that I was not responsible for his daughter's pregnancy? In the end I decided that if Maggie confided in me and told me the truth, I would cover her shame and admit to the father that I was the person responsible. If she did not confide in me and still stuck to her lies, then I would refute her allegations. While still in Birifu, I was reliably informed that the very day I left for Kumasi, Maggie had left my quarters and went down to live with Jɔvaa in the teachers' quarters. My informant swore me to secrecy and because of this I could not ask him. But on one occasion, Jɔvaa gave himself away when he asked me an intimate question about Maggie. Maybe when Maggie moved down to his room he might have attempted to have sex with her and she might have refused and told him she was still in her menstrual period. Otherwise how could he have known that I went against the taboos of the Gandah house etiquette by eating food together with Maggie and sleeping on the same bed with her. For the Kukpɛnibiɛ rules forbade any adult male to eat food prepared by, accept drink from, or drink from the utensil used by, a woman passing her menses. Consequently all adult women must carry their own drinking calabashes when they are in such a condition. I would have suspected Jɔvaa as being responsible for Maggie's pregnancy but for the reliable stories I heard about Chief Dombo's involvement with her in Accra. It was hard to accuse either of them until the child was actually born. All I knew was that one of them was responsible. But I was known to the family as her future husband and she indeed stayed in the palace while I was there.

On one Lawra market day, I rode to Lawra to spend the day there. I was told that Maggie was in town and was staying in her father's quarters provided by the Native Authority, first in his capacity as Native Authority Clerk and later as Sanitary Overseer. During the evening, to kill two birds with one stone, I went with my cousins, Nitii and Dapla Nũũi, together with Tom Tang from Eremon to drink pito at Nitori's quarters so I could confront Maggie to see if she would confide in me who was fathering her baby. We met Jɔvaa with his friends there. The party became larger than we had anticipated. After the party had consumed a few pots of pito, I decided to have a quiet word with Maggie behind their house where no one could see or hear us. I went out, followed by her and when we were alone, I told her that I knew I was not responsible for her pregnancy but that I was prepared to stand by her lies and shield her from her father's wrath if she confided in me. She began to weep and had Jɔvaa not appeared suddenly to disturb our privacy, she would probably have confessed the names of the number of men she had slept with since her last menstrual period before her pregnancy. With Jɔvaa's presence, I could get nothing out of her and decided to return to join the party, hoping to get her alone another day. One day Nitori wrote me a letter accusing me of being responsible for his daughter's pregnancy and threatening to take me to court to claim damages for the cost of her education from the beginning of primary school to the time when she became pregnant. The tone of his letter was very rude and that really got my back up. I wrote back telling him that I was not responsible and he was at liberty to do what he liked but advised him to ask his daughter to get the truth of the matter before rushing into rash decisions that could land him in deep waters.

As time went on, I later became Chief Dombo's private secretary. I am not sure if Maggie had accused him of this pregnancy or whether it was because of his love for Maggie that he wanted to marry her. At any rate he was not sure if I was still in love with her and so he sent chief Baloroo as his emissary to come and consult with me, even though I had already told him personally that my love for her was non-existent. I was in Kumasi when Chief Baloroo came down and was looking out for me. By this time Chief Baloroo had replaced my brother, the Birifu Nũũ, as Chairman of the Lawra District Council. I did not know what errand brought him to Kumasi but it could be he had come down to collect his new Vauxhall car. In Kumasi Chief Dombo usually lodged with his cousin, Sunpuɔ, in Asawasi. After chief Baloroo and I had visited Chief Dombo, Baloroo offered to take me home in his car. Half way to my lodgings in Amanhia, Baloroo parked his car by the roadside and told me that he had been asked by Chief Dombo to find out from me if I was still in love with Maggie and still wanted to marry her. I told Chief Baloroo that my marrying Maggie was out of the question since she had already betrayed me twice and there was no guarantee that she would not be unfaithful to me again if we got married. Besides, my business carried me away from my station most of the time and she could be unfaithful to me any time I was away. But if Chief Dombo wanted to marry her, he was welcome to do so and I would not be offended. Baloroo should tell him so. From then on Maggie was known as the wife of Chief Dombo and her relation with me or with the family became nothing but one of sisterly love.

Debomo as I mentioned won a government scholarship to study building construction in the UK and was enrolled at the Bristol College of Technology. Although he had two wives at home, Debomo befriended a young Bristol girl, Lily Brock, during his studies and before he could return to Ghana, he and Lily had a baby girl born to them on November 2, 1953. Prior to this when Lily was expecting, David wrote to me to go to his maternal uncle, Fanyɛ, the headman of Baapar, and ask him to sell one of his bulls and remit some money to him. Still maintaining my father's principle that his children should not depend on their maternal uncles, I immediately made a cable transfer of the money to him followed by a letter explaining the money was from me. For because of our late father's stand, I couldn't go to his uncle and demand money from him. According to David, the money was for the wedding in a registry office. I understood he wrote a similar letter to our brother, the chief, entreating him to let his uncle sell one of his bulls from his kraal and remit the money to him. Faanyɛ obliged but the Birifu Nũũ never remitted the money. I don't think that even when the chief went to the UK for the Queen's Coronation, he offered his brother, Debomo, a penny. But that would be Nana all right; he loved his money more than anything. I often believed it was the curse of his senior brother, Sɔrkumɔ, made when we were at school that followed Nana to his death. About December 1953, I received a letter from Debomo saying that he would be sailing on one of the boats of Elder Dempster Lines, the S.S Apapa, and docking at Takoradi harbour in mid February, 1954. After attending one of the New Year Schools in the south at Holy Child I hurried back with my merchandise to sell and then return to meet him at Takoradi. I was in Kumasi about the first week in February and bought the goods for my shop as quickly as possible and paid for them before going to Takoradi with a total sum of more than £400 in my pocket.

My business was booming and I could afford to splash out lavishly on my favourite brother returning home. I arrived in Takoradi in the evening of February 13 and booked into a hotel called the "Cassava Farm" and guarded my cash with great care. The next morning I hurried down to the docks to await the docking of the boat.

Between ten and eleven in the morning, the boat docked and about half an hour later Debomo appeared on the deck with a friend. As soon as I saw him, I waved to him and he waved back.. He came down to greet me and we both went back into the boat for drinks and later for lunch. At lunch Debomo asked me if I had enough money on me. I asked him how much he wanted and whether £200 was enough. He told me that it was as his European friend was going on to Nigeria and had asked him to lend him some money. That is "Gandah generosity" for you! Debomo had known the man on the boat for only twelve days and trusted him enough to lend him money. After lunch we left the boat and half an hour later it sailed off for Nigeria, the last destination, as we waved Debomo's friend goodbye. We then went into the luggage hall to retrieve his luggage before calling a taxi and going back to the hotel where I had reserved two rooms for the night. Comparing the first class fares for two on the train from Takoradi to Kumasi and the cost of chartering a taxi, I found there was very little difference. I decided to charter a taxi, which took us very early in the morning from the hotel to Kumasi arriving at Ashanti New Town before dusk. The next day, Debomo went to the Government Transport yard and took a lorry to Tamale to report to the Authorities whilst I loaded my merchandise for Tumu.

From about the early forties onwards more scholars in the Northern Territories were beginning to be politically aware and stood their ground for their rights in front of their colonial masters much better than their forerunners. No wonder northerners were prevented from going to southern schools, because it was believed we would be influenced by them. This awareness accelerated with the opening of the Tamale Teacher Training College in 1944 which was then the highest educational institution in the region, and because of the end of the war in 1945 with its mass demobilisation. Despite their political awareness, there were no organised groups except youth associations that provided amenities such as football and tennis in villages and towns. These were formed by enlightened youths but soon fell apart if the enlightened person who was the motive force behind the formation of the association was transferred from or left the district. The moment mention was made of the introduction of fees and membership cards often boded the death knell of that association. The members, comprising mostly chiefs, of the Northern Territories Territorial Council (NTTC) which was inaugurated in December 1946, were non-party. The NTTC was the forerunner of the Northern Territories Council (NTC). Three members from this body, J.A. Braimah,

Yakubu Tali, and S.D. Dombo, were added as extra-ordinary members to the Legislative Council to debate the Ewart Committee Report. We have seen that even in 1951 when the North was given nineteen seats in the Legislative Assembly, candidates sent to the electoral college were not party members but were nominated and selected by the District Commissioners. The only people who claimed to belong to the parties but did not hold party cards were southerners working in the district administration in the north, and as a matter of pride they tried to show they belonged to one of parties in the south. These people I call sympathisers, just as I was a sympathiser of the United Gold Coast Convention (UGCC), the forerunner of the Convention Peoples Party (CPP). In effect there were very few northerners who held party membership cards before 1954, and these few were notably in Tamale town just before the dissolution of the Legislative Assembly.

Before Parliament dissolved, most members from the north, S.D. Dombo (the Duori Nũũ), Mumuni Bawumia, L.R. Abavana, J.A. Braimah (the then Kpembe Wura), and Yakubu Tali (the then Tali Nũũ), among others, decided to form a party with northern interests in mind and to fight the elections collectively. They found out that as a collective group in the Assembly, they were very effective on issues concerning the north. Because of the reactions of their paramount chiefs, both the Kpembe Wura and the Tali Nũũ declined to take a leading role in the formation of a party but supported its formation whole-heartedly. At the same time some northern members of Parliament, especially those few who already held ministerial posts, were enticed to join the CPP, and some others were promised ministerial posts if they stood and won the next elections. Persons such as J.H. Alhassani, Ayarna Imoru, Abavana, Asumda Ayeebo, Akantiɛsi Afoko, all decided to the fight the elections on the CPP ticket. In the end S.D. Dombo and Mumuni Bawumia were left to become the leaders of this new party that was to be set up. As soon as parliament was dissolved, Mumuni was given the task of convincing the chiefs and people in the Mamprusi District, which at that time comprised the Kusasi, Frafra and the Mamprusi districts. The Duori Nũũ was given the task of convincing the chiefs and people of the North-west district of Bole, Wa, Lawra and Tumu and the Kasena-Nankani confederacy and Builsa areas. I was in Lawra when chief Dombo addressed the youth in the Lawra District. I went to this rally with my brother, Nuɔnatuo Gandah, the Birifu Nũũ, who was then Chairman of the Lawra District Council. Chief Dombo outlined the aims of the party whose name was to be ratified later at a conference in Tamale. At that time I was not drawn to this idea of forming a party, partly because I found it difficult to shift my allegiance from the UGCC to a new party, the NPP, even though I did not possess a membership card of the UGCC. Nana, my brother, on the other hand objected not because the idea was bad but that he would stand no chance of becoming a candidate on the party ticket. He believed that the selection of the candidate would be based on nepotism.

I returned to Tumu to continue with my daily work. Then one day, Chief Dombo drove up in his Hillman van to my shop. I asked my wife to take him and his entourage to the house and entertain them while I handed over the shop to my brother, Dɔdulɛ. After the entertainment, Chief Dombo told me he had come to establish the NPP in Tumu. I had still not decided to join this new party and was therefore reluctant to take an active part. After a while, when he could not convince me to make up my mind about the new party immediately, he told me he would like me to go with him and have an audience with the Tumu Koro, Luri Kanton, Kanton II. I was still in the good books of Chief Kanton and so we set off for the palace. We were at the Tumu Koro's palace from about 8pm until about 11pm during which time Chief Dombo explained the party's aims and views. The Tumu Koro embraced it immediately and gave his support. We returned home and he left for his next destination. Then in April 1954 the NPP was inaugurated in Tamale with Chief Dombo as its Chairman and Mumuni Bawumia as Vice-chairman. The General Secretary was Fuseini Dramani, while Imoru Salifu was the Propaganda Secretary.

The Easter School for 1954 was held at St Augustine's College, Cape Coast, and from the north only Bagyirɛ and I attended. After two weeks' deliberations, the school ended. As we returned home on the train to Kumasi en route for the north, I saw in the papers that my friend, Mr Imoru Egala, was to stand for the elections as the CPP candidate for the Tumu constituency. When we got to Tamale, Mr Egala, who was then teaching at the Tamale Teacher Training College, met me at the Government Transport yard and asked if I could start canvassing for him when I got to Tumu. There and then I told him that he knew that both he and I despised the CPP and what it stood for at the time. Why was he now standing on that ticket? Of course Mr Egala called Dr. Nkrumah all sorts of names and told me that he never offered his name to him as his party's candidate. If I did not believe him, I should consult the records at the District

Commissioner's office in Tumu and I would see he was standing as an independent candidate and not on the CPP ticket. When I got to Tumu, I went to the District Commissioner's office to verify the veracity of Mr Egala's statement. I was told by Mr Pepys Cockerell, the DC, that it was true that Mr Egala's name was registered as an independent candidate for the forthcoming elections but that the CPP had paid his deposit for the election fees. On paper there were five candidates contesting this single seat in Tumu, all of whom were standing as independent. They were Alidu Kanton, the outgoing MP, Abu Nankpa, a Native Authority Dresser, Imoru Egala, a college lecturer, Hilla Limann and Mumuni Dimbie, both certificate B teachers. Of the five, I would have preferred Imoru Egala to be our prospective MP, had it not been for his political stand. But since I found out from Pepys Cockerel that Egala was a CPP candidate in disguise, my next preference was for Hilla Limann.

At Tumu I was first approached by Alidu Kanton to be his Polling Agent in the Zini ward and later that week Hilla Limann also asked me to be his Polling Agent for the same ward. I was in a quandary. Do I turn down Alidu's request although he was the first to approach me and accept Hilla's, or turn down Hilla's whose candidature I preferred and accept Alidu's? That was the rub! Once the decision was taken to help Hilla, I tried to assist him as much as I could. Apart from the Gwollu and Zini areas and Tumu town, Hilla was not very well known. However, he had allies on whom he could rely, Bawol the headteacher of the Zini Day School under whom he had taught and Bagyirɛ Daŋnikuu, the headteacher of the Fiɛlmuŋ Day School and a mate of his. I asked for Hilla's current photograph, took it to Kumasi and had some handbills printed of him at the Ashanti Pioneer Press. This was to let the voters we were canvassing know whom they were going to vote for. A few days later I was also approached by DC Pepys Cockerell who wanted to appoint me as a presiding officer at one of the Polling Stations. He was surprised when I turned him down in favour of becoming Hilla's Polling Agent. As a presiding officer, I would have been paid from Government funds for the job while as a polling agent the job was being done free of charge for a friend. Pepys tried to convince me to accept his offer but I refused. I told him money was not the most important thing.

In the Lawra District, there were two constituencies, namely, the Lawra-Nandom and the Jirapa-Lambusie. In the Lawra-Nandom constituency, there were five candidates contesting that seat, namely: my brother, Nuɔnatuo Gandah, the Birifu Nũũ and Native Authority

Dresser, Abayifaa Karbo, a Certificate A teacher and the son of the late Lawra Nũũ, J.A. Karbo, Polkuu Konkuu, a trained teacher and a brother of the then Nandom Nũũ, A.P. Sarvero Tɔrmaɣri, a Local Council Clerk and Silvester Sanziri. Abayifaa Karbo stood on a NPP ticket whilst Nuɔnatuo Gandah, the Birifu Nũũ stood as CPP. The other three stood as independent candidates. Nuɔnatuo had never been a CPP follower but just like Mr Egala in Tumu he was bribed with an offer of a ministerial post in the Ministry of Health. I wondered what would have happened had they both won their seats. Indeed the Birifu Nũũ was not attracted to the radicalism of the CPP, as Dennis Austin put it, but by monetary and egoistic motives.[a] He had never been radical but an eccentric and a tease, mocking people at their expense. In the Jirapa Lambusie constituency, S.D. Dombo was opposed by Bapɔɔyiri Yelpoi, a teacher at Sabuli at that time, and the son of the then Jirapa Nũũ. With Baloroo Yesibie, headteacher of Lambusie and nephew and heir to the Lambusie Koro as an ally, Chief Dombo had the voters of Lambusie in his pocket. In the Wa District there were two constituencies, Wala-South and Wala-North. B.K. Adama of the Medical Field Unit (MFU) stood as NPP candidate in Wa-South against the interpreter of the DC whilst Jatoe Kaleo stood as NPP in the Wa-North constituency.

The NPP was barely two months old when the election campaign began in earnest. There were altogether 80 candidates contesting the 26 seats for the north. Of these there were 44 candidates that belonged to the various parties. The CPP entered candidates for all the 26 seats and the 18 other candidates were registered by the NPP and the Moslem Association Party (MAP).

On the election day in Tumu, which was June 10, after the votes had been counted, Egala was proclaimed to be duly elected by the Returning Officer whilst in Lawra there was a close contest between the NPP and CPP: A. Karbo who was elected polled 2,764, but Nuɔnatuo Gandah came a close second polling 2,434, a majority of 330 votes. In Jirapa-Lambusie Chief Dombo was elected and in Wala-South and Wala-North, B.K. Adama and Jatoe Kaleo were respectively elected Members of Parliament.

---

[a] See Dennis Austin, *Politics in Ghana*, p.247 note 58.

CHAPTER NINETEEN

IN THE NORTH-WEST DISTRICT there were four NPP Members of Parliament, with one as CPP. But in the north there were 18 MPs elected with one on MAP/NPP ticket making a total of 19 NPP and pro-NPP MPs. For although C.K. Tedam, J.A. Braimah and Yakubu Tali, the Tolon-Na, stood as independents, they were pro-NPP. W.A. Amoro, who won his seat as an independent, also joined the NPP as an opposition member in Parliament initially. In the country as a whole the CPP won 72 seats and the Opposition 32 seats. In Ashanti, of the 21 seats, only Dr K.A. Busia among the opposition won. The other twenty seats were taken by the CPP and some independents. True to his word, when all the votes were counted a few days later, and Dr Nkrumah was called upon to form a Government, Mr Egala was called to Accra and offered the post of Minister of Health. The NPP was the largest opposition party in Parliament and by British Parliamentary practice should have been recognised as Her Majesty's Official Opposition. When Parliament was convened on the 29th of July, 1954, Emmanuel Quist was re-elected the Speaker of the Legislative Assembly, with the Speech from the Throne being delivered by His Excellency the Governor, outlining the Government's programme for the session, this time with an all African Cabinet. There was some friction when Chief S.D. Dombo was proposed as the Leader of the Opposition and Dr Kwame Nkrumah objected. The members of the NPP had to walk out, boycotting the sitting of Parliament. Although the members of the Opposition in Parliament were only thirty-two in number, they were very vocal both within and without the Assembly, especially with eminent lawyers such as Justice Nii Amaa Ollenu and J.B. Danquah giving them legal ammunition from without to fight the government from within. At last the Opposition members marched to the Castle and presented their petition, quoting to Governor Charles Arden-Clarke from Erskine May's "Parliamentary Practice", as to why the NPP should be recognised as Her Majesty's Opposition. With reluctance and with good advice from his aide de camp, Arden-Clarke relented and advised the Speaker who over-ruled Dr Nkrumah's objection and the NPP was recognised as the Official Opposition party in Parliament. S.D. Dombo was immediately recognised as the Leader of the Opposition in Parliament with a salary of £1500.

After settling down in his ministry for a while, Mr Egala came on a tour to the North when the Parliamentary sitting came to a close, and visited Tumu for the first time since his election. The traditional council of chiefs all met to welcome him. We the educated young lads in Tumu also met and decided to welcome him and bury our electoral hatchet. We bought a few bottles of beer to do this and waited in the school where most of the lads resided as teachers. He fixed an appointment to meet us at nine o'clock in the evening. We assembled in the school before nine on a cold harmattan night but he did not turn up at the appointed time. Several messages were sent to the Tumu Koro's where he was, but any time the message came back, it was to say he was still busy and would be with us very shortly. But the time he gave would always pass without his word being honoured. Ten o'clock passed but still he was not with us. I felt he was trying to snub those of us who had had the audacity to contest the elections against him. I was getting agitated since I was the only person in the group to have to ride back to the Zongo and did not want it to get too late to do so. However, the young lads persuaded me to stay until he made it. We were there waiting until after eleven when he decided to grace us with his presence, being driven to us in his official car. At this gathering he gave a very short speech and, in trying to justify himself for standing as a disguised CPP candidate, said he was not prepared to subject himself to the leadership of a Certificate B teacher. That was by implication referring to the Duori Nũũ who led the NPP into the elections. That remark knocked me for six partly because the lot of us were Certificate B trained and partly because his logic failed in that not all highly qualified trained personnel are necessarily good leaders or good organisers. For if that were the case, persons such as Dr Danquah would have appealed to their parties as leaders.

Mr Egala did not know at that time that he had committed political suicide by alienating all the young, educated men in the district with his arrogant utterances and actions in a way that would cost him his seat in the 1956 General Elections. John Oseini, who was a schoolmate of Egala, had left the Police force and returned home to settle. With Egala's help he was employed by the Native Authority as the Traditional Court Registrar, a post Alidu Kanton had relinquished to become an MP. With the introduction of the Local Government and the establishment of Local and District Councils in the country, he became an employee among other District Council personnel. When Egala became Minister of Health, John Oseini resigned from the Council services and was appointed as his propaganda secretary. He was provided with a motor bike to do his job properly. I believe John's appointment as Mr Egala's propaganda secretary was a factor in Egala's downfall in the 1956 General Elections. For John never went outside Tumu to canvass or recruit members into his party, even though he had the means of transport to do so. Due to Mr Egala's arrogance and his alienation of all the young lads in the district, I felt this was now the time to form an NPP branch in the District to prove to him that Certificate B teachers can organise parties. All the young lads agreed to join the party. As most of the educated lot came from the villages, once they joined the party they carried its flagship into their respective villages and pervaded the nooks and crannies of the District. As time went on I had the support of all the important lads from these villages, especially those from the populous areas.

We have seen that it took time before the NPP was recognised as the Official Opposition in Parliament and S.D. Dombo was officially acknowledged as the Opposition Leader. When Parliament closed for recess after the first meeting and Chief Dombo returned home and met me in Lawra, he told me that the Opposition members had advised him to appointment me as his Personal Secretary. They were aware I had a business of my own to run, and I could still do this and be his personal secretary on a part-time basis on a salary of £15. He also told me that the Government had decided to form a National Shipping Line and the minister in charge was about to set up a committee and had approached the Opposition to appoint a member, and that my name had been put forward to the Minister. He told me that I would soon be receiving a letter direct from the Ministry of Transport and Communications about this appointment.

At one of the PEA Schools at Holy Child, I was able to get the address of a Tutorial College in the UK through one Mr Ofori, an acquaintance who was once the headmaster of the Tumu Primary Boarding School. Mr Ofori relieved Mr Egala in 1952 from his post so he could enter the Institute of Education for a further course in the University College of the Gold Coast, Legon. When I got this address, I wrote to the Principal of this Tutorial College in Sidcup, Kent. Within a few months I received a reply with the prospectus and an application form of the College. I immediately filled the form enclosing the deposit of £25 which the college requested before a place could be reserved for me and before I could receive a letter to enable me to get my passport for travel abroad. I showed this prospectus to Mr Afewu, who had relieved Mr Ofori as the Headteacher in the school, and to Hilla Limann as I normally joined them at the school to study together. Hilla was particularly interested. I left the brochure with him so he could write to the College on his own behalf.

When Hilla lost the election his ambition to go abroad for further studies increased. He wrote to the Greatwood Tutorial College and got himself registered. As soon as he received the letter of acceptance from the college I urged him to apply to the District Council for a once and for all financial help. The Tumu District Council was not a rich council like the Lawra District Council or the Mamprusi and the Dagomba District Councils. When Hilla put in his application it was referred to the Finance and Staff Committee and when this committee met, his application was on the agenda for discussion. Although Hilla was a committee member, by the Standing Orders of the Local Government Act he could not participate in the discussion since he had a personal interest in the matter. When he left the room while his application was discussed, I moved that his application be accepted. This proposal was seconded and accepted unanimously, that he be given a lump sum of £200 to help him with his education.

The National Liberation Movement came into being when the CPP government made a U-turn on their promise to increase the price of cocoa to the farmers, who were predominantly Ashantis. They were not only annoyed about the price being pegged at the previous year's level of 72s a load of 60 lbs., that is, about £134.40.0 per ton, but worst of all the price was being fixed for the next four years. Such an action only helped to inflame the cocoa farmers, especially when world price had risen to £450 per ton. This action in Gbedemah's budget proposals united all the farmers from the cocoa farming regions just as the north was united together because they did not believe in the CPP slogan of Freedom and Self Government Now! Critics of the bill seized upon the argument that since the Government in 1951/52 was able to pay cocoa farmers eighty shillings per load when the world price was only £245 per ton, then the Government could easily have paid the farmers over £5 with the present high world price. The NLM was soon formed under the Chairmanship of Bafuor Osei Akoto and its aims and slogan spread like wildfire throughout the Ashanti region. On Sunday September 19, 1954, when I happened to be in Kumasi for the purchase of my stores, there was a grand meeting of chiefs and people at an open park popularly known as Kejetia, but officially known as the Prince of Wales Park. This was used as a lorry park and lorry mechanics area during week days but was deserted on Sundays. This day however, there was pomp and pageantry in the traditional Ashanti fashion. War songs and drumming echoed through the length and breadth of the park as the chiefs and people gathered, and when Bafuor Osei Akoto was proclaimed chairman of this new movement, the noise drowned the announcement. I was terribly afraid as my nephew, Batan, and I looked on and my hair stood on end as the proceedings progressed. As time went on prominent Ashanti members such as R.R. Amponsah, Joe E. Appiah and Victor Owusu, who was my lawyer at the time in Kumasi, resigned their membership of the CPP and joined the NLM.

R.R. Amponsah had resigned as an Education Officer and a liaison officer for the Cocoa Marketing Board in West Germany, and Joe Appiah was Dr Nkrumah's personal representative in Britain who had returned home about November 1954. When they all declared themselves for the NLM, its stature went up while that of the CPP declined in the eyes of the people in Ashanti, especially since Joe Appiah was the son-in-law of a former Colonial Secretary and former Chancellor of the Exchequer in the Labour regime, Sir Stafford Cripps. He was also the son of J.W.K. Appiah, the Chief Secretary to the Asanteman Council. Not long after resigning from the CPP, Joe Appiah sent a message to Chief Dombo seeking to have a meeting with him. It was unanimously decided that I should first go as Mr Dombo's personal secretary to meet Joe and then bring back whatever message he had for the chief. This was to preserve Chief Dombo from any personal harm in case it was not genuine but rather a plot to get him out of the way. Joe was a man we had never heard of until he returned from Britain and we knew that he had been Nkrumah's representative there. He had suddenly introduced himself in a letter, wanting to have private audience with the Leader of the Opposition. The choice of intermediary was appropriate in that I stayed in Ashanti for nearly six years and still had accommodation in Kumasi. I was not afraid to meet Joe and travelled to Kumasi the next morning, arriving there by Government Transport about five in the evening when I took a taxi to my lodgings in Ashanti New Town.

After dinner I took a taxi to Asafo where he had his lodgings in a beautiful mansion. I was led in to the lounge by his steward boy, who was a northerner so when I told him I had come to see his master, Joe Appiah, I was shown a seat. He then went out while I sat there, only to return with Mrs Joe Appiah, the daughter of Stafford Cripps. She introduced herself as the wife of Joe Appiah and I also introduced myself as Personal Secretary to the Leader of Opposition. I told her the purpose of my visit and she told me that her husband had gone out and should be back shortly. She offered me a cup of coffee and vanished, leaving me alone in that vast sitting room. It was not until about nine or ten that Joe returned home, to be briefed by the wife. After another hour or so Joe came in to see me and to introduce himself. He was a very small man, compared to me at the time. I told him the purpose of my visit, that it was in response to his request to see Chief Dombo that I had come. And whatever he had to say would be carried back to the chief. Joe sat down and began to reveal the evil and murderous plans which Dr Kwame Nkrumah had mapped out for his political opponents when self-government was attained. There were to be, among other things, political executions and imprisonment without trial for some of his leading opponents as well as for some of the chiefs; that chiefs would run away and leave their sandals behind and others who were not killed or imprisoned would be exiled. I listened intently as he unfolded Nkrumah's evil plans and as he continued a sudden chill ran through my spine and into my bones. I suddenly began to shiver as if I had been shut in a compartment filled with ice or was suffering with an acute ague. I could not believe my ears that a civilised human being could conceive such barbarous plans for his fellow human beings. I was still shivering when I left Joe's house and caught a taxi back to my lodgings. When I entered my place, I had to have a Turkish bath to warm myself up before I went to bed. Of course political skeptics would scorn such tales as political opportunism on the part of Joe but some of these claims which he had made did come to pass during Nkrumah's Independent Ghana. Most opposition members were jailed in Nsawam prison and others ran away into exile until they returned after the coup of 1966.

However, during the 1954 General Elections, as the NLM was not yet formed and could not participate, they had no member in the Assembly to fight their cause for them. For the CPP had won 18 of the 21 seats in that region. On its formation the NLM had become a formidable opponent to the CPP in Ashanti and both sides soon began to try to intimidate each other with violence, even though the NLM had claimed as one of its aims the desire to eradicate violence among the young. In Kumasi, for instance, it was very frightening for any CPP member to visit Ashanti-New Town and similarly it was very daunting for any NLM member to visit places such as Krofufrom or New Tafo on the Kumasi-Yeji road. Indeed these were no-go areas for their opponents. The slogan for the NLM was "we separate ourselves (from you)", which soon became the cry for federation. When Parliament reopened and I travelled with Chief Dombo to Accra and met Mumuni Bawumia, he also confirmed that my name had been put forward to the Minister of Communications, Mr A.E. Ofori Atta. Unfortunately neither the Leader of the Opposition nor the Opposition whip, B.K. Adama, had offices allocated to them in the Assembly Buildings where we could do our research or receive representations from the public. Had we been given offices I would probably have done my job for my leader much better than I did. As it was I depended solely on the Parliamentary reports, the Hansard, and news reported by the Ashanti Pioneer, which was against the Government, and the Obuasi Times printed by the Ashanti Gold Fields Press. As soon as the Parliamentary session finished for the day, we normally returned home for lunch. After lunch there was nothing I could do but sit around and prepare one or two questions in the name of the Leader of the Opposition. Of course sitting in the lobby and listening to the debates every day gave me an insight into the British Parliamentary system on which the Ghana system was modelled. Having engrossed myself in politics I neglected my business, and left the running of it to my young wife and my brother.

Towards the end of 1954 a branch of the newly formed United Nations Educational, Scientific and Cultural Organisation (UNESCO) was to hold its first meeting in the Gold Coast under the auspices of its first Secretary, Miss Ogilvy, at the University College of the Gold Coast, Legon. This was a conference to be attended from the whole of the West African colonies, but mostly dominated by the English speaking territories. Dennis Austin, the resident tutor of the Extra-Mural Department in the north, told me about it and urged me to convince some members of the PEA in Tumu to attend. Bagyirɛ and Hilla had attended the New Year School in Kumasi a year before and consequently I had no problem convincing them to attend this conference. But it had occurred to me to ask why the NT Council failed to send delegates to this important conference or why MPs from the north were not encouraged to attend at least the open lectures in the evenings. After all, Parliament was still sitting at the time. It turned out that Hilla, Bagyirɛ and I were the only delegates from the north to attend. My wife was very pregnant with my second child and as there was no hospital in Tumu where she could be admitted I sent her to the Jirapa Mission hospital where there was a maternity ward. She was due at any moment and I instructed a friend and a teacher in Duori, Bayuo from Ulu, to notify me at the University College in Legon the very day my wife gave birth to her child. Because of this, I asked Hilla and Bagyirɛ to meet me at my dwelling in Kumasi when we could travel together to Legon since I had been there previously on one of these New Year and Easter Schools. On the eve of the conference, Hilla and Bagyirɛ arrived in Kumasi and came to stay the night at my house. We went into town to find out the cost of the journey to Accra by road and by air. I discovered there was not much difference but we could gain time and arrive at Legon before reporting time. I decided to treat them to their first experience of travelling by air and booked three seats for the next day's journey to Accra.

At that time there were regular helicopter flights from Kumasi to Accra. So the next day I called for a taxi that took us to the little airport where we boarded this helicopter for Accra. From there I hired a taxi that took us to where Chief Dombo and Mr Karbo lodged which was not very far from the Assembly House at the Government Transport Transit Quarters. I reported my arrival to the chief and told him where he could find me if he wanted me urgently. When it was getting to the time to report, we went to the College bus stop, waited and when it arrived we hopped on. The bus took us to the College where we alighted and reported at the porters' lodge with our luggage. The chief porter was a Dagarti man from Kaleo area whom I had known from my previous visits. He welcomed us, booked us in and asked the porters to take us to our respective rooms. Representatives came from as far afield as South-west and Central Africa. From Sierra Leone, we had as delegates the brother of Dr Milton Margai, the then Prime Minister, Siaka Stevens, the then Leader of the Opposition and Dr Davidson Nicols, the then Principal of Fourah Bay College. From the Gambia came a Trade Union Leader, whose name I believe was Jawal. I can still remember these people because I was in the same seminar with some of them while one or two were guest speakers. Two days before the close of the conference, I received a telegram from Bayuo informing me of the birth of my baby girl (now Mrs Agatha Palmer). About the same time, the National Liberation Movement (NLM) were forming a branch in Obuasi in the Adansi area and Chief Dombo was given an invitation to be a guest speaker. Chief Dombo approached me as his personal secretary at the campus and requested me to represent him at that gathering. I decided to return to the north and give a name to my baby girl before anybody else did. I approached Dennis Austin to inform him of my intention to leave the conference earlier than the closing date. He told me that he would have to consult David Kimble the Director of Extra-Mural Studies and see if he would agree to my leaving early. He returned and told me that David Kimble had refused me permission to leave and gave an ultimatum that if I left of my own accord, I would not be reimbursed for my transport cost to and from Accra. David should have known me better and realised that I was a young man that never accepted an ultimatum.

The next day, after breakfast, I bade farewell to Dennis, Hilla and Bagyirɛ and the other friends I had met and made at the conference, and left for town where I caught an afternoon flight for Kumasi. After my evening meal, I went off to the house of Bafuor Akoto (the chairman of the NLM and chief linguist to the Asantehene) to acquaint him with Chief Dombo's message and to let him know I was representing him at their rally in Obuasi. When he knew that I was living just about two hundred yards from his house and only about fifteen to twenty-five yards from the house of Alex Osei, he told me to meet him for a lift to the rally. Alex Osei was a professional photographer and became the leader of the "Action Group" when the NLM was formed in Ashanti, and we were already acquainted. The members of this group propagated the ideas of the NLM with its slogan of "we separate ourselves" with two fingers pointing into the air like a victory salute. The next morning I walked down to the end of our street to a T-junction where Alex Osei's house stood. There was a truck ready to take us to Obuasi, led by their propaganda van blurting out music through the loud speaker that was mounted on top. We arrived in Obuasi between ten and eleven o' clock in the morning and drove straight to the park where the rally was being held. I was led to the podium where the other speakers sat. Among the guest speakers were Dr K.A. Busia, who was the only Ashanti in the opposition in Parliament, and myself, representing Chief Dombo. As I did not have the chance to prepare a speech, when it came to my turn I appealed to the northerners in Obuasi, a mining town where many from the Dagara area were working down in the mines, to support the NLM. After that short speech the rally came to a close and I returned to Kumasi on the truck of the Action Group. But it seemed I had made my mark on the leaders of the NLM in Kumasi.

I was to attend the New Year School at St Augustine's College after the UNESCO conference in Legon. A week later I travelled to Cape Coast for the opening. The next day, I approached David Kimble to see if he could re-imburse me for my expenses to the UNESCO conference in Accra. But David was as stubborn as I was and refused to do so. When the school came to a close and I received the reimbursement for the cost of my travel to the New Year School in Cape Coast, I stopped at Kumasi to buy goods for my shop in Tumu.

As soon as the goods were purchased and loaded on to an available truck, I returned to Lawra allowing the driver to travel to Tumu to deliver the goods at the shop and be paid by my brother while I travelled by another vehicle to Lawra. In Lawra, I picked up my wife and the little baby girl and returned to Tumu with them. In Tumu I found a letter waiting for me at my shop. It was from the Minister of Transport and Communications and signed by A.E. Ofori Ata appointing me as a member of the committee to advise the Government in the setting up of a National Shipping Line, later to be named the "Black Star Line". The first meeting was a formal one under the chairmanship of A.R. Boakye, the Ministerial Secretary to the Minister. The majority in the committee were pro-CPP and I was the only Opposition member plus Mr Wheeler, a non-party member and the Managing Director of Elder Dempster Lines in Accra.

Before the Christmas recess when we returned to Accra, I had applied for a passport and my application form was witnessed by two persons, Chief Dombo and J.A. Braimah. I was supposed to have my papers processed and my passport issued to me in no time. But nearly a year had elapsed and I had heard nothing from the passport office in Accra. It was when Hilla applied for his passport long after I had done so and received his, that I began to wonder whether something had gone wrong with my application. On one of my travels to Accra I fell ill with severe malarial fever in Kumasi. Had this happened in the north, I could easily have been cured with my father's herbal treatment. As I was severely affected, I sent a message to Chief Dombo about my illness and entreated him to check with the Passport Office about the cause of the delay in the issue of my passport. At his investigation, he was told that I had a criminal record, namely, possessing a gun without a valid licence. I could not believe my ears when he came down to Kumasi and told me this. As I was still ill and very weak, he drove me to Dr I.B. Asafu-Adjaye's clinic and paid for an injection to be administered for my fever. This treatment immediately did the trick for I was soon up and going. This charge related to a criminal offence which had been committed by one of my senior brothers, Tiisip Gandaa (at that time S.W.D. Tiisip Gandaa, later B.S.T. Gandaa). During my father's lifetime, he owned two double-barrelled and one single-barrelled guns in his name as well as over ten capguns. He gave one of the double-barrelled guns which he had bought from a European for £75 to Tiisip and the single-barrelled one to John Dɛri Gandaa without officially transferring the licences to the names of his two sons. Tiisip travelled with this gun to Nandom and on his return was stopped at the Lawra police station where he sat with his gun at the front in the driver's cab. He was challenged, charged by the police and sent to court. He was found guilty and cautioned, but it went against him in the criminal records. I am sure that had Tiisip oiled the palm of the constable, which probably was what the latter was after, the case would have been dropped. I was surprised that the passport office could not differentiate between our initials in that one was S.W.D.K. and the other was S.W.D.T. Besides I spelt my surname differently, according to the pronunciation of the Birifu people, whereas my brothers followed the pronunciation of the Dagaar. Anyway, the error was pointed out to them and within a month or two I was issued with the passport.

The North-west Districts used to organise inter-district games called the North West Games. This was introduced and organised on the same basis as the Highland Games in Scotland by the Government Agent, Westland Adams, himself a Scot. It was held between Wa, Lawra and Tumu in the North-West. The Games this year were to take place in Lawra for they had taken place in Tumu the previous year when the Lawra Nũũ came with a contingent of dancers who performed the sɛbri dance at the Tumu Koro's palace. Being the chairman of the Lawra District Council, my brother, the Birifu Nũũ also attended and I put him up. As they were both chiefs from my area, I gave my brother a ram and another to the Lawra Nũũ but my brother violently objected to my giving one to the Lawra Nũũ, an objection which I ignored. It might have been at that meeting that the Lawra Nũũ invited the Tumu Koro to visit Lawra when it came round to the turn of Lawra to host the games. When the time came for the Games to take place, the Tumu Koro travelled ahead with the Government Agent of Tumu, leaving his driver to bring up the rear with his two wives and his younger brother, Issaka Kanton. I had wanted to travel to the Games by the Government Transport lorry which normally arrived from Lawra at about mid-day and returned an hour later, but when I realised there was room in the Tumu Koro's car, I asked the driver if he could give me lift. He was at first hesitant, afraid of what his master would say if he picked me up without authority, but Issaka urged him to give me the lift. We set off between nine and ten o'clock in the morning and met the Government Transport at the junction town of Han. Han is about 32 miles from Lawra and by eleven we had travelled a further eight miles and passed the village of Ulu.

As we went down to the Kaani valley, there was a blind and acute bend before we could reach and traverse the bridge. At the speed at which the driver was going, it would have been impossible for him to manoeuvre the bend. I opened my mouth to warn him of the dangerous blind bend and to let him slow down, and had hardly finished my sentence when all of a sudden we found ourselves plunging deep into the dried bed of the dam. I shut my eyes as we rolled down some yards from the road before stopping, and when I opened my eyes again we had stopped in front of stubble. There was a brief silence in the car, then the driver called out my name and I replied. He called out to Issaka sitting next to him at the front but there was no reply from him. Both the driver and I got out of the car and I carried the two wives of the Tumu Koro from the deep valley on to the road as the driver was a little man who could hardly lift them. Issaka had been wedged in by the door on his side. When we eventually forced it open, he slumped to the ground like a log. I believed he had fainted. Issaka was one and a half times my body weight and I tried to revive him on the rugged surface in the valley but without success. I asked the driver to assist me to carry him to the road side but his help made little impact. With great difficulty, I managed to drag him up the valley on to the road. Here, he at last came to, but I was totally exhausted. We waited at the road side for the return of the mail lorry and by about three in the afternoon, it pulled up as I hailed it down. He let us go on his vehicle and we travelled the rest of the eighteen mile journey to Lawra. There he drove us straight to the hospital where I saw to it the injured were admitted while the Tumu Koro's driver went to alert him of the accident.

After the Games we returned to Tumu. As I learnt some years later, Issaka who had passed out while I was evacuating them from the car, told his audience in Tumu that I had vanished as soon as the car crashed and that he later saw me returning to the scene of the accident from a distance to give help. This implied that I either used black magic to escape before the accident occurred or that I used the art of witchcraft to do so. I believe the latter was in his mind since he was in Lawra school when I was stigmatised as a wizard.

In April 1955 we were to have the first annual NPP conference in Tamale. The new General Secretary was one Ziblim Cockra and the Propaganda Secretary was Imoru Salifu. When the NPP was formed a year before at the weekend of April 10 and 11, we did not have any funds. Our first van was donated to us by an Accra lawyer, Kwasi Lamptey. Unfortunately the North-West saw no propaganda work done with this van even though the four MPs were paying their dues. As a source of income it was decided after the General Elections that all MPs in the party donate at source the sum of £10 a month into the party coffers for the efficient running of the party. At this conference it seemed the two paid officers of the party had been spending the money without any audit being made of the accounts. I therefore suggested that their books ought to be audited from time to time to see that the money, which came only from the MPs, was well spent. Jatoe Kaleo agreed with me. But Imoru Salifu and Ziblim Cockra disagreed, accusing us of not trusting them. However, I have always agreed with the maxim that "he who pays the piper calls the tune," so it was suggested that Jatoe and I should audit the books. Despite the meeting appointing us as auditors, the two officers failed to present the books to us for auditing before we left Tamale after the meeting.

CHAPTER TWENTY

THE NLM'S SLOGAN LITERALLY STOOD for separation but it had been transformed to mean Federation or Federalism in order to encompass the other opposition parties in the country. We met in Kumasi at the Prempeh Assembly Hall where all parties opposed to Nkrumah were represented. We spent the whole weekend debating the complicated issues of federalism and thrashing out any disagreements that occurred. Prior to that, I had had a lengthy debate with Dennis Austin on this subject while travelling from Tumu to Lawra and the next day we continued this debate from Lawra to Wa and then on to Damongo arriving there at midnight. Dennis tried to convince me that Federalism was not good for the north, and that the NTs could not stand on their own. British politicians and writers on politics had always believed that the centralised Westminster type of parliamentary system was suitable for their colonies and therefore for the Gold Coast at that time. Consequently, Dennis Austin, whose knowledge I respected, tried to convince me about that. But the British colonial system did not lend itself to a unitary system. Theirs was to divide and rule.

I vehemently countered his arguments and when he could not convince me he promised to lend me two books written by K. C. Wheare namely, *Government by Committees* and *Federal Constitution*, from the library of the Department of Extra-Mural Studies of the University College of the Gold Coast. True to his word he brought these two books to me in Tumu the following week. These books were at that time heavy reading and I tried to work my way through them. Reading them also armed me for any discussions at the conference on the Federal Constitutional proposals, which was now taking place in Kumasi. I was glad to agree with the views of most constitutional lawyers such as J.B. Danquah. The Northerners present at this constitutional conference included S.D. Dombo, Mumuni Bawumia, Salifu Imoru, B.K. Adama and myself. After the meeting when signatures were required from delegates I declined to sign but Chief Dombo insisted that I did since I had participated in the debate. After the meeting, Bafuor Osei Akoto offered Chief Dombo and myself a lift in his car. On the way, I happened to mention that in the north we did not believe in the CPP slogan "SG Now!" and of course he thought that it was political suicide for me to say so. This was because most southerners were drawn into the false belief that independence would bring "milk and honey" to all and sundry. Of course it did bring milk and honey to a few but not to all and sundry. He tried to convince me all that evening in his car, but since we had different political platforms he was unable to get me to accept his views. I told him it would also be political suicide if I went to the North-west and canvassed on the slogan "Self-government Now!"

Chief Dombo's Hillman van was in the workshop while we were at the conference and after it was over, the engineer advised him to get a new car as his was nearing the end of its life span. Dombo saw a Humber Sunbeam car that was in the show room and wanted to buy it on hire purchase. However, the chief was asked to provide two guarantors. The payment would then be met by those person should he falter in his repayments. Of course Chief Dombo had no one in Kumasi of financial substance who could stand surety for him. I told him that I would speak to R.R. Amponsah to feel out if he would stand surety with another person. He told me he had nothing to use as surety but he would consult Bafuor Osei Akoto to see if he would oblige. They were hesitant at first, which is not surprising as the chief had not been known to them for long. However they later agreed to stand surety for him and the next day we went to the Hillman garage where all the papers were signed and we picked up the car the next morning. This engineer could have given him the car as an Opposition Leader and he would sign an undertaking with the Speaker's Office so the money could be deducted at source. But this white man could not find in his power to do so.

The MP for the Atwima Nwabiagya constituency had a fatal accident which left a vacant seat in the Assembly. The bye-election for the constituency was scheduled for July, 14, 1955. B.F. Kusi was nominated as the NLM candidate for the constituency. It was one of the most memorable bye-elections I ever had the opportunity to witness. During the canvassing both the CPP and the NLM swarmed into the area with their agents. There was antagonism between the NLM Action Groups and CPP Action Troops. Pepper was sprinkled into the eyes of opponents. But one incident would have marred the bye-election had it been allowed to be carried out. The CPP sent their heavy guns into the constituency including three cabinet ministers, Welbeck, Botsio, and Aaron Ofori Atta. Some members of the Action Group who knew the route these ministers would pass, went and placed some explosives in the middle of the road and waited to detonate them as they came through. It was with luck that R.R. Amponsah was informed; for he immediately ordered these boys to go and remove the explosives before the two ministers, Welbeck and Botsio, were wiped out. According to Mr. Amponsah, the explosives were removed seconds before the ministers passed.

Hilla decided to leave for the UK in October 1955. The Tumu District Council had already voted a lump sum of £200 during our financial estimates which had been approved by the office of the Chief Regional Officer. News of Hilla's departure for the UK soon spread in town and in the entire region like an inferno. John Oseini, Egala's propaganda secretary in Tumu, was bragging that Egala had promised to prevent Hilla and me from leaving Accra for Britain. I had not heard this from Egala himself but it was said he would prevent us from leaving the Gold Coast for the UK. Hilla resigned about a month earlier from the teaching service to get ready and leave for the south en route for Britain. As a servant of the Council, that body should have been responsible for the transport for him and his family to Gwollu. But when the day came for him to leave, there was no transport made available. We held a farewell party for him in the yard of the house in which I had my lodgings. So after the party I asked his direct cousin, Aduna Issifu, the Clerk of Council at the time, why the Council had refused to sanction transport for the move. My friendship with Hilla had become so close and intense that I could not sit aside and have his cousin humiliate him in that manner. I ordered the Council truck to take Hilla and the family to Gwollu at my cost, which was only £17. When Hilla saw his family well settled in the village he returned to Tumu and we left together for Kumasi. In Kumasi, we went to confirm the air ticket which he had made me reserve a month or so earlier. Being known to Nancy Tsiboe and the proprietor husband, John, of the *Ashanti Pioneer*, I went to ask if we could have a lift on one of their delivery vans going to Accra that night. The editor of the paper, Dumolga, a political ally, was present and told one of the drivers to give us the lift. We were given a free lift and by early morning we were in Accra. We stayed at the Government transit quarters till evening when we moved to the airport where we booked into the Lisbon Hotel. Luckily we met a young boy, a cousin of Meliga Bamford, whom I knew during our college days at Bole but who was now working at the hotel as a steward. I told him to take good care of my friend. The next morning after giving him a good tip we found our way to the airport where Hilla checked in and took off an hour or so later. I returned to Kumasi, purchased my goods and returned to

Tumu by the earliest available transport. On arrival I told John Oseini that Hilla had left for Britain and there was no one at the airport to stop him flying.

When I saw Hilla off and returned to Tumu, I took it upon myself to organise the NPP in Tumu. First of all, I tried to unite the young lads against any possible defeat by the CPP in any future General Elections. Not only were the young lads alienated by Mr Egala but some of the chiefs were also alienated by the Tumu Koro who was then the President of the Traditional Council. I was told that he threatened to destool all those chiefs who supported their sons or relations against Mr Egala during the 1954 General Election. The chiefs in question were the Zini Koro, the Gwollu Koro, the Pulma Koro and the Wallembellia Koro, all of whom supported their relations who were candidates in the last General Election, although the Zini Koro who supported Hilla was an exception. Armed with my knowledge of the oral history of the area, I told these chiefs they had nothing to worry about since they were on equal par with the Tumu Koro before the advent of the Native Authority system. So I had gotten allies in the form of these chiefs and they did nothing without first consulting me. The only obstacle was to select a prospective candidate whom the majority of the electorate in the constituency would support. I organised a meeting and asked each of them whom they would like to have stand on an NPP ticket since most, if not all of them, now supported the NPP and its aims. Although I would have liked George Nandzo to be the candidate for the Tumu constituency, the majority of the young lads settled for Mumuni Dimbie. Mumuni was a virile young man who was both a great womaniser and a spend-thrift. One or two of his mates had slight misgivings on that score. After he had been accepted by these young lads, my immediate advice to him was that he should refrain from womanising with the wives or girl friends of his supporters lest he antagonise them. But it seemed he paid no heed to my warning as we shall see a few months later. Having convinced the young lads to nominate Mumuni as the prospective candidate to oppose Egala in any future elections, I wrote to my friend, Hilla Limann in Britain about our decision. I received a reply from him confirming our choice and informing me he had written to his uncle, the Gwollu Koro, asking them to support me.

On November 4, there was an important visitor to Tumu, Sir Arden-Clarke, whom the chiefs and people were asked to gather to welcome. In the evening I held a rally behind my shop to launch a branch of the NPP in Tumu. It was well received and I approached the chiefs such as the Wallembellia Koro, the Zini Koro, the Gwollu Koro, the Pulma Koro and the Fielmon Nũũ who had given their support to my prospective candidate. After the meeting and my rally to launch the NPP branch, John Oseini and a few small boys came to heckle and interrupt our speeches but without much success. One day, after the inauguration of the branch, John Oseini, who usually came into my shop for a drink and a jest, entered and after drinking a bottle or two of beer, started arguing about party politics with me. I told him with my tongue in my cheek that during the next general election, my candidate was going to win and if we failed, I would go and hang myself. This was meant as a joke between John and myself. But when Egala came on one of his trips from Accra to Tumu, I understood John blurted out to Egala what was meant to be a joke between us. Egala took an exception to what John told him about me. He went on his soap box and made derogatory remarks about me and at the end of his speech, threw me a challenge saying that he heard that if during the next election my candidate failed to win, I said I would hang myself. He was giving me a warning that if at the next election my candidate failed to win and I did not hang myself, he would let the youths in town beat me to death. When I returned from Kumasi with my merchandise, my worried wife told me of Egala's threat to my life. The next morning when I woke up everybody was telling me of Egala's threat, but I paid no heed to it. Anyway towards evening, I also went on the soap box and told my audience that what I told John Oseini was meant as a joke, but since Egala had personally challenged me I was taking up his challenge. If at the next elections my candidate failed to win and I did not hang myself, then I was not the son of my father but a bastard. In other words I swore by my father in the grave to hang myself if my candidate failed to win (this is a very serious Dagara oath and can only be rescinded by sacrifices to the ancestral shrine). I urged John to tell his master that what he had heard from me was the truth and no longer a jest.

The NLM had promised to donate a van to the NPP for our political propaganda. They had bought a new Peugeot van with loud speakers mounted on it and one day when I was in Kumasi it was decided to hand the vehicle to me so I could take it back to the north and hand over to the chief. It meant employing a driver to drive the vehicle there. Luckily, my brother Sunkuol, for whom I had managed to obtain a driving licence, was staying with me at that time and working at Kingsway Hardware shop where I usually bought cement and iron rods. As there was already a driver, Sunkuol worked as a store assistant. So I did not have to look far for a driver and I went to Kingsway after my brother had reported for work and spoke to the Stores Manager, Mr Menu, after talking to his assistant, Mr Ocran, to ask if he could release my brother to drive the van for me. With reluctance Sunkuol was released and I went with him to take delivery of the van. At the same time, there were two girls from Nandom studying at the Holy Child College, Cape Coast, who were on their way home for holidays and asked for a lift. I agreed and by dusk we had arrived at Wa. As I was passing to Tumu, I took them to show the van to B.K. Adama. I asked him if he could accommodate the girls for the night and find transport for them the next day. He agreed to house them and to drive them to Nandom the following day. Sunkuol and I left for Tumu arriving there between nine and ten in the evening.

The next day after lunch we drove sixty-nine miles to Lawra arriving early in the afternoon. I presented the van to Chief Dombo and A. Karbo and the next day we went to Nandom and held a rally for the people at the market after the majority had come out of the church from Mass. My brother was confirmed as the driver for the van with Adamu Wala who was the propaganda secretary. The van was stationed in Wa but was to travel round from constituency to constituency in the area. After the rally Sunkuol drove me back to Tumu and the following day I despatched him to Wa to report to B.K. Adama. After that I saw very little of the van as it was mostly used in the Wala South constituency. In Tumu things were heating up as the young lads and some of the elders in town turned hostile to me. Prior to that, when I was in the good books of the Tumu Koro, John's father Oseini was one of the elders of Tumu whom the chief had authorised to mark out two plots in the Zongo, for which I paid the traditional fees so I could put up some buildings. Now Oseini elder had decided I was not entitled to the plots at all. I had already put up a building on one of them and the other which still lay vacant was given to a Gũ man who was working in the District Administration as a carpenter. Even the plot on which I built five rooms, he gave it to one man, Bawa Frafra, popularly known at that time as Bawa Fitter and threatened to burn down the building. The building cost me nearly a thousand pounds, about £960 to be exact. I was even told to pack my things and go back to my country as I was an alien. But the one I pitied most was my young son, Kofi, who was only five at that time. He was very good for his age and I felt he could benefit if he went to school. Anyway the headteacher felt he was too young but told me he could go to the school as a visitor. Every day Kofi went to school he was ambushed by the boys from the chief's compound and thrashed. When I heard of this I tried to stop him from going to the school. Yet every day he would cry until he had his way.

That year in April the NPP were having their annual conference in Bawku. Chief Dombo had given me his old Hillman van to use in my constituency. Joe Appiah, Victor Owusu and Nancy Tsiboe were touring the North-West constituencies on their way to Bawku to attend the conference. It turned out that the day they were to visit Tumu was to be on the market day. In Tumu the Postmaster, one Mr Ntim from Akim Abuakwa area, was a personal friend of mine and joked with my little two-year-old daughter, Agatha, about becoming his future wife. I supplied some yams and meat for Mr Ntim's girl friend to prepare food for my visitors while Ntim's fridge was stocked with beer and soft drinks for their refreshment when they arrived. As soon as they came and I saw them settled in Ntim's quarters, I took my van and drove to the market to broadcast the news of the evening rally in the Zongo and to announce the arrival of my guest speakers. Unfortunately, some small boys in the Tumu Koro's compound were incited to throw stones at the van. One of them, Basuɔlo, shattered the screen with a stone and ran off. Luckily at this time there was now a police post in Tumu manned by a sergeant who was a Dagara like myself. I reported the case to him and when he took action against the boy, Issaka Kanton turned this into tribal feud. He accused this police constable, one Sgt. Kaŋmina, of practising nepotism or tribalism. Anyway Joe Appiah and the others were frightened and decided not to speak at the rally so to my disgust it was cancelled. I left with them for Bawku. We passed the night on the road at Chiana and the following morning we left for Bawku arriving there at about two o'clock where Imoru Salifu showed us our lodgings. I met Adamu and my brother with the van. Indeed my brother was driving Imoru Salifu around as he broadcast through the loud speakers the news of our arrival as well as of the conference as a whole. However I was disgusted when I saw Adamu (Wala) soliciting money from some of our guests from Ashanti to buy cigarettes. I immediately told him he was a disgrace to us all and he should desist from this disgraceful act. As he pushed me out of his way, he told me I was not his boss and that only Ziblim and Imoru could tell him off and not me.

At that moment, a grudge I bore him a few years back returned to my mind. When my driver, Tang, falsely reported me to the Asantehene's police for having falsified his signature and collected his money, Adamu, whom I did not know and had never set eyes on before, testified to the police that he could bear witness that I had done it. I felt this was the time to take revenge on him; I held him by the hand, which he used to push me away, and whipped him to the ground, to use the wrestler's term, and then stamped on his chest whilst he struggled beneath my foot. Some of the members of the NLM Action Group who came in attendance and who knew me very well in Kumasi, begged me to leave him alone which I did. But I was ashamed of myself for losing my temper in front of them. It soon became the gossip of the evening and came to the ears of Chief Dombo. He asked me why I had to fight Adamu and when I told him the disgraceful attitude of Adamu, he also rebuked him for it.

Apart from that the conference went well all through the weekend. After the conference we and our distinguished guests went from Bawku along a south-east road to Nalerigu, the seat of the Nayiri (chief of the Mamprusis), to pay homage to him. Although most of the roads in the north were muddy ones, this particular one was really perilous, especially ascending and descending this scarp which we had to traverse before entering Gambaga. The Nayiri was very pleased to see our guests from Ashanti. This was the first time I had ever passed that way and the first time I had ever been to Nalerigu or Gambaga. From Nalerigu we went to Tamale for our guests to proceed to Kumasi. I returned to Tumu to see about the case I had earlier reported to the police about the vandalism caused to my van. Although a juvenile the boy was charged with this vandalism and brought to court. He was cautioned and not sent to a remand school, which did not exist in the north at that time.

After the case, I travelled to the south to have the van completely overhauled and also to buy my merchandise and drums of petrol, which I had begun to sell in Tumu. At that time petrol was sold in 44-gallon drums and dispensed through hand pumps at petrol stations. As I bought all my petrol from John Holt, the firm had supplied me with a hand pump as well as drums of petrol on credit which I sold and paid back every month. This trade became handy when the 1956 General Election campaign became active. While in Kumasi the NLM executive did not only agree to pay for the cost of the repair to my van but they decided to buy a new loud speaker to fix to the top so I could use it in the campaign. In Bafuor Osei Akoto's house the executive of the NLM were discussing the strategy of their campaign when I went to bid them goodbye before leaving for the north. Bafuor Osei Akoto promised me that if I managed to defeat Mr Egala he would give me a ram. This would be worth between £10 and £15 in

Kumasi at that time depending on its size. One other person, Mr Osei Baidoo, an Organiser of the Department of Extra-Mural Studies who knew me at Peoples' Educational Association conferences and at the New Year and Easter Schools, also promised me a ram if I defeated Mr Egala.

In the north-west the CPP candidates were Hamidu Yakubu, my school chum and an Agricultural Assistant who had only recently been gazetted as a Government civil servant, who stood for the Wala-South constituency, Daramani Dagarti, a District Council driver who was for the Wala-North constituency, my brother, Nuɔnatuo Gandah, the Birifu Nũũ, who was standing for the Lawra-Nandom constituency, Gbari Gariba, Clerk of Council for the Lawra District Council, who was for the Jirapa-Lambusie constituency, whilst Imoru Egala was for Tumu. The NPP on the other hand had Jatoe Kaleo and B.K. Adama standing for Wala-North and Wala-South respectively, Abayifaa Karbo for Lawra-Nandom, S.D. Dombo for Jirapa-Lambusie and Mumuni Dimbie for Tumu. When Nkrumah came round to nominate his candidates, I was at Birifu when he nominated my brother and promised him a ministerial post in health. I told him that he was wasting time on nominating my brother, for he would never win the election. He wanted to know who I was and Nuɔnatuo fobbed him off and called me his mad brother. When I learnt that my school chum whom I greatly adored was standing in Wala-South as a CPP candidate, I wrote a letter to him trying to persuade him not to stand in the election on any party ticket. Being a government civil servant, the election regulations at the time meant that he would lose his post that he had trained for if he stood and lost the election. When Hamidu replied, he told me that he did not believe the letter he received was genuine since he thought that my handwriting was none others than Kaleo's. I did not understand why he should mistake my writing with that of Kaleo's. Anyway I felt that if I persisted to argue with him, I might be accused of persuading a CPP candidate not to stand because my own candidate was standing. However that was far from my mind since I knew he was no contestant for B.K. Adama.

A year earlier the Wa Nũũ had given a lift to his personal friend, the Dorimon Nũũ, but met with an accident in which the Dorimon Nũũ died. He was sent to jail for the crime, but his cousin B.K. Adama appealed on his behalf. I was in Kumasi when B.K. Adama came and sought my help to recommend a good lawyer for him. Mr Akainya had just returned from the UK as a qualified barrister and a promising one at that. Rumours had it that prior to going to Britain, he was a police officer who used to prosecute. I introduced B.K. to him and he was hired. Anyway Lawyer Akainya petitioned and got the Wa Nũũ freed. This riled some of B.K. Adama's supporters in Wa. It seemed that members of the Ahmadiyya Movement in Wa blamed B.K. Adama for helping his cousin to be acquitted and decided not to support his candidature. They wanted to put up one Sidiki as the candidate.[58] At that time Malam Issah had won a contract from the Tumu District Council to build the Middle Boarding School and he spent most of his time in town. Indeed, he hired the whole block of my new house for his accommodation. Anyway when he learnt that the NPP was nominating B.K. Adama as our candidate for Wala-South, he confronted me in Tumu and told me that they the Ahmadiyyas would not support his candidature because he helped arrange for his cousin to be acquitted and saved from destoolment. I told Malam Issah that he was confusing religious conflicts with politics and family matters. I told him I was NPP and my brother pro-CPP but if he was in jail, I would not stand aside and let him be jailed. I would do all in my power to get him out of that jail. If I approached him as a friend, would he help me get my brother out or refuse to do so because he was pro-CPP? Of course he saw the folly in their argument and said he would return and speak to their head, Malam Salih.

When the Legislative Assembly was dissolved and the election papers filed, the campaign began in earnest. I had five constituencies to cover. In Tumu my candidate was a man of very little means. He was a Certificate B teacher paid only five pounds a month with two pounds headteacher's allowance, who was facing a minister with ample means apart from what the CPP had pumped into the district. For according to my brother, the Birifu Nũũ, Mr Egala was given £2,000 for the five constituencies, so that he expected £400 from Egala to run his campaign. When he did not get his part of the campaign money, he started to grumble about it. He did not know that Egala had a lot of trouble to cope with in his own constituency. For the first few days of the campaign, Egala's new Rover 2000 car got stuck several times on the muddy roads and needed to be dug out, partly because his driver was not used to the roads up north and partly because the Rover was a heavier vehicle than my Hillman van. Any time my van got stuck on the road, between the three of us we would get down and lift the back of the vehicle and place it on dry ground, then would lift the front and place it on the dry ground and drive off. It seemed God was on our side as far as mishap was concerned whilst all the mishaps befell my friend, Mr Egala. For within a week his new engine had burst whilst my old van was working like clockwork. We went into the villages I had never been to before. But after a few days, I found my campaign was not getting to the electorate, so I decided to change tactics by campaigning at night, and that worked.

This was the farming season and the rains at this time of the year were always very heavy. By dawn everybody was at the farm until dusk. It was difficult to get to canvass the ordinary voters during the day. We therefore decided to stay at home to rest during the day until late afternoon about four o'clock, when I would send my driver to Wallembellia to pick up Mumuni Dimbie if the campaign was in Gwollu, Zini, Fiɛlmon or any villages west of Tumu. However, if the campaign was around Sakai along the road to Wallembellia and beyond, then I would go with the driver to pick up Mumuni so we campaigned from there. I was surprised that any time we went out at night to remote villages where I had never been, the villagers recognised me as soon as they heard the music blurting out from my loud speakers. We often played the music for some time and when we had gathered a sufficient crowd of villagers we delivered our message and moved on to another village. The campaign was not whether we wanted self-government now or self-government at our own pace but whether we wanted to be governed from the south as a unit or governed in the north by our own people in any kind of federalism. The majority of these villagers had been to the south and seen how they were being discriminated against as inferior beings. Consequently, Nkrumah's "self-government now" was obviously rejected in favour of federalism and the gradual development to independence at our own pace. After campaigning all night, we normally returned home at dawn to sleep out our tiredness. Sometimes if we were going to campaign during the day, we brought Mumuni to town to sleep at a friend's, and set out after a late lunch at about two thirty in the afternoon.

I was informed that Mr Egala was dishing out money to the chiefs in the villages to gain their support. As the majority of the northerners at that time were very honest, those who were given such money by Egala approached me to advise them about what they should do with it. The lowest amount some of these chiefs received was a five pound note, and most chiefs or headmen had never been paid that much by their Local Councils; and even if they were paid at all, the amount would have been far less than five pounds. For instance the Birifu Nũũ, who was paid by a wealthier Local Council, was at that time receiving three pounds ten shillings. It would therefore have been politically suicidal to tell a chief or headman not to accept such moneys. I had to visit all these villages where our support was greatest advising them to accept the money received from Mr Egala even though it was against the electoral law to bribe any person to vote for you. I told them that my candidate had not a penny to bribe any of them to vote for us and even if we had we would not offer it; our only bribe would be to tell them only the truth. So if they believed in our campaign they could spend the money and still vote for NPP, and there was nothing anyone could do about it. In other words the decision rested with their conscience and they had the final say.

In the 1954 campaign I had found it difficult to convince the Fiɛlmon Nũũ to support Hilla Limann because the Tumu Koro had already got on to him to support Mr Egala, and as I was a Dagara, since the illiterate ones especially hated to have "forked tongues", the Chief told me to campaign to the people direct as he had already given them his word. However, in this 1956 campaign he was all out for my candidate and received us very cordially any time we went there.

Though not a paid official, I was responsible for the five constituencies in the North-west and I planned my strategy in such a way that I could visit each of them at least once or twice a week before the election date. Jatoe Kaleo and Chief Dombo did not have stiff opposition, but B.K. Adama, Mumuni Dimbie and A. Karbo had. I therefore concentrated more in the Tumu constituency than any of the five, only visiting the two constituencies in the Lawra District on the Babile market days and Sundays and I went once or twice to Wa town to canvass for B.K. Adama. On the Babile market days I was not only campaigning against the Birifu Nũũ, who was my brother, but for S.D. Dombo, B.K. Adama and Jatoe Kaleo, some of whose constituents used to congregate at this focal point on these days. Both Karbo and I usually spoke on the same platform. At Babile I tried to convince the voters, especially the people of Birifu, that this was not a battle between the people of Birifu and those of Lawra; for if it had been, I would take up my bow and arrows and fight on the side of my brother and not on the side of Karbo. My brother, I told my audience, could not even represent them in the District Council where he was elected the Chairman but had drunk himself stupid and lost any chance of his re-election as chairman. I was canvassing against him because he was not the right candidate and Karbo was. Besides, the Birifu Nũũ had never been a CPP supporter but was an opportunist. If he was elected he would get drunk in the Accra drinking bars instead of acting on their behalf in the Assembly. Of course, just as he disowned me in front of Nkrumah when he came to select him as his candidate for the constituency, he disowned me as not being his brother but a Wangara from the Upper Volta. The election campaign was often covered by the CID constable who would take down any inflammatory speeches that might lead to a breach of the peace and on this particular day it was being covered by Mr. Sori, who was in the CID of the Gold Coast Police but is now a retired diplomat.

CHAPTER TWENTY-ONE

AFTER MY POLITICAL DEBATE WITH my brother at the Babile market, Karbo and I together with members of his party drove about half a mile to Kofi Nsiah's bar opposite the Agricultural Station to buy some drinks to quench our thirst. There I met my brother carousing. I teased him suggesting he offer my party some drinks since he had made us thirsty with his heckling and to this he agreed. After we had finished drinking what he had offered to us, Karbo also bought some drinks for all of us to consume. There was no animosity between the members of our political parties, unlike in some other parts of the country where politics divided families and brought hatred through its activities.

On Sundays we always had a very heavy schedule of campaigning. We often left Lawra before eight in the morning for Nandom where the majority of the mission teachers, as well as those of the District Council, were our supporters. Where the support for the Birifu Nũũ and for Karbo was divided, I harped on the same message which I delivered at the Babile market, that were it a family battle between the Karbos and the Gandahs, I would be on my brother's side. After the morning Mass was over I attracted a large crowd to the platform with my music played over the microphone. The microphone itself was novel to them at that time and within a short while, we had a crowd of about ten to twenty deep intently listening to our speeches. After my short introductory speech, I handed the microphone to Karbo and Chief Dombo. It was at this meeting that my two brothers, the Birifu Nũũ and his agent, Biz, were booed out of the gathering when they came to heckle me during my speech. After our speeches we drove down to Lambusie where we paid homage to the Busie Koro, Salifu Dy-Yakah, after which we retraced part of our steps to the Koo market where the mission there had finished with the morning Mass and people were enjoying the market. We delivered our speeches and campaigned on the way through Zimuɔpari to Lissa until we arrived at Doŋmini where there was a funeral in progress. We went to the funeral parlour to pay our respects to the deceased and then to the xylophone area to sympathise with the mourners. We then moved on to Jirapa through Tizza before the market there could pack up. Here Chief delivered his speech and then we went and paid homage to the Jirapa Nũũ, Bapɔɔyiri Yelpoi, who was now our ardent supporter.

In the Wala-South constituency, I met my school friend, Hamidu Yakubu, busy campaigning in the town and I went to wish him good luck in his campaigning, and hoped that the best man might win. While I was canvassing for my candidate in Wa town, I was approached by an arrogant and eccentric middle-aged woman, Assana Wala, popularly known as Assana Gyaŋgyaahũũ (literally, "Assana the crazy lady"), who proclaimed herself to be the leader of the CPP women in Wa. Even before the advent of the CPP, Assana had proclaimed herself the leader of the Wa market women and was feared by all the women who went to the various markets around Wa. Assana questioned my audacity to be on the other side of the political fence from that of my senior brother. When I tried to explain to her that no one was obliged to join a particular political party or any party at all because their relation joined it, she threatened to remove the dirty underwear (mungana) she was wearing underneath her cloth and stuff it in my mouth. The word *mungana* (literally, a cover for the vagina) is a Wala word that describes the sort of underwear worn by most women in the Gold Coast before underpants became popular in modern Ghana. This was a strip of red poplin sold to women and in the north, it was popularly given a nickname, "the Union Jack". I dared her to do so, saying it would be the end of her life. At that juncture, her supporters were pleading with her to get away from me as they had other places to visit in order to cover their campaign for the day.

When Bapɔɔyiri failed to win the 1954 General Elections in his constituency, he returned to the teaching field and a year or so later his father died. Bapɔɔyiri combined his teaching with that of acting as regent. Had tradition been followed, the Sabuli Nũũ, Gariba, being second in command to the Jirapa Nũũ, would have acted as chief for the Jirapa division, as Gandah did when Bini of Lawra died or Gyiɛlɛ of Guo did when Konkuu of Nandom died. But it seemed that Gariba's position was hijacked by the two literate chiefs in that division, the Tizza Nũũ and the Duori Nũũ. For these two chiefs had elevated themselves to the subchief status. I am not sure whether this was officially recognised by the Government or not, but if it was not, it could pose chieftaincy problems in that division in the future. Being Chief Dombo's personal secretary, I found myself involved in the organisation and preparation for the installation. Kofi Nsiah was now an established building contractor in the district and was commissioned to make a big chair resembling a throne for the occasion. On the day of the installation all the important chiefs in the division had assembled awaiting the arrival of the other divisional chiefs and people, especially the Lawra Nũũ, who was then the President of the Lawra Confederacy Native Authority. The chiefs of Duori, S.D. Dombo and of Tizza, Dakura Ŋminwule, with myself in attendance, led the heir apparent, Bapɔɔyiri Yelpoi, to the centre of the congregation where his throne had been placed for his installation as the Jirapa Nũũ. His hat was brought by the teŋdana and placed on him before the medallion was hung round his neck by the Lawra Nũũ.

After the installation there was mirth and jollity in the town with music and dancing. From morning to evening I had eaten nothing all day apart from a few cups of tea and by evening I was very tired and hungry. After finishing my duties of seeing that all the distinguished guests had been entertained, I returned to Babile Imoru's house in Jirapa to get something to eat, as I was to pass the night there. After an evening meal, I stretched on a mat on the floor hardly knowing when I passed out in a deep slumber. When I woke up it was nearly midnight and the music and dancing still continued. The brass band which was brought from Wa was still playing when I got up. The girls in the band were led by Babile Imoru's sister-in-law who was married to one teacher and a school mate of mine, Kenneth Mumuni Bɔmɔ, the son of Wa Nũũ Bɔmɔ (now a chief and an Education Officer in Wa). In fact they were the people who entered the room and woke me up with their noise. As I was still clad in my attire, I went out to join the music and dancing till the early hours of the morning when I retired to put in a few hours of sleep before daybreak. I woke up very early in the morning to get ready and return to Lawra with Chief Dombo. The part played in the installation by Chief Dombo and the Tizza Nũũ must have endeared them to the Jirapa Nũũ, for they became his right hand men in the traditional council.

IN BRITAIN THE WORKERS EDUCATIONAL ASSOCIATION (WEA) sent their members to Ruskin College, Oxford, for further studies. When the PEA was formed in the Gold Coast, just like Ruskin College in Oxford, Fircroft College, Selly Oaks, Solihull in Birmingham offered a place to members of the PEA every year to study a social science subject. The first recipient of this award was the chief of Kejebi (Kejebihene) in British Togo (then the Trans-Volta region, now the Volta Region). However when I became an active member of the PEA in the north, at one of our Easter School Conferences I was elected to the executive of the Association as an Assistant Treasurer, which I had Dennis Austin to thank for. Dennis was the Resident Tutor for Ashanti in 1951/52 and from the 1952/53 to the 1955/56 academic year he was the Resident Tutor for the Northern Territories. He knew most of the Ashanti and the Northern delegates who frequented these conferences. Prior to this conference, in about March or April, 1955, Dennis had organised a weekend school in Lawra with members of the PEA from Tumu and Wa congregating there. Miss Lalage Bown, the Resident Tutor for the Trans-Volta region, travelled to the north and came with Dennis to Lawra for this weekend school. At the school on one evening, we organised an open forum where I managed to invite a few dignitaries to attend. We appealed for funds for the three PEA branches and at the close of day we had promises of over two hundred pounds from these dignitaries. The secretary for the Lawra Branch of the PEA was detailed to collect the donations and send the amounts for the Wa and Tumu branches to them. As far as I know we never had our share in Tumu.

At this conference Dennis knew that neither delegates from Ashanti nor from the North would command a majority if they contested for the national posts independently. On his suggestions, the Ashanti delegation was to fight for the post of Assistant Secretary while the north fought that of Assistant Treasurer. Dennis nominated me and in his nomination speech mentioned how I had managed to raise over two hundred pounds at a weekend school and if I could do that at branch level, I would be an asset at the national level. When the votes were taken, all the Ashanti votes came to me as well as from some delegates from other regions including those lecturers and organisers whom I had met and known over the years of attending the Easter and New Year Schools. Similarly in the case of the Ashanti delegate, the northern delegates voted for him. So it was a good tactical ploy adopted by Dennis. At this conference, instead of the usual puzzle, three persons were chosen to speak off the cuff for five minutes to describe the work they did daily. My friend, Walter Birmingham, a lecturer at the University College, myself and another person, were the speakers; the other two volunteered willingly while Dennis egged me on, with forceful persuasion from David Kimble. After we had returned from this Easter School I received a telegram from McGregor Mamattah, younger brother of Newlove and an assistant to David Kimble at the Department of Extra-Mural Studies, University College, Legon, asking me to attend an interview for an award to go to abroad for further studies. I was surprised as to the best of my knowledge I had not applied for any scholarship nor answered any advertisement.

All applicants were supposed to bring with them an essay of a certain length chosen from some set topics. At the Department, when David Kimble asked me for my essay, I told him that I had not received any notice of the topics that I was supposed to write about and therefore I had not written one. There and then I was given the paper, told to choose a topic and to write an essay on it. This was an unfair advantage for the other candidates, how many I did not know, who would have had time to collect material and prepare their essays. One or two months later I was told I was unsuccessful. But this mishap of mine must seem as if it was an omen that followed me all through my life; since I was never successful with free offers. While in the north Dennis and I worked very closely together and at one time he tried to convince me not to go abroad for further education but to take up an appointment with the Department of Extra-Mural Studies as an Organiser for the north on a salary of £650 a year which was more than graduates were receiving at that time (£400 a year), if I graduated and returned. I told him it was not the money I wanted but the quest for further knowledge. I believed he wanted me to take over from Mr Newlove Mamattah who was being transferred to the south.

Returning to the election campaign of 1956, recall my confrontation with Assana Wala in Wa, although I had never believed in political violence and had never encouraged my supporters in the north-west to adopt such attitudes in all my political campaigns. But I later learnt that in the Mamprusi area, especially in the Bawku area, such violence did take place. I understood one schoolmate of mine, Duglɔnyuɔlɛ (nicknamed Dugums), lost his life through this political violence. If these rumours were true, then I do blame Imoru Salifu who was our propaganda secretary and my good friend Bawumia, the party's vice-chairman, who should have stopped it. It could have been the reason why the NPP lost more seats in the Mamprusi area than we had anticipated.

On the last few days before the election day, I left the candidates in their constituencies to complete their last campaigning whilst I returned to Tumu to put on the finishing touches. We put polling agents in all the wards where we had the majority support to urge a good turn out. Instead of the five boxes for each ward for the five independent candidates in the 1954 election in Tumu, there were now two boxes for each ward for the two candidates. The slogan of the CPP was "Freedom" with its sign, the picture of a red cockerel, pasted on the box of each CPP candidate. The slogan of the NPP was "Unity" with the clenched fist as its sign on the candidates' boxes. The slogans were never pasted on the ballot boxes however.

In open spaces in the Tumu constituency, many temporary round huts were constructed as polling booths where there were no permanent structures that could be used as such. The ballot boxes were placed in these booths for the voters to enter one by one and cast their votes. These served as polling stations and the presiding officers sat outside under the shade of a tree with their books containing the ballot papers. On the eve of the voting day, July 12, 1956, I had travelled to Fiɛlmon where I expected heavy polling from supporters. I passed the night there and rallied my supporters very early in the morning. As polling agents, we were not allowed to canvass within two hundred yards of the polling booth. I only approached the polling area occasionally to see that the presiding officers were complying with the electoral rules they were supposed to follow. When polling came to a close and the two boxes had been sealed in my presence, I allowed my van to pick up those polling agents of mine returning to Tumu for the count while I travelled on the official vehicle carrying the boxes, guarded by a constable. We arrived at Tumu at about six thirty in the evening and when the boxes were safely locked up in the DC's office, I dashed home to have a quick wash and dinner so as to return on time for the count. When my candidate arrived from Wallembellia, I advised him to rest at Malam Dodo's house where he usually lodged when he was in Tumu and, if we were winning, I would send for him. If on the other hand we were losing, I would let the driver take him to his village while I stayed to face the music. After a quick wash and dinner I went back to the DC's office and after not very long Mr Pepys Cockerel, the Returning Officer, arrived and opened his office that was guarded by a police constable.

John Oseini, being Mr Egala's agent, and I, being Dimbie's, followed Pepys into his office together with the counting agents. George Dasent, a Veterinary Assistant for Tumu at the time, was a friend of both Mr Egala and myself, and did not take sides all through the campaigning. As soon as we took our seats the first two boxes were opened and almost all votes went to Mr Egala. Not very long after Mr Egala arrived and took his seat to the left of me. He was briefed by Pepys as to the position of the count. A few more boxes were opened and Egala's lead jumped by the hundreds but I was not perturbed since those boxes that had been opened came from neither of the wards where I had canvassed seriously nor in which my supporters had been numerous. The Presiding Officer provided beer for the refreshment of the counters and the candidates with their agents. At that time I had given up drinking and drank only mineral water. When I refused the beer offered to me, Pepys asked to know what I would prefer to drink and realising that the count would go into the early hours of morning, I asked for coffee so that it would keep me awake and alert all through the proceedings. Pepys sent to his bungalow for his wife to have coffee prepared for me. Within half an hour, his steward boy came with a two-pint flask of coffee and some sausages, which were offered to me. More ballot boxes were opened and as the counting continued, Mr Egala's lead widened into several hundreds. I could see some glee in the faces of both Egala and John as they consumed more of the beer that had been offered to them. Even George Dasent who was supposed to be neutral gave them once in a while an encouraging glancing smile. All this time I was still undaunted and returned them a sly and cheeky grin instead. As the boxes of the wards which supported Mr Egala had almost all been opened, his lead seemed not to be increasing in that exponential leap but the reverse. As the boxes of wards supporting us began to be counted, the gap began to narrow by leaps and bounds.

The boxes of our supporters so far opened were those from Wallembellia, Bugbellia, Duu and south Wallembellia areas. There were still boxes from Pulma, Gwollu, Zini and Fiɛlmon to be opened and counted. At this juncture, Egala began to smoke profusely as the counting continued and our speed gathered momentum, cutting his lead by the hundreds. When there were only a few boxes to be counted, I went out of the office to inform my driver, who was with some of our supporters in this cold rainy season weather, to go and bring Mumuni to the office where the counting was taking place. When Mumuni arrived and entered, he sat by me and wanted to know how the counting had gone so far. I told him we were now in the lead by a couple of hundreds. After the last box was opened and the votes counted, Mumuni had won by a majority of 341 votes and was duly declared the MP for Tumu before the small crowd that still waited outside to hear the declaration of the results. I knew that there would be trouble in town, so I asked my driver to drive Mumuni home to Wallembellia while I waited in Tumu to sense the atmosphere the next day and see what would happen to me. Going to bed about four o'clock in the morning, I woke up at nine only to be told that some boys from the chief's compound were outside threatening to kill me if I did not return to "my country", meaning Birifu.

It was a good thing I had sent Mumuni to Wallembellia. My landlord, who was called by his rank, Regimental Sergeant Major in the last war, and Adama, from Gwollu, the district driver and also a tenant, both loaded their shot guns and were prepared to defend my life. As much as I would like to keep a gun, I did not trust my anger enough to have a weapon on my person. I pleaded with them not to take the law into their own hands and to unload their guns for I did want them to mar our victory with bloodshed. My younger brother, Dɔndulɛ, who was running my shop with my wife and who had a much shorter fuse of anger than I had, wanted to go out and confront them as they chanted abuse at me and called me to come out of the house so they could kill me. I ordered him to stay put in the house while I went out to meet my supposed assailants. As I went outside, I saw Issaka Kanton's younger brother, Luriwie, who at that time would be about seventeen years old. He was with some other small boys from the chief's compound ranging between eight and twelve years old. It was a laugh when I saw them yelling insults at me. I told them I was there for them to kill but none of them dared to come forward to lay their hands on me, not even Luriwie, the eldest of them all. I told them to clear off lest I reported them to the DC for causing a breach of the peace. As I was addressing them one of them sneaked to the front of the house and pulled down a party flag that had been hoisted and set it on fire. I was incensed when my attention was drawn to this but when I went round the culprit had vanished.

I controlled my temper and tried to act according to the law. I walked across towards the DC's office to report the arson as they followed, about fifty yards behind me, casting stones which missed me by a mile. Anytime I turned to confront them, they would retreat and run as far away as they could. That was how this "cat and mouse" game continued until they were told by one of the elders and Debomo's in-law to clear off and stop their silliness. He was the orderly who formerly worked in the old dispensary but was now employed in the Health Centre. I went and reported the matter to the DC at his office and he told the Constable in charge to keep the peace in town. When I returned from the DC's office many of the people in the Zongo, who saw how I stood against these hooligans, thought I was heroic. But to me they were cowards playing the buffoon.

I had only about three months left before I left for the UK. I had to clear my shop and sell the few goods that were remaining. I had two fridges at that time that were run on kerosene which I had to get rid of. I sold the small one to Adama, the district truck driver, on credit for £75 and the other to Alidu Kanton from whom I had bought it in the first place at £45 for £30 also on credit. I might as well have given these to them free of charge, for neither of them paid a penny to my wife after I left the country. After the elections, I tried to make my wife and my brother, Dɔndulɛ, account for the sales in the shop and my uncle, Miiru, for the sale of the petrol. They could hardly account for these.

I travelled to Walewale where Debomo was doing some construction work to bid him goodbye. He gave me £30 as a farewell gift and towards the cost of my air fare to Britain which was £80. I had ordered a course of French Linguaphone records costing £17. 10s. from the UK and before I left, my brother, Tiisip was interested in them. When I went to bid him goodbye in Jirapa, he also gave me £15 as I handed the records to him. Chief Dombo also gave me £15, which I took to be my remuneration as his personal secretary, the payment of which had been very irregular. I was short of at least £30 to make up the air fare of £80. This would have been no problem had Mumuni contributed for part of the cost of the petrol for the campaign. He had practically nothing to offer immediately after the elections. Reluctant as I was to borrow, I had to approach my friend, A. Karbo, for a loan of £30 which Mumuni Dimbie promised to repay on my behalf when he got his first pay packet as MP from the Assembly. I travelled down to Kumasi to book my flight for Britain before returning to bid my friends in Tumu the final goodbye. Again, before I left Tumu finally, I warned Mumuni to guard himself against flirting with supporters' wives or girl friends as this would cause friction amongst them, and to be careful never to spend beyond his means. I also asked him not to forget to pay the £30 back to Mr Karbo as soon as he got his pay packet. In addition I advised him to get a branch propaganda secretary and pay him at least £10 a month, so he could continue with the work we had started.

The Governor was scheduled to visit the Northern Territories to meet the chiefs and people and to tell them that the British Government would sever its relations with the north as soon as the Gold Coast became independent. That was British or Colonial Government loyalty for you! For over fifty years of Colonial rule, after the treaty of 1901, the Northern Territories was ruled and treated as separate entity with its own laws passed in the Legislative Council. Indeed the Gold Coast was ruled under four different entities – the divide and rule principle of the Colonial Government – when it suited them but when it did not, the north was cast aside and offered a Hobson's

Choice. It was the selfishness of the British Government and that of Arden-Clarke that left us to the whims of Dr. Nkrumah and of Arden-Clarke who aspired to be made the first Governor-General of Ghana if the country became independent. At his palaver, however, the chiefs from the various districts met the Governor in this open air arena which could accommodate three to four football pitches. He informed his listeners that Her Majesty's Government was rescinding its obligation to the north and abrogating the treaties of 1901. In other words, in the eyes of the British, the north could go to hell if it did not want to unite with the Gold Coast before we were reasonably and fairly educated and ready to join on equal terms in an independent Ghana. For however good the northerner was in his job, he could go nowhere without a paper qualification. Indeed, at the time of this declaration, there was only one graduate in the whole of the Province. Historically, the British Colonial Administration held us back even from being in contact with our southern brothers except for providing labourers for their mines or for the construction of the infra-structure of the country and for staffing the army and the police.

After his speech, disgraceful in the eyes of some of us, the chiefs and people who sat in a horse-shoe round the perimeter of this huge park, got up followed by their subjects in order to present themselves to the Governor, the "biggest white chief of them all". It seemed the durbar was pre-rehearsed in each district by the Government Agents and at the regional capital by the Chief Regional Officer for the benefit of their big chief. For each chief was accompanied by music and drumming as they proceeded round the perimeter in a sort of orderly file to present themselves to His Excellency. The Lawra District brought two types of xylophones used during the procession, the *gbin*, the "war xylophone", and the *Bɔɔ-gyil* played at Bɔɔr performances or dances of mirth and jollity. The Lawra Nũũ's nephew, Laayaar Bini, was the player during the procession but he needed some drummers to accompany him as he played the xylophone which was borne by two persons and held to waist height. I asked my cousin, Nuyaa, a very good drummer accompanying the Birifu Nũũ, to play one of the drums, but my brother, Nana, refused to allow him to oblige. I was very upset with the chief and decided to play one of the drums myself. I led the Lawra contingent on the drum as Laayaar played a marching tune on the xylophone followed by all the chiefs and their followers in the district.

I mentioned earlier how a schoolmate, Yahaya Wala, had conned me into supplying him with building materials such as timber and cement by telling me he would pay for them as soon as they were delivered at the site. A year and a half passed, and I more or less wrote off this amount of £200 as bad debt. Immediately after the durbar, I returned with the chiefs from Lawra to Kofi Kpɛb's house where most of them normally stayed when in the capital. There was music and dancing to the big xylophones in front of the house. I joined the dancers enjoying my dance when I was approached by a young man who introduced himself to me as Issifu Kumbugu, the son of the chief of Kumbugu. He told me he was a friend of Hilla and was about to leave for Greatwood Tutorial College in Britain and thought that he could get more information from me. As soon as I finished with Issifu and went back to join the dance group again, out of the blue came Yahaya Wala with the surprising news that he had come to pay me his debt of £200. I was knocked for six with that news. I left the dancing area and asked him to follow me with the money to the bank. We went straight to the British Bank of West Africa (now Standard Chartered Bank) where he gave the money to the cashier to check. I immediately authorised the manager to transfer the whole of that amount to the Lombard Bank, Fenchurch Street, London, which at that time was advertising in the papers to pay six percent interest on deposits. Indeed had Yahaya not paid this money at that time I could not have got money from another source to leave for the United Kingdom as I intended.

I had learnt a year or so earlier that the Lawra Local Council, on hearing that the Tumu District had given a lump sum of £200 to Hilla, also voted £400 as a lump sum to help me go abroad. However, when it came to the time to approve the payment of this sum, there were two persons from the Finance and Staff Committee, together with the Government Agent, Mr Wallace, who objected to the council helping me financially. The two persons were none other than my two brothers, the Birifu Nũũ and Biz. They objected on the grounds that they felt the money was being donated to me on party grounds. Mr Wallace's objection was that I was too old (29-30 years at that time) to study. We had never met at all for him to know my age even though he was in Tumu for a short while of about six months. Besides, coming from a place like Britain he should have been aware that persons aged over 60 still studied for their GCEs at that time. I believe the Department of Extra-Mural Studies was paying him £2 an hour to take extra-mural classes. Was I older than all the members in his class, I wondered. I would not have had any money problems had Mr Wallace not vetoed the council decision. So in Lawra the youth gathered and organised a farewell party for me on the Lawra tennis court on the eve of my departure south en route to Britain. At this party, besides the drinks provided, I was given the sum of fifteen pounds. Biz was nowhere at this party although he was teaching in the Middle School in Lawra which was about a mile away from town. On the afternoon of September 15, 1956, he had promised to come and bid me goodbye before my transport took off but he never did so. I think he was ashamed to face me for his part in preventing the Local Council donating the £400 to me.

As usual I spent three days on the way to Kumasi arriving there on September 17th. After one or two weeks in Kumasi finalising my trip, I travelled to Accra to collect the papers for my various inoculations. My landlord in Kumasi must have heard some rumours about my travel to Britain, for when I left for Accra he assumed I was on my way abroad. The very day I left for Accra, Kuffuor, the landlord, managed to con his way into my lodgings with quack bailiffs and threw my illiterate nephew, Batan, and his wife, together with all my things, out into the street. He then locked the place securely and vanished from the scene altogether. I was amazed that my nephew was so stupid as to allow them to do this without any court order. I was so livid with him that I didn't bother to take any remedial action to reclaim my tenancy. After all I had only a week or so left to stay in the country. This young man had stayed in that accommodation for nearly six years without paying any contribution to the rent or paying for his food any time I was around, even though he was earning enough as head-labourer, about six shillings to seven shillings and sixpence a day. Before I left Lawra, I had promised my four-poster bed that was in Kumasi to Dibaar Kuuyele (W.K. Dibaar), a brother-in-law, who was appointed as the District Education Secretary for Lawra. I asked my nephew to dispatch that to him.

Besides the British Overseas Airways Corporation (BOAC), which flew Accra-London at a cost at that time of £102, there was another light aircraft that flew from Accra to London but took three days to arrive there. It was by the same airline that a year ago I had booked for Hilla to fly. This line was run by Hunting-Eagle Star. On the evening of the 10th October, I travelled to Accra arriving there on the morning of the 11th and booked in at the Sea View hotel, near Ussher Fort, until the morning of the 12th October. The services provided in those days were excellent compared to some of the top hotels in Accra today. After breakfast, I took a taxi to the airport, then at the old site, and after checking in, boarded the plane and was ready to take off.

At this time there were no agents of Mr Egala nor he himself to stop me from leaving the Gold Coast. It had again been an empty threat on their part. We took off soon after boarding and by about one o'clock, after flying over Liberia, landed in Freetown, the capital of Sierra Leone, where we were to have our lunch. Being a small aircraft with no catering facilities on board, we had to land at convenient airports for our main meals. While we were having our lunch in the open air, Mr Siaka Stevens, the Leader of the Opposition, whom I had met two years earlier during the UNESCO conference at Legon, was at the airport travelling to America. We chatted for a few minutes before he took off on his plane. Not long after we also took off for the Gambia, our destination for the day. We landed at Bathurst, the capital of the Gambia. This was a very small town and I was able to walk through the length and breadth of it in no time at all. Everybody seemed to know everybody in the Gambia. I asked to be taken to the house of a trade unionist whom I also met when he attended the UNESCO conference at Legon. After he had shown me some of the important places of the Gambia, I returned to the hotel that was situated by the beach. It was a beautiful beach with white sand and silvery little pebbles that stretched along the coast. I admired every bit of the coast as I gazed at the sea enjoying the evening sea breeze, returning at dusk to the hotel, which was also called the Bathurst.

We soon had the evening meal and some moments afterwards I retired and fell asleep. At dawn the next morning, we left the hotel between four or five o'clock driving through the heavy morning dew that covered the road with its silvery drops. As the sun peeped above the horizon painting it golden, we were borne up in the air heading for our next destination. By nine o'clock we landed at a very cold, dusty desert airport, Agadir, where we had a short break for breakfast at this Moroccan town. Being a small airport, there was hardly anyone around except the few employees refuelling the plane or serving us our breakfast. After thirty minutes' rest or so, we took off for our next destination. The weather was unbearably hot at times, as we flew over the desert displaying its mountains of sand and its occasional green patches of vegetation around the oases. The sea of sand expanded across the horizon with dunes rising into the sky and above the horizon like anthills, only much bigger. From time to time we crossed little settlements in this scorched earth until we at last landed at another airport, Rabat, for lunch. After lunch we took off again for our destination for the night. Towards the late afternoon, we were flying over Tangiers and landed at the airport. We were driven to our hotel for the night. This was the age of African nationalism that was spreading across the length and breadth of colonial empires, and we were met with slogans such as "Vive la Sultana" and "Algerie française". With such opposing slogans reminding me of the NLM and CPP, I was loath to venture outside. I was travelling with two other people from the Gold Coast who were keen to explore the city but could not convince me to go out with them. I did not want to be caught in a melée in a foreign country where I would not be able to get myself out of trouble. I stayed in the hotel preferring to read. I had seen enough political agitation at home and did not want to be caught in any other. After dinner, I went into my hotel room to read and rest after viewing the town from within.

At dawn on the 14th of October, we were driven off to the airport where we boarded the aircraft and travelled along the coast noticing the meandering of the Mediterranean sea between the two coasts like a big python moving slowly through its path as the pilot told us in his commentary of our position as we crossed the Straits of Gibraltar. At about nine that morning we landed at a Spanish airport, Cadiz, on the west coast of Spain. Here we were served with a sumptuous breakfast of fish and salad with plenty of Spanish wine. After an hour or so on land, making pigs of ourselves with this meal, we took off again along the Portuguese mountains on the west coast across the Spanish mountains into France where we landed at the airport in Biarritz, a coastal port near Bayonne for a late lunch. After lunch we boarded the plain again for the last lap of the journey to Britain. We soon flew north over Nantes and then the English Channel and over the Kent coast into Britain. It was a dull and cold autumn afternoon, but as I was wearing big thick northern attire, the *badakeri* with another smock underneath, I did not feel the cold when I landed at Heathrow. As we approached London and the plane prepared to land, I was disgusted with the sight of the place. The houses were all grey and dull, covered in the autumn smog, so there was very little to see in the form of beautiful houses. I was not impressed with London since most of the houses, from a bird's eye-view, were blackened with soot or the smog of those days. We approached Heathrow and had permission to land. We alighted and were lead to the customs area, where because of my chiefly attire, I was being saluted by police constables and doors opened for me everywhere I went at the airport. I was greatly impressed by the politeness of the British police and of the workers at the airport, and thought that every Londoner was like that in the capital.

I must have been mistaken for a VIP, since in those days West Africans were very few passing through Heathrow in such attire and those who did so were usually important visitors, presumably from Nigeria. Indeed one of the constables did ask me if anyone from the High Commission had come to meet me but I said no, as a friend was coming. I thought that the Principal of Greatwood Tutorial College would have sent some one to meet me at the airport or the air terminal if Hilla did not come. Of course my friend Hilla knew the date of my arrival and had promised to meet me but he was not there. When I did not see him I became a little worried, especially when we were being driven out of the airport to the air terminal at Gloucester Road, Kensington, where he was in fact waiting for my arrival. As I approached the air terminal, I saw Hilla and and his friend, Issifu Kumbugu (now lawyer Issifu Alhassan) waiting to receive me and to take me home. Before my arrival in Britain, Hilla, Issifu and one Alexander, from British Guiana (now Guyana) who was a classmate of Hilla at the time, had combined to rent a complete two-bedroom house, so that on my arrival, I could share it with them. After picking up my suitcase we left on a bus, a no. 29 that took us to Harringay where my life in Britain began.

CHAPTER TWENTY-TWO

ARRIVING ON THIS COLD AUTUMN evening, the place soon became pitch dark and the streets and houses littered with electric lights that looked like the constellations in the skies. I hardly knew to where we were heading. When we got to the house, Hilla and Issifu shared the upstairs room whilst Alex and I shared the back room downstairs. I believe the landlord was a Polish GP. The next morning, immediately after breakfast, Hilla took me to a men's out-fitters to look for some warm clothes for us to buy. As my money, which had been transferred from Tamale, was at the headquarters of the Bank of British West Africa in Fenchurch Street, London, we first had to go there where I could be issued with a cheque book. This allowed me to do my purchases and also to get cash at any bank if I wanted to. After finishing with the bank, I withdrew some cash to do the little shopping needed. My friend, Hilla, bought me a tweed jacket which cost about four pounds ten shillings and I bought a pair of grey trousers to match for about two pounds ten shillings. The pair of shoes cost about one pound ten shillings and a couple of shirts did not cost more than fifteen shillings. After the shopping we returned to the house where Issifu and Alex had prepared lunch awaiting our arrival.

After lunch, Hilla, Issifu and Alex sat down to do their homework. They had been registered for their courses and were over a month into them. Schools and Further Education Colleges in those days opened about mid-September. As I had been coaching myself in maths and French from textbooks while in the Gold Coast, I also fetched out my textbooks on these subjects and joined them in their study. I had thought I would be going to the Greatwood Tutorial College where I had paid my enrolment fee, but was convinced by Hilla and Issifu not to go; for Hilla spent over a year there and Issifu a few months. I was advised that I would be better off finding a school in London than going to Greatwood Tutorial College, for there were only a couple of tutors, the Principal and one other. I was, at first, hesitant to accept their advice, because I felt morally obliged to Mr Gosling, the Principal of that College for my entry into Britain.

The nearest tube station to where we lived was either Manor House or Turnpike Lane each of which was about a quarter of a mile in either direction. It was easier to pick up one of the trolley buses that served the area into town and which passed a few yards from a T-junction in our street; it was a choice of catching the trolley buses into town or walking the distance to either of the stations. We opted for the former. Hilla had decided to find a school for me in London and on my first Monday, the four of us went to the end of our street and picked up a bus for town. When we got to Camden Town, Issifu Kumbugu alighted to go to his college whilst the three of us proceeded to Westminister College of Commerce on Victoria Street where Hilla and Alex had enrolled to study for the GCE O'Level and A'Level subjects. Hilla first took me to the reading room to wait for him whilst he went to have his morning lectures. After the lectures, Hilla and I travelled to Aldwych to see the Ghana Education Attaché and ask if he could procure a school for my course. He was one Reverend Matterson who I believe hailed from the Cape Coast Province. In the High Commission, which was housed in India House at Aldwych, and directly opposite the London School of Economics, Hilla introduced me to the Reverend, and asked him if he would assist me to enrol in a College of Further Education where I could study for my GCE exams. Hilla thought that in his official capacity the Reverend would have more muscle and could find me a school much quicker than he and I trying on our own. The Reverend agreed to help us and asked me to return home and wait to hear from him during the course of the week. We returned home that day and I waited. The week passed, but there was no word from the Education Attaché; another week passed by and still no word from the noble Reverend.

While waiting for Mr Matterson's letter, Hilla advised me to register for the autumn exams, which were normally taken in November, with one or two of the Examination Boards. The closing dates for most of the examination centres where the registration took place had expired; but I was lucky to get one in Wood Green that was still taking late entries for the Oxford Examination Board. I registered for three subjects, Maths, English Language and French, for the examinations with this Board. There was also another centre that took students registering for the exams on the London University Board, so I put my name for the same three subjects, making sure that the dates for the examination did not clash. For about three weeks, I was at home studying and revising the exams for these papers. To help me in my revision I bought some booklets of past exam papers of both the London and Oxford Examination Boards. These booklets became invaluable during the revision as I was able to sample the most likely questions which examiners delight in setting. I was both my own student and tutor.

While at home, and not having heard from Mr Matterson, I decided to look for a school for myself. But the problem here was knowing where to get the information and having done so, how to get it. Such information was normally available in the daily and weekly papers in August and early September and so by October or November such information was non-existent. Anyway, I ventured out on my own in search of a school with which to register. However, as a JJC, a jargon used by West Indians or West Africans for their fellow new arrivals into Britain which stood for "Johnny Just Come", I found myself losing my way all the time. For instance, any time I wanted to go to a place in Chiswick, I would find myself somewhere in Southgate; or while in town, I might want to go to Nottinghill Gate, and suddenly find myself in Harringay. As I had not yet travelled by the underground, I found it easier to use the buses than the tube. Travelling by bus was more expensive, as I later realised. On the tube, you could use the same ticket to retrace your steps if you went the wrong way, but this was not feasible on the bus. So I gave up my search for a school in order to concentrate on my revision as it was costing me too much time and money.

When I first arrived in Britain, there were only a handful of students from the Northern Territories of the Gold Coast who I knew were studying in Britain. Bukari Yakubu and C.Y. Mahama who had been awarded Cocoa Marketing Board scholarships to study abroad were here; Issifu Ali and Bukari Nambe had been helped by a Government Agent, Westland Adams, himself a Scot, to go to Scotland for further studies; and Issifu Alhassan, Hilla and myself who were here as private students. Almost all these students were past pupils of the only Middle School in the North and later on students of the Teacher Training College in Tamale. There were two other persons from the north, who went through the same middle school as us; these were one Andani Andan (now Dr Andan and the chief of Sanerigu) and Ludwig Henkel (the late Dr Henkel). They were here studying medicine. All in all there were about nine students of northern extraction in Britain. More than half of these were private students or assisted financially by expatriates who had served in the north as colonial servants.

About the time of my arrival in Britain, the BBC at Bush House, London, was about to open a branch of the Radio ZOY in Wa. They approached the High Commission here under whose auspices Bukari was studying to solicit his help in finding a Wali speaking person in London. Bukari was a pro-CPP member of Parliament in the 1951 Legislative Assembly but lost his seat to an NPP candidate in the 1954 General Elections, and I learned Nkrumah had given him a scholarship to come to Britain. As Bukari was a Kusasi-speaking person and could not speak Wali, he contacted Hilla who put my name forward; for Bukari had no idea I was in the country. Anyway, a few weeks later, I received a letter from the BBC Overseas Department inviting me to call at their office and contact a certain lady. When I got there, the lady told me that I was to prepare my speech in Wali with its translation in English so it could be broadcast to the people of Wa town on the opening day of the station. Without even giving me any guidelines to work on, this lady asked me return home and prepare this speech and bring it back to her.

After preparing the speech, I took it back for her approval. Even though she fixed the time for us to meet, I had to wait an hour or more before she attended to me and this happened at subsequent visits. I began to disbelieve the myth in the Gold Coast that punctuality was the forte of the white man, whereas that of the African was unpunctuality. Of course I soon learnt the falsehood of this statement when I worked in industry a few years later. At our first recording she felt my broadcast was jerky in parts and not flowing, and she even became livid with me at my first performance. Maybe she thought I was one of her colonial employees who were sent here from time to time to work under her. She told me to take the speech back home and learn it by heart. I was preparing for my exams, and I thought to myself that I had better things to learn than listen to this lady's instructions. I nearly told her there and then to stuff her job and where to jump and that I was not prepared to continue with her programme; but for other reasons, I held my peace. If I had discontinued with the programme, I would have been letting down my friends, Hilla and Bukari who put my name forward.

When I got home, I put the speech aside not bothering to learn it by heart, but concentrated on my revision for the exams. I was at Bush House the next day, prepared to tell her to stick her job if she was as rude to me again as on the previous day. In those days the recordings were made on large discs like gramophone records and played back again and again until they were satisfactory enough to be relayed to the public. At this recording session, even though I did not learn my speech by heart as she wanted me to, she thought it was performed much better than the day before. We spent the whole day recording over and over again and after about three sessions, she felt it was satisfactory for broadcasting. I was then paid a meagre £5 for all the effort I had put in. If I had known that after spending three or more days travelling between Harringay and Bush House I was only to be paid £5, I would not have bothered and would have concentrated on revising my papers for my exams.

It seemed that British colonial institutions abroad tended to exploit nationals of those countries where they have established their overseas branches any time they wanted their services. They often tried to underpay their colonial nationals for their services, forgetting that in Britain the cost of living was much higher than for those born and bred here. For instance a British student at that time could go into digs for only fifteen shillings a week. Whilst a colonial student, if he was lucky to get a similar type of digs, would be paying between £2.10s to £3.10s a week not including lighting and heating. Those who lived with their parents only contributed a pound or two a week towards their upkeep.

Apart from my experience with the BBC, I had similar one with BOAC a few years later when they wanted to advertise their flights to West Africa and approached the Ghana Education Office for volunteer students to partake in their project. I was approached by one of the officers in the High Commission whom I knew and had met during two of the New Year and Easter Schools held by the Department of Extra-Mural Studies in conjunction with the PEA at Cape Coast; he was then the music master at St Augustine's College. I agreed to volunteer for it; and on the Sunday when the shooting was to take place, I arrived at the airport to meet with the other participants. There were about five other Ghanaians and Nigerians with some five or eight white men. One of the whites took to me like a duck to water; perhaps he was fascinated by my Northern Ghanaian attire and so we chatted all through the filming any time there was a short break. At one of these conversations, he asked how much I expected to be paid; and when I told him that I had been told it would be five pounds, he showed some astonishment and exclaimed, "Is that all!" I obviously took that to mean that I was underpaid.

After the exams in November for which I had registered, Hilla took me to see the secretary to the Principal of his college to see if I could gain admission there. As good luck would have it, there was a vacancy as someone had dropped out, and she booked an appointment for me to see the Principal at two o'clock that same day. After lunch when the afternoon classes re-assembled, the secretary led me into Mr Moon's office and left the two of us alone, so he could prepare a time-table for me. To do so, he wanted to know what career I intended to pursue after the GCE. I told him that I had the intention of reading law. At that time, the necessary subjects for reading law were passes in History, Latin, English Language, and British Constitution among other subjects. I also added subjects such as French, Geography, Economics and Maths, which I had been pursuing on my own. Bearing in mind these subjects, Mr Moon prepared my time-table and by the time this was done, he did not allow much lecture time to each subject at all. I was enrolled that day on November 30, 1956 and I began my classes from then onwards. Not very long afterwards the college closed for the Christmas Holidays for three weeks.

I did not know that Hilla had placed my name with the GPO near the college to do some Christmas work. Luckily for me, I was placed inside the GPO sorting office to sort letters and parcels as I was still a JJ and lived miles away from the Westminster area. I started at 11 a.m.and finished at 11 p.m. We were only employed for ten days and were then paid off. For the rest of my holidays, Hilla and Issifu advised that I go to Greatwood Tutorial College and make use of part of my deposit, and then to return when my college re-opened. I toyed over the idea and considered it morally wrong to do so. I was hesitant in carrying it out but eventually I had to go against my own moral conscience.

On the day of my departure for Greatwood Tutorial College, Issifu and Hilla saw me off at the railway station Charing Cross. At the station, I rang the college to let them know which train I was taking. When I arrived at Sidcup Station, a German girl was sent to meet and collect me from there. She was at this college with some other girls who, I later learnt, were au pair girls studying English whilst working for their upkeep in the kitchen and making the beds, cleaning and dusting in the dormitories.

The college premises was situated in a large area which housed both the staff and the students. As the students were also on their holidays, it was hard to tell how many the college could accommodate in such a confined area. Anyhow, I could only see about a dozen persons at meals at any one time, including the Principal, his wife and one or two lecturers. Most of the students whom I met belonged to rich families whose parents came from the Middle East. From my short stay with them, I had the impression that they were not serious students. Some of them were there for over two years and I understand had not passed any exams at all. None of them read a book while I was there; but it could be that they were enjoying the holidays after a hectic last term's work and therefore were taking a break from reading or studies. Of course, I came to Britain with a promise to my wife that I would be back in the Gold Coast within the next three years as a qualified barrister. But this was a tall order to aim for at that time. For at best, I could do my O' and A'levels in one year; at worse it could take several years to qualify to enter the Bar School which also took at least three years if one passed all the exams and completed one's dinners at his Inn of Court. For however clever one was in his course, one had to take twelve dinners a year at the Inns of Court for three years. Nevertheless, I tried to aim towards that goal. All through my stay there, over the Christmas and into the New Year, I stuck tenaciously to my books from morning till evening, stopping only to have my meals and then resume. So all those who were with Hilla a year earlier saw me as a bookworm by comparison.

There was a TV in the common room but the only time I took much interest in it was when there was a news broadcast and also when the Queen broadcast her Christmas Message to the peoples of the Commonwealth. At New Year's Eve there was a party when the New Year was seen in. I spent the Christmas and the New Year here and at the end of my fortnight, and a few days before my college reopened, I told Mr Gosling, the Principal, that I was going to London to visit Hilla and Issifu whom I had not seen since my arrival to Britain so I could stay a few days with them. This was a white lie so that I could get back to London before the opening date of Westminster for the winter term. Hilla and others were pleased to see me back, although I had another hurdle to overcome – to tell Mr Gosling when his college re-opened that I was not returning there. I had again to wrestle with my conscience as to how to tell him of this decision. A few days after their college reopened, I telephoned Mr Gosling and told him that while in London, I had found a college in which the tuition fee was only £30 a session compared with his 240 guineas inclusive of board and lodgings.

It was long after the examinations that the GCE results were released by the various Examination Boards. As soon as I returned to the college on the opening day, my results were given to me and they were worse than I expected. For after the exams I knew I had not done very well but had expected just to scrape through at least in the English Language and the Maths papers; however to fail in all the papers, even though it was by a very narrow margin, was hard for me to take in. Since this was the first time I had ever failed an exam, the effect of this initial shock was devastating and took a toll on my confidence, which affected my future studies, especially exams. I was in a state of despondency as if I had lost a very close relative. Hilla's words of consolation did nothing to appease my grief and I was in this despondent mood for weeks.

I suppose the result of Alex's exams were very good for him to gain entrance into an Inn of Court. At that time one did not need to have a University Degree as a prerequisite to entering the Law School. Once one had matriculated and also satisfied the Law School's extra requirements, one could enrol to do the barrister's course, unlike today when a degree is needed as a pre-requisite.

When Alex matriculated, he enrolled with one of the Inns of Court to read law and wanted to find accommodation nearer to his Inn and to the Law School. This meant the break up of our tenancy agreement with the current landlord. At that time law lectures were given at the Inner Temple and this meant Alex would have to find accommodation in the vicinity of that area. This must have been planned between the three of them before I returned from Greatwood Tutorial College and when they had their exam results. Hilla and I moved to the Earls Court area to be nearer to our college so as to cut down on transport costs, whilst Issifu Alhassan also found accommodation nearer to his college. For it would have been foolish for him to move in with us. At Earls Court our new landlady was an elderly woman from Sierra Leone, living there with her husband and a son. Their son was studying in the same college as us and a class-mate of Hilla's. It could have been through him that Hilla got the information about the accommodation, since I knew nothing of this arrangement until we moved into No. 16 Wharfdale Street, SW6, before the college reopened. This house was directly opposite the Princess Beatrice Hospital and behind the hospital and towards Fulham on the Old Brompton Road was a big graveyard.

When college reopened for the winter term, the lecturer in our maths class had left to teach at the University of Manchester; a young Irish lady who had just graduated and was majoring in Biology was asked to take us in maths. It was a bore listening to her struggling to solve some of the mathematical problems, especially in geometry. Within a short space of time, many of the students turned to me for help in arithmetic and algebra with which I was at ease. There were especially two girls from Nigeria in the class, one, an Ibo, from Eastern Nigeria, and the daughter of a judge, and the other, a Yoruba from the West. At that time, Nigeria, just like the Gold Coast, was still a British colony divided and ruled in three regions, North, East and West. Initially I sat alone in the front row and the two girls sat directly behind me. But as time went on, the way I answered the lecturer's questions made them assume that I knew the subject and they moved themselves to join me in the front row, sandwiching me between them, so I could help them with the exercises which the tutor usually set after the remainder of the period.

After about a month or two the head of the Maths and Science Department, Mr Cassell, decided to take over our class. It was then that we were coached properly in geometry and trigonometry. I found the theorems in geometry too theoretical to comprehend just by reading from the textbook; by the time Mr Cassell took us, I had taught myself and covered only the first four theorems.

In the Gold Coast, in the Primary and Middle schools, I could do most of riders connected with these theorems but was not taught to prove them. I could remember when I was in standard six, Yakubu Tali taught us how to solve the areas and volumes of triangles and cylinders but not to prove how they were arrived at. When Mr Cassell took over, I could not still see the wood for the trees as far as geometry and trigonometry were concerned, especially topics on "locus" or "loci". Even though I bought myself a textbook on geometry entitled *A Geometry for Schools*, by Cassell (not my lecturer), I was getting nowhere with it. This was because of how my individual timetable was made; I had to fit my Maths into my other subjects such as English, Geography, French etc., and I found I could only attend one period a week on geometry. As a result when I attended a topic one week then by the following week, I would find I had lost two or three lectures on that subject. This is because most of the classes were organised into groups of students of the same ability in every subject.

In Tumu, I had bought myself a set of French records from the Linguaphone Institute from which I was teaching myself French. So when Hilla and I moved into Earls Court, we decided to buy a set of French records from the Linguaphone Institute for our French studies, especially for the oral side of the exams. Hilla bought a radiogram on which we could play and listen to the records whilst I bought the course from the Linguaphone Institute on Regent Street. Prior to that we were learning the subject from a textbook supplied to me by Bennet College, Sheffield, for their correspondence course, entitled *Hugo's French Grammar Simplified*. When we had the records, I continued to learn from the textbook and allowed Hilla alone to use the records. When Hilla had become sufficiently proficient in the subject both oral and written, he joined my class taught by one Mr K.W. Knight, whom Hilla and I nicknamed the "professor". Professor Knight was a good tutor in the subject and seemed to know it well; so I never liked missing any of his lectures even by a few seconds. However, one of his students who hailed from Greece would probably disagree with my statement; for the professor took great delight in making this student look very small. He teased or mocked him in class. Any time he set us homework and marked the papers, this young man would be the subject of his humiliating ridicule. For should this student get a zero mark, the professor would put ears and a mouth to the mark, depicting a face. At lectures, if he wanted this student to answer a question, he would call him by the name "sausage" instead of by his real name. This amused the students in the class, but I am sure the student was not the least amused. When Professor Knight eventually retired from teaching and returned to his home town in the west country, he published a French textbook *Living French*, sending me a complementary copy as his best student in French at Westminster. I was so proud that he should consider me so.

At Earls Court, Hilla and I always studied together far into the early hours of the morning before retiring, only to wake up at about five and continue till about six or seven or until the money for the gas or the electric meter ran out. We had to put money in the gas meter for heating and in that of the electricity for light. As time went on, I became mentally depressed and worried about my monetary problems—how I could cope with financing my course and maintain my pregnant wife and two children at home. I would find it degrading if people back home learnt I had stopped studies and taken up full time employment. I also did not realise that I was suffering with some stomach gastritis, which made me eat very little and yet feel as if I had overfed myself. I often went straight to bed any time I returned from college and had finished eating my meal. The moment I had finished eating, I would look like an overfed serpent, unable to crawl, and would go straight to bed until the next morning. So after every evening meal, whenever Hilla asked me whether I was studying for the night or not, I often told him I was too full to do anything by quoting this Dagaar proverb at him: *waab ma tiɔɔ liɛ vu?* lit: "can an overfed serpent crawl?". All this was taking a toll on my studies. Feeling uneasy about my health and the way it was affecting my studies, I went to see the doctor, my General Practitioner (GP), who was a Pole. He diagnosed my ailment as gastritis when I had told him all my symptoms. He prescribed some green tablets for me to take three times daily; and that I should drink a lot of fresh milk, at least two pints, a day. The treatment did the trick; for within a year or two, I did not experience those symptoms any longer. But it nevertheless affected my studies, especially during revision periods.

As the course progressed, I found out that my timetable did not allow me enough time to attend lectures on all the subjects I was supposed to study. I decided to register for only four subjects for the GCE O' level summer exams. In order to concentrate on these subjects, I re-adjusted my timetable to accommodate just the four subjects namely, French, English language, Geography and Mathematics, allowing me to spread my time to accommodate some of the periods of these subjects which I had been missing. In doing so, within a few weeks I began to see the wood for the trees in all of these areas I was studying and could appreciate and comprehend each lesson without looking dim and aloof as before.

At the beginning of the winter term, Hilla and I had placed our names for a forthcoming excursion to the colleges of the University of Oxford, stopping at Stratford-on-Avon. This trip was organised by Mr Moon, the Principal, and a former student of Oxford. It was to take place during the Whitsun recess. It was a very good thing that I had paid in full for the trip much earlier when Mr Moon's secretary had asked for deposits to be paid. I would otherwise have been unable to meet the cost when the full bill for the trip was being demanded.

Although I was finding it hard to concentrate on my revision due to the many worries on my mind, I still tried hard to persevere with them with the help of Hilla and the two Nigerian girls as my revision mates. Being with them, I forgot my worries as we discussed past questions. It is only when I was left revising alone that the worries kept flooding back to my mind. Hilla was taking French at the O' level and so we could revise that subject together. He also enrolled for the A' level in Geography whilst I enrolled for the O' level in it. Since the topics overlapped, we were able to study together without much disruption to each other's plan of revision. As for the Nigerian girls, one of them, the Yoruba girl, dropped out of the maths class as the exams drew nearer, leaving the Ibo girl and I to revise together at college. I still found the proof of the theorems on loci difficult and too theoretical to comprehend, even at this stage of the studies. From the past papers, it was invariably one of the compulsory questions included. I therefore made it a point to master this concept before the exams. Despite my effort on this topic, I could still find no way forward in it during the Easter break. Indeed during the mock exams, I fared very little better in it, which brought my aggregate mark into the lower fifties. By Whitsun, I was still as ignorant in this topic as before.

On the day we were to go to Oxford, I took with me a booklet of the GCE O' level past papers on maths with model answers, set by the London University Examination Board. I read these model answers all the way to Oxford, still not understanding any part of the topic. Hilla too was busy revising his topics and even though we sat together on the coach we seldom disturbed each other with conversation. I persevered to read the model answers on the various questions on this topic on our return to London, still without a clue of what it was all about other than that it was a topic on geometry.

On our way to Oxford, we stopped at Stratford-on-Avon for a short break to have our elevenses on the bank of the river. After an hour or so listening to the historical lecture of the place, which was of special interest to those students studying literature or interested in Shakespeare and his place of birth, we boarded the coach again for Oxford. It was the only time I put my booklet aside and listened to the history of the place. At the University we went round all the colleges and two or three hours later we had our afternoon tea at one of them. We left the University by a different route for London via Stratford-on-Avon again where we stopped at Shakespeare's village. It was the first time since coming to Britain I had seen thatched roofs. I persevered reading the topic in maths on our return to London, still not unravelling the maze of this topic. I glued my eyes to this little pamphlet and tried hard to concentrate; as we were about to enter London, eureka! my eyes lit up, for I had at last discovered what all this topic of loci was about. I was pleased with myself when we got home and I practised proving several theorems on this theme and solving the riders connected with them. By the time college reopened, I was conversant with this topic and was also able to teach and explain it to my mate, the Ibo girl.

The date for the Gold Coast becoming independent was fixed for March 6, 1957. Lawyer Asafu-Ajaye was sent to relieve Joe Mercer as the High Commissioner in London and to prepare the way for an independent Ghana, but was relieved by Hutton Mills shortly afterwards. On the morning of March 6,1957, Hilla and I went to the High Commission to witness the new Independence flag being raised and replacing the old one, the Union Jack. By the time we got to Belgravia, the ceremony was over and so we returned to our lectures at the college.

There was to be an Independence dance organised by the Students' Union and headed by pro-CPP students at Seymour Hall. Hilla and I went to see how these dances were run. But unfortunately we could not find the place and so after many hours searching in vain, we returned home. As soon as the Independent Constitution of Ghana was published by Her Majesty's Stationery Office in London, I secured myself a copy to see if it contained some of the proposals that we put forward while I was still in Ghana. The new constitution did not meet all the points raised by opposition parties' federal proposals. However there was a clause that was entrenched prohibiting the amendment of any matter relating solely to a particular region without the consent and approval of the Regional Assembly or Council. Thus matters affecting Ashanti or the Northern Territories could not be changed without those regions concerned first discussing and agreeing to the new amendment in their Regional Councils.

The summer exams started immediately after the Whitsun recess and spread to the end of the college session. Before the exams started, Hilla and myself had applied to the NAAFI for holiday jobs. Luckily we were both accepted and posted to the Pirbright Military Training Camp near Woking. As I was writing only four O' level subjects for the exams, I finished my papers before Hilla and immediately left for Pirbright a week or so earlier as he still had some A' level papers to write.

A week later Hilla came to join me at the camp and we worked all through the summer holidays. We were told that our pay would be £5 per week before we even took up the appointment. For those students on grants, this was a good supplement to their grant; but for Hilla and myself who were private students, this was a means of earning income to pay for our courses. At Pirbright we were accommodated in a dormitory at the Canteen with all the other permanent workers except the female cook who stayed in town and came very early. In any case there was a resident male cook who provided the breakfasts in the mornings. We got up very early in the morning to clean our dormitory and by 7.30 the cook had prepared our breakfast. By 8.30 we had finished our breakfast and started to arrange the cakes on the counters and to brew the teas, ready to open the shutters for the soldiers when they had finished with their morning drill. By nine we were all ready and raring to go. The canteen opened at 9.15 when the other ranks occupied the main hall whilst the NCOs occupied a side room for their refreshments. By mid-morning the canteen was shut to the soldiers whilst we started to put away the remaining cakes and sweep and mop the floors. As Hilla and I normally served the teas and the cakes, we helped Mrs Lyman who was in charge of the cakes to put them away. We then mopped the floors, cleared the tea urns for cleaning and by twelve lunch was ready.

At Pirbright, the first thing I learnt about the British working class was their indulgence in gossiping about and backbiting against one another the moment one of them was out of sight. Such backbiting irritated me very much but I ignored this at first, partly because I was still new to the place and partly because I had not more than eight weeks to stay there. About a week before the re-opening of schools and colleges, Hilla and I returned to London. I believe Hilla had applied to enter the LSE pending his results in the summer exams. We had given up our accommodation in Wharfdale Street before we left for Pirbright; otherwise we would have been paying our weekly rent while we were there.

CHAPTER TWENTY-THREE

ON OUR RETURN FROM PIRBRIGHT we had to find new lodgings and Hilla found a temporary place for us to rent somewhere in Camden Town. The accommodation was so awful that neither of us stayed there for more than three weeks. Hilla found a place which was nearer to LSE whilst I moved back to 16, Wharfdale Street where I was offered a single room. When College re-opened, I found out I had passed all the four papers in the summer. I enrolled at the College for 1957/58 to study A' level in Economics and British Constitution and also to improve my grade in English Language at the same time. I registered to write these two papers privately at the Autumn Exams in November. The college would not have done so as I had had no previous tuition with them and they often want good exam results from their students to boost the college name.

I had previously had some introductory lectures in Economics during my attendances at the Easter and New Year Schools in Ghana, conducted by the Extra-Mural Dept of the University College of Ghana; for I usually chose to attend economic lectures and seminars whenever I was able. Whilst in Ghana, because of my association with politics and as founder of NPP in Tumu and being also the private secretary to the then Leader of the Opposition, Mr S.D. Dombo, I had some practical insight into the workings of parliamentary democracy during my attendances at the Legislative Assembly and my fieldwork in the running of the NPP. Because we advocated a federal constitution for Ghana, I was also helped by Dennis Austin who brought me books on Federalism to broaden my mind on the theoretical side of politics. Consequently I was at ease with both of these subjects.

I was put in Mr Collin's class for both economics and British constitution and in a revision class in English with Mrs Gwen Lansdell. Since most students normally chose to do these subjects at A' level without first studying them at O' level, the class I was placed in went at rather a slower pace than I would have liked. I therefore enrolled with the Rapid Results Correspondence College and got their lecture notes to work through. I would not otherwise have met my ambition to sit the autumn exams in November. I had to burn the midnight oil in order to attain my ambition and I was able to do so because the cure of my gastritis was beginning to work and I could read into the night without feeling giddy or tired. I took the exams in November and when the results were released in the New Year of 1958, I found that I had passed in both subjects. My ambition to pass my GCE O and A levels in one year had materialised. I also found that I had matriculated for both the London and Manchester Universities. I applied to both Universities for a place to read Economics; the London School of Economics (LSE) of the University of London and to the Department of Economics of the Manchester University, which I knew was at that time headed by Professor Arthur Lewis. Manchester was my first preference because I had heard Professor Lewis lecture during the UNESCO conference in Ghana in 1954.

When the LSE got my application and found out I was a Ghanaian, they wrote to the Ghana Education Attaché for a sponsorship for my course. Without even consulting me, Rev. Matterson wrote back to the School refusing to sponsor me. I was surprised to get a letter from the LSE telling me my application would not be considered unless I got someone to sponsor my course as the Ghana Education Attaché had refused to do so. I showed this letter to Mr Collin, my course tutor, who in turn showed it to Mr Moon. Both Mr Moon and Mr Collin had previously recommended me very highly on my application form regarding my academic ability. When Mr Moon saw this letter, he immediately decided to sponsor me himself and wrote to the LSE accordingly.

Some months later I had a letter from the school asking me to call for an interview at a certain date and to confirm that I would be attending it. I immediately replied confirming my intention to do so. As both Manchester University and London had accepted my application and had asked me to call for interviews, I felt it was no longer necessary to remain at Westminster College and to read more subjects or to repeat those I had passed in order to get higher grades. Consequently I immediately left the college and started applying for jobs. When I found I was getting nowhere, I decided to apply to NAAFI again and lo! and behold, I was sent to the Pirbright Military Training Camp as before. Here I met a drum-major from the Sierra Leone army who was also there for further training and was later to head the first coup in Sierra Leone. We became bosom friends for the duration we both were there together. Before taking up my appointment with NAAFI, I had earlier applied to join a college trip to France for a week's holiday at the Easter recess, for which I had paid four pounds. This was to cover all my expenses while in France.

At Pirbright, when the time arrived, I asked for a week off work so I could travel with the school group. Peter, the chef, had lent me his box camera, which I took along. The group was a hen party; the only men in the group were the two lecturers, a Mr Melor and one other who organised the trip, a student from Westminster, and myself. From London we went by train from Victoria Station to Dover where we took the ferry to Calais. We then took a train from there to Paris, arriving at about five o'clock in the afternoon. Here we took another train to a school in Versaille where we were housed. We then travelled all over Paris visiting important places of interest. The week soon went by and I returned to my base in Pirbright.

In those political days in Ghana, some of the leading opposition members wanted to boycott anything that they did not believe in, whether what the Government or what the CPP was doing, and this even included the boycotting Local Government Elections. So in 1958 there were to be some Local and District Council as well as Regional Council elections and the leaders of the opposition ill-advised their supporters to boycott these. I was still at Pirbright when my friend, Mr A. Karbo, wrote informing me of the intention of the Opposition to carry out the boycott. I immediately wrote back imploring him to tell the NNP leaders not to comply with such a decision. I told him the consequences of the action vis à vis the effect on the constitution. He wrote back informing me that the elections had already been boycotted. The outcome of this boycott was that CPP candidates went unopposed, and at the Regional Council the only clause which prevented the Government from taking any action which would affect that region without its consent was removed. This enabled Parliament to legislate and amend the constitution and by the time the Republican Constitution of the First Republic was written, there was no such clause protecting the special interests of each of the regions.

EDITOR'S POSTSCRIPT

KUM GANDAH NEVER FINISHED HIS autobiography before he died, since he did not touch upon his later life in London nor his many visits back to Ghana, where many of his friends eventually held important posts.

I had first met him at the Final Funeral of his father and later at a Bagre performance in 1950. I only met him again in the 1960s when I had translated a version of the Bagre myth which I was about to publish. I needed to sort out some points and consulted him in London. At that time he was working as a statistician with Guiness the Brewers in Park Royal. They had helped him raise a mortgage on a house in Clevely Crescent, Hangar Lane, West London. By that time his first wife had died and the two children, Kofi and Agatha, came to join their father in London, where they found work and established their own families. But the great interest Kum continued to have in Ghana became diluted with the generations; at various times he planned to return permanently but they had become solidly based in Britain.

He returned to Ghana with me in 1969 to make a tape-recording of the Birifu Bagre and we went back again in 1979 to visit the settlement. He returned more regularly and on one occasion arranged to be followed by Florence, the daughter of his friend, Chief Dombo. They married at a South London mosque and she bore him two children, but the marriage did not last long and Kum was again living on his own. But he had his consolation at the Guinness Club (for his version of the Muslim faith no longer prevented him from drinking beer), his TV, his Ghanaian interests. He was very proud when his close friend, Hilla Limann, became the first northern President of Ghana.

Between the time that his narrative ends and the time that we met again, Kum had continued his studies, initially while working as a clerk with British Rail. There he studied a variety of subjects, including statistics and the philosophy of science. That qualified him for the better-paid job with Guinness.

He took early retirement from the firm and planned to return to

Ghana to set up some business there, perhaps working for a brewery, perhaps building a dance school attached to thc hotcl built by his brother, Debomo, in Bolgatanga, and there were many more possibilities. None came to fruition because when he did go back, not necessarily for good, he had a terrible accident in his new Land Rover on the road between Accra and Kumasi in 1982. He would certainly have died had not his longstanding friend, Polkuu Kũnkuu, who had become Chief of Nandom and a member of the Provisional National Defence Council (PNDC), been able to call upon the help of an army helicopter to evacuate him from the scene. He spent a spell in the main hospital in Accra (Korle Bu) before being sent back by air as a stretcher case in virtue of his travel insurance. He was first in a hospital in St John's Wood, unable to move, unable to feed himself, unable to talk. Then he was sent for rehabilitation to Stanmore Orthopaedic Hospital where they did a brilliant job of rehabilitating him in mind and body, including teaching him to operate a word processor, which gave him the means to write his autobiography. At the same time he continued to do translation for, or sometimes together with, me and thus kept himself very busy. The Social Services adapted his house so that he could sleep and work on the same floor. A Home Help came in twice a week and his daughter, Agatha, arrived with her family on Sundays to prepare northern Ghanaian dishes (saab or fufu) out of ingredients available in London which Kum would eat during the week. He had visitors but inevitably his life became thin and isolated compared to earlier times. But he had his Land Rover in Ghana adapted for his handicap and went back on more than one occasion, for he remained intensely interested in his native land and in its performances and customs. Indeed he was in Accra when he had a fatal heart attack and died on June 12th, 2001.

He was buried in his native settlement, Birifu, but after a year, his daughter Agatha arranged a splendid memorial service at St Mark's Church Pastoral Centre in Kennington, London, on 15th June 2002 to which many friends and relatives came to pay their respects to the silent rebel.

EDITOR'S NOTES

1 The people in the Lawra division of northwest Ghana are known variously as Dagarti (a spelling no longer used), Dagaare, Dagaaba, and Lobi. The situation is complicated because many groups that see themselves as different use these terms in a relative way to describe themselves. Dagaare is a general term for the various dialects. I use the term LoWiili for the group into which the author was born (see J. Goody, *The Social Organisation of the LoWiili*, London 1956).

2 Tamale is the capital of the Northern Region, and formerly of the Northern Territories.

The third part of the book was left unfinished at the author's death.

3 Lopiel, "White Lobi", is how the neighbouring people of Lawra are referred to by the people of Birifu.

4 The Lawra Bagre is being published as *A Myth Revisited: The Third Bagre* by Carolina University Press in 2003. The myth itself and the association and ceremonies to which it is attached are described in J. Goody, *The Myth of the Bagre*, Oxford 1972, and in J. Goody and S.W.D.K. Gandah, *Une Recitation du Bagre*, Paris 1981.

5 In pre-colonial times there was no chiefship of a political kind in Birifu; Gandah was appointed by the colonial authorities and his assistants were appointed by him.

6 Kyaa is the flat inhabited area by the river Volta; Bataan is the open area to the north.

7 The idea of scarring such children is widespread in the region.

8 These "cudgels" are what I call "throwing sticks", heavy pieces of wood that are thrown at the bird or animal to stun it.

9 Each clan has its own hunting shrine, with its own medicine, cry, and in the case of the Naayile, songs.

10 Chief Gandah was one of the few people to have a muzzle-loading gun in the settlement. The horn was made from the horn of a large antelope. The hunting described here takes place during the period of the Bagre ceremonies and all the animals killed belong to the shrine. But similar expeditions take place at other times.

11 The male crown bird is often associated with the Bagre but here apparently with the clan.

12 Women who have passed the menopause are said to have changed to men and can participate in many of the rituals hereto forbidden them.

13 "Territorial boundaries" because Birifu is very close to the border with Burkina Faso.

14 "Farming for the Chief" had been practised by the centralised states of the area and when chiefs were appointed in the "tribal" areas, they too began this practice. By this means, some of them became quite rich.

15 If the diviners pronounced it to be a "bad death", the funeral would not continue, at least until some sacrifice had been made.

16 A hole is made in the wall of the house so that the body does not pass out by the normal way. The funeral stand is erected outside the house and the body, dressed in the best cloth, is displayed there for three or four days so that the mourners can say their last farewells.

17 "Carrying the mat" on which the deceased had slept used to be a common method in West Africa of attempting to diagnose the cause of death. It has often been condemned by the authorities.

18 "Wangara" is the Hausa name for Mande-speaking traders from the Niger bend.

19 Togo was a German colony until the First World War when it was mandated to France and Britain by the League of Nations.

20 Tiisep became Chief of Birifu after Nana's death until he too died in the late 1990s.

21 Eyre-Smith had served in the northwest as a District Commissioner and had written an interesting booklet on the pre-colonial system.

22 Water divination is one of the methods of Islamic divination in West Africa.

23 Such quantities of meat would be unheard of in most local diets.

24 The Earth shrine protects the members of the parish against witchcraft and other calamities.

25 This shrine, a structure surmounted by mud sculptures of animals, is situated outside the Chief's compound. It was this shrine that had so prospered in Ashanti and brought wealth to Birifu, in the shape of the lorry that formed the basis of the family transport business and paid for the brass band to come to Chief Gandah's funeral.

26 Builsa is the name of the ethnic group to the east of the Sisaala. Grunshi is a vague word but probably refers here to those living around Navrongo.

27 Fuseini Daramani later became Headmaster of the Salaga school and subsequently was put in charge of the District.

[28] The marriage transaction included 20,000 cowries, eventually several cows, plus the obligation to bring a body of farmers to work for the wife's father. That obligation literates were seen as less likely to fulfill.

[29] The beer bar was run by an Ashanti trader.

[30] The Kũbinɛ dance is performed in the market place at the end of the hoeing. Young men then show off their dancing skills in front of the public, sometimes travelling to neighbouring markets.

[31] Hamile is the roadstop on the border with Burkina Faso.

[32] These are quarters of Kumasi.

[33] Apprentices are frequently made to work as unpaid labour.

[34] The Linguist is the office of Spokesman found in Ashanti but adopted by chiefs elsewhere.

[35] Gyiripuo and Kpaari were two of the brothers not sent to school; the latter later acted as my assistant, before becoming an assistant in the fisheries, and later acting as Regent for the chiefship.

[36] The Société Compagnie Occidentale Africaine was the French commercial society for West Africa.

[37] Nikara from Tongzu was the best xylophone player in the settlement.

[38] Lambusie is the major town for the Sisaala people in the Lawra district.

[39] The area surrounding Bawku, the main town in the far north-east of Ghana, was noted for attempts to introduce plough farming.

[40] Dibaar Kuuyele was from Nandom and married a sister.

[41] UAC, the United Africa Company, owned by Lever Brothers.

[42] Ghanem and Halaby were Lebanese traders based in Wa, some fifty miles south of Birifu.

[43] As distinct from the local Ashanti collectors.

[44] The Tolon Na (Chief) of Dagomba, like the Duri Naa and J.A. Braimah, Kanyasiwura of Gonja, were among the first major political figures from the North in Parliament. All were chiefs. The ban on spirits was much resented by the educated inhabitants and was therefore soon abolished.

[45] "Station" refers to the government buildings.

[46] Moor-Darling later became Director of the Royal Anthropological Institute in London for a short while.

[47] This Bagre (Bũũr) ceremony was one of those I used as the basis for my account in *The Myth of the Bagre.*

48 Victor Owusu was a well-known lawyer in Kumasi who became a prominent member of the opposition to Nkrumah.

49 The Chief of Asante's police station was the one attached to the Native Authority of Kumasi.

50 Tordoff later became a lecturer in Politics.

51 Egala became MP for Tumu and later a Minister under Nkrumah.

52 Adisadel is an old-established Anglican school.

53 Koro (or kuro) is the word for "chief" in Sisaala.

54 Gardiner was a noted educationalist who later worked with the UN.

55 That is, Tumuuli, a variety of the language of the Sisaala people, belonging to the Grusi group of Gur (Voltaic) languages.

56 Edward Nasser was the name of a Lebanese store in Kumasi that prepared locally grown coffee.

57 Upper Volta is now Burkina Faso.

58 The Ahmadiyya movement is a modernising Islamic sect that had become established in Saltpond and was brought to Wa by a police officer, where it became very successful. Sidiki and Malam Issah were among its members.